PROTOTYPES OF PEACEMAKING

PROTOTYPES OF PEACEMAKING

The First Forty Years
of the United Nations

Compiled and written by
MARY ALLSEBROOK

Foreword by Lord Caradon

StJ

ST. JAMES PRESS
CHICAGO AND LONDON

PROTOTYPES OF PEACEMAKING, THE FIRST FORTY YEARS OF THE UNITED NATIONS

Published by Longman Group UK Limited, Longman House, Burnt Mill, Harlow, Essex CM20 2JE, United Kingdom.

Distributed exclusively in the United States and Canada by St. James Press, 425 North Michigan Avenue, Chicago, Illinois 60611, USA.

ISBN 0-582-98701-6 (Longman)

0-912289-72-4 (St James Press)

Published in association with the United Nations Association of Great Britain and Northern Ireland

British Library Cataloguing in Publication Data

Allsebrook, Mary
Prototypes of peacemaking: the first forty years of the United Nations.
1. United Nations — Armed Forces — History 2. Security, International — History — 20th century
I. Title
341.5'8 JX1981.P7
ISBN 0-582-98701-6

Typeset by Tradeset Photosetting
Printed by Butler & Tanner Ltd.

CONTENTS

LIST OF ABBREVIATIONS

ECOSOC	Economic and Social Council
FAO	Food and Agriculture Organization
GA	UN General Assembly
HR	Human Rights
ICJ	International Court of Justice
ILO	International Labour Organization
IMF	International Monetary Fund
OAS	Organization of American States
OAU	Organization of African Unity
PLO	Palestine Liberation Organization
SC	UN Security Council
S-G	UN Secretary-General
SWAPO	South West Africa People's Organization
TC	UN Trusteeship Council
UNDOF	UN Disengagement Observer Force
UNEF	UN Emergency Force
UNFICYP	UN Peacekeeping Force in Cyprus
UNHCR	UN High Commissioner for Refugees
UNICEF	UN Children's Fund
UNIFIL	UN Interim Force in Lebanon
UNRWA	UN Relief and Works Agency for Palestine Refugees in the Near East
UNTAG	UN Transition Assistance Group
UNTSO	UN Truce Supervision Organization in Palestine
WHO	World Health Organization

UN Secretaries-General, 1945–85

Trygve Lie	1 Feb. 1946 to 10 April 1953 (tendered resignation 10 Nov. 1952)
Dag Hammarskjöld	10 April 1953 to 17 Sept. 1961 (killed in plane crash)
U Thant	3 Nov. 1961 to 31 Dec. 1971
Kurt Waldheim	1 Jan. 1972 to 31 Dec. 1981
Javier Pérez de Cuéllar	1 Jan. 1982

PREFACE

An earlier version of this compilation first appeared in duplicated form in 1974 and was well received at the time by a necessarily limited audience. At the suggestion of a number of people I have now updated and expanded the original work to cover the first four decades of the UN's efforts in the field of peacemaking.

In gathering material for the present book I have been greatly assisted by the UN Information Centre in London, whose weekly summaries, special reports and press releases have proved invaluable. Other important sources have included the monthly *UN Chronicle, Everyone's* (formerly *Everyman's) United Nations* and other material published by the UN Department of Public Information as well as the press releases and background information issued for the International Court of Justice. (A select bibliography of relevant published works is given at the end of this book.)

I am grateful for the encouragement and help I have received from my family and various individuals and also for the support given by the United Nations Association of Great Britain and Northern Ireland (see page x). I should stress that any errors of omission or commission in the book are entirely my responsibility, as are the views expressed in the Introduction on what steps might be taken to improve the UN's peacemaking capabilities.

Prototypes of Peacemaking is intended to be a contribution to the UN's International Year of Peace and is dedicated to peacemakers everywhere.

MA
May 1986

About the author
Mary Allsebrook, a US citizen who has lived in Britain for many years, is a former Central European correspondent of the *Washington Post* and from 1977 to 1984 covered United Nations affairs for the *Annual Register*. She has held several offices within the UK UNA and contributes a regular column to its publication *New World*.

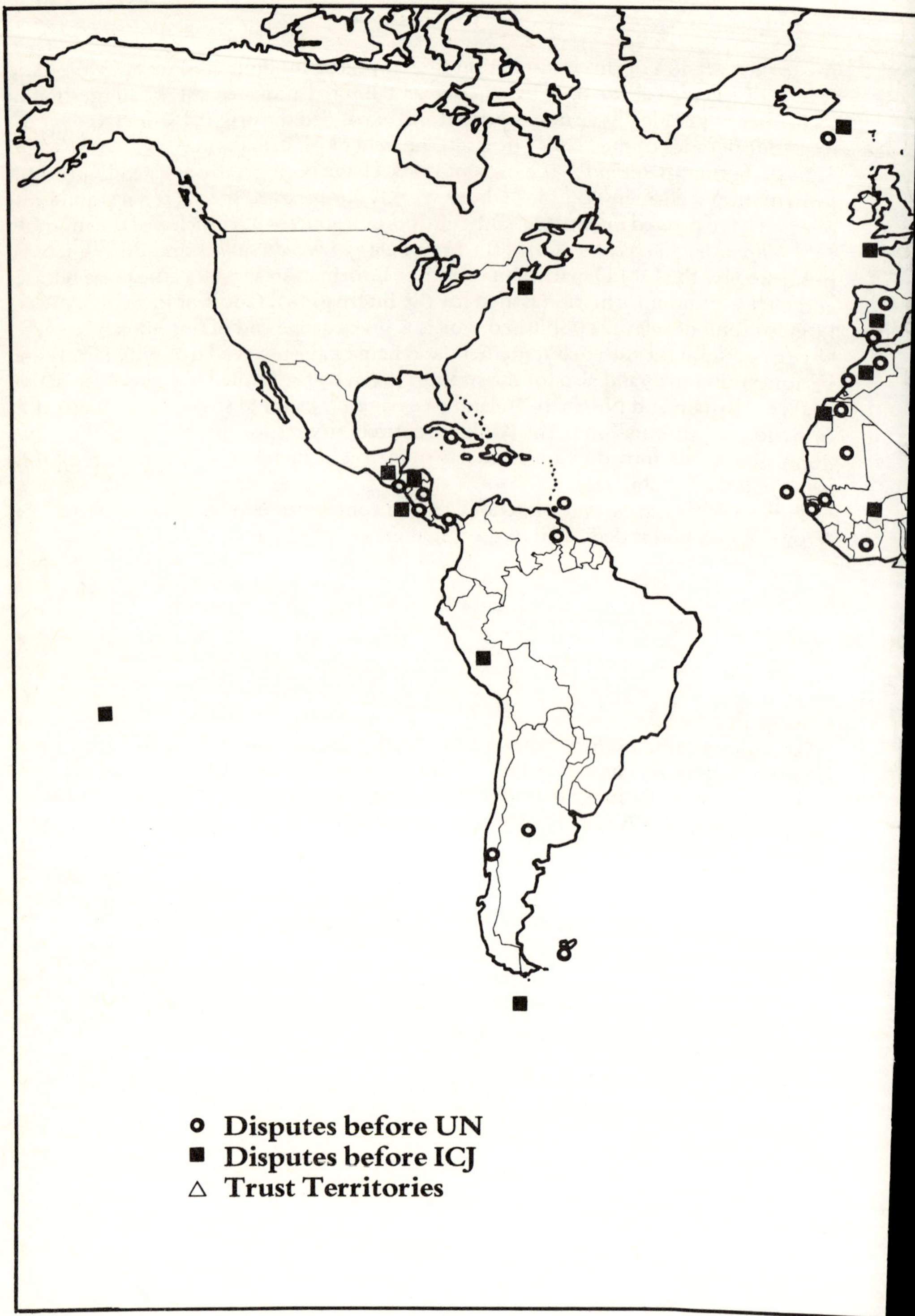
Disputes before UN
Disputes before ICJ
Trust Territories

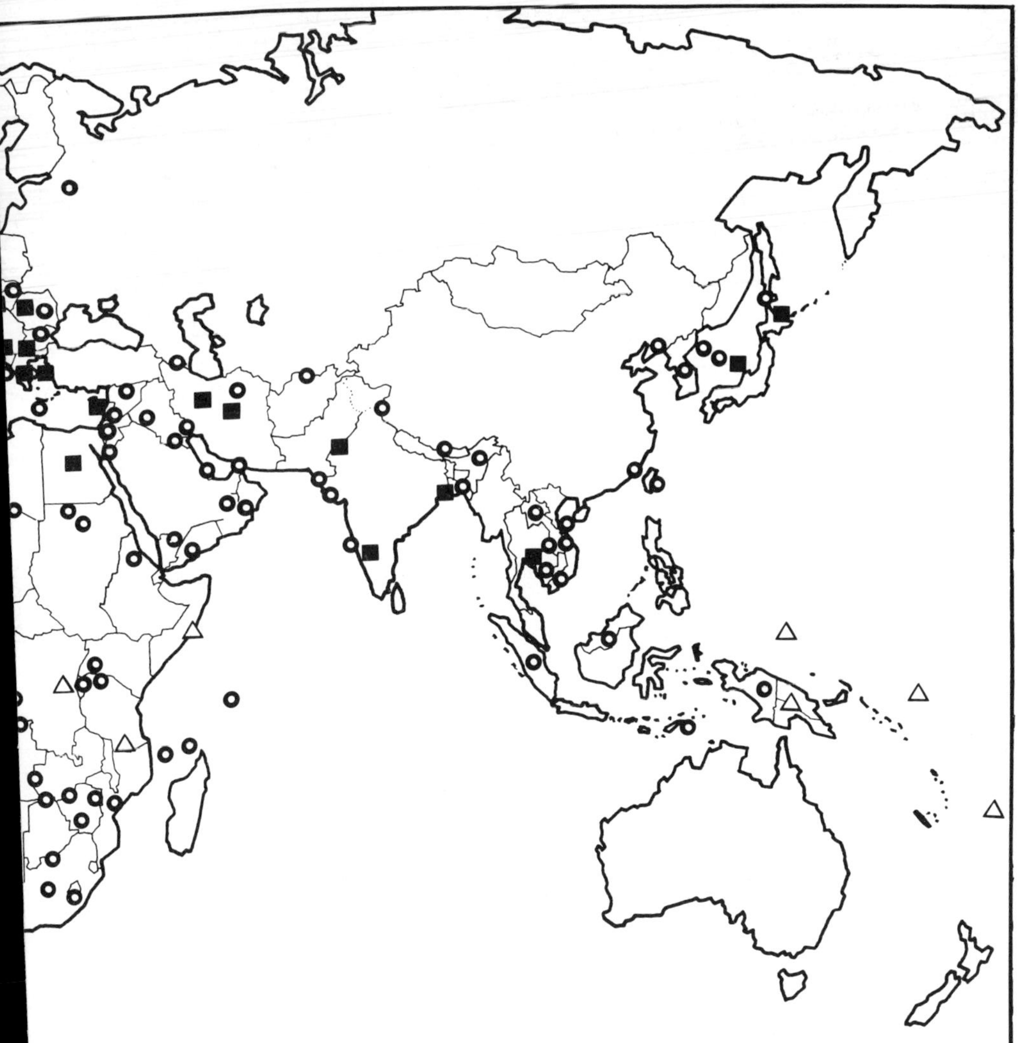

Map of UN and ICJ cases

UNITED NATIONS ASSOCIATION OF GREAT BRITAIN AND NORTHERN IRELAND

Chairperson: David Ennals
Director: Malcolm Harper
Deputy Director: Myriel Davies

The United Nations Association (UNA) exists to promote a further understanding of the potential and actual roles of the United Nations in global affairs, how it seeks to operate and where successes can be built upon and failures assessed. It argues for a developing of the UN's role in international life and for reforms in those areas where its performance needs to be strengthened.

To achieve these aims it campaigns to influence British foreign policy in favour of fuller use and support of the UN's machinery for conflict resolution, peacekeeping, refugee work, improving human rights standards, economic and social development, environmental care and all the other activities in which the UN becomes so deeply involved. By behaving thus the UNA believes that the member states could help to make the world safer and more just for *all* and not only for the lucky few.

UNAs exist in over 60 countries and the UK Association tries to strengthen practical international understanding through active membership of the World Federation of UNAs and through direct links with UNAs in particular countries.

The UNA's educational work, both inside schools and colleges and outside the formal structures, seeks to increase understanding of the UN and its comprehensive role in global life. And its International Service volunteers work with some of the world's poorest communities and assist them practically in their efforts to achieve their emancipation from poverty and injustice.

In short, the UNA seeks to develop in practice the ideals of the UN Charter of a just world for everyone.

For a UNA publications list and membership form, contact:

UNA
3 Whitehall Court
LONDON
SW1A 2EL (tel. 01-930-2931)

FOREWORD

*By Lord Caradon**

Mary Allsebrook has given us an important book. It is a unique record and a searching challenge. By taking major international disputes in the forty years of the history of the United Nations, summarising the source of each dispute and the action taken to deal with it, by reviewing the record of the past, the book provides invaluable guidance for the future.

The story told provides both a justification of the principles of the United Nations Charter and some explanation of the failure in so many instances to give them practical effect.

Amongst most of the 159 UN member states there is still faith in the peacemaking capacity of the United Nations. It is therefore of vital and urgent concern to study the detailed record, and to search for solutions where settlement of disputes has so far been unsuccessful.

The main obstacle to international agreement in the past forty years has been the antagonism between the two major powers. In the early years of the United Nations the Soviet Union often used the veto in the Security Council to prevent effective action. In recent years the United States has taken over the lead in the use of the obstructive veto, particularly on the Middle East.

There were hopes that the negative policies of the two super-powers would diminish after the apparently cordial meeting between Reagan and Gorbachev in Geneva November 1985; but these hopes have not been sustained by subsequent statements and attitudes.

And now it cannot be denied that the outlook for successful international agreement at the United Nations is more discouraging than ever, with the United States indicating its opposition to effective UN action in UNESCO and on such questions as the Law of the Sea, as well as making drastic and severely damaging reductions in its financial contributions to the United Nations.

But while not underrating the serious situation now existing, mainly due to the new US opposition, the record in this book does lead us to remember and to welcome a number of encouraging factors. Though the super powers may falter, most of the rest maintain their faith and confidence. For instance, in the long and complicated discussions on the Law of the Sea it was the delegates from the small countries, particularly Malta, Sri Lanka and Singapore, who made the most constructive contribution. Another encouraging factor is the great readiness of the Secretary-General to join in peacemaking endeavours by himself giving a lead, as he has been doing in the discussions on Cyprus. The general membership is much more in support of a progressive Secretary-General rather than are the reactionary major members.

---

*Lord (Hugh) Caradon, PC, GCMG, KCVO, OBE, had a distinguished career in the British Colonial Service before being appointed UK permanent representative to the United Nations in 1964, with the unprecedented rank of minister of state for foreign affairs (in Harold Wilson's first Labour government). He held that post until 1970, during which period he achieved the major success, referred to in this Foreword, of securing the unanimous adoption by the UN Security Council in 1967 of Resolution 242 on the Arab-Israeli conflict.

Let me go back some way in my own experience to sustain my hopes for the future. After the 1967 Middle East war we needed a working plan for the future, and after much hard negotiating work I, as British Ambassador at the United Nations, thought I had won the nine votes necessary for the important Security Council Resolution 242. I went down to the Council that Monday morning expecting to maintain my resolution against Soviet opposition. When I arrived at the Council the Soviet special representative, Mr Kuznetsov, said that he wanted to see me urgently alone. We went into a small room by the Security Council and he said to me at once: "I want you to give me two days." I hesitated. I did not know what he wanted to do in the two days. I anxiously wondered what my Government, and what my delegation, would say. But I knew Mr Kuznetsov well and I trusted him as he trusted me. I went back into the Council and asked for a postponement of the vote till the following Wednesday. I do not forget the moment on that Wednesday morning when I turned to my right and to my delight I saw Mr Kuznetsov with his finger raised voting for the British resolution, thus making it unanimous.

I tell the story to show that in spite of all disappointments and delays and suspicions it is possible, where there are men of courage and good will like Mr Kuznetsov, to get results, to get agreement, to get success.

I claim to be the only representative at the United Nations who ever spoke in verse in the Security Council. Here is the verse I used in the Council after that unanimous vote in 1967:

When prospects are dark and hopes are dim
We know that we must send for him.
When storms and tempests fill the sky
'Bring on Kuznetsov!' is the cry.
He comes like a dove from the communist ark
And light appears where all was dark.
His coming quickly turns the tide
The propaganda floods subside
And now that he has changed the weather
Lion and lamb can vote together.
God bless the Russian delegation.
I waive consecutive translation.

I hope that that old story will give us some encouragement as we study the few successes and the many disappointments which this book presents.

Hugh Caradon
May 1986

INTRODUCTION

This compilation of cases considered in the United Nations, including the International Court of Justice, from 1945 to 1985, is a review of the past, but its purpose is for the future. Often it is claimed the UN has a good record in the humanitarian and economic fields, but a poor one in the political. It was to analyse why the UN appeared not to succeed in settling disputes and to investigate how it could be made more effective that this study was undertaken, so that others can use it for the same purpose. It does not cover efforts outside of the UN to settle the disputes, or the interaction of other events. These were often vital to the course of the dispute; but this study is intended as a reference source of UN involvement.

The prime purpose of the UN is 'to maintain international peace and security'. Consideration of disputes is an important factor of this goal. It is often called 'peacemaking', and will be termed that here, despite the confusions that can arise. Firstly, it is necessary to clarify this use of the term 'peacemaking'. It is the resolution of a dispute, but in its broadest sense; it does not presuppose that hostilities have occurred. In fact, the most successful settlement is usually the one initiated when the dispute is in its infancy before a conflict breaks out, just as industrial peace can best be negotiated before there is a strike. In this sense 'peacemaking' includes the process of airing, good offices and, when relevant, depends on holding the ring with peacekeeping operations.

Taking this broad view of peacemaking means that peacekeeping, or policing – necessary *after* hostilities or possibly if hostilities are threatened – is complementary to peacemaking, but not necessary to it. In many cases peacemaking forestalls a conflict.

This concept – that peacemaking can take place as soon as a dispute arises and in its very early stages – changes the past perceived political record of the UN, and the whole direction that peacemaking should take. Considering the past, one thinks of the wars in the Middle East, between India and Pakistan and the conflict in Cyprus, and judges the UN's efforts as unsuccessful: but placed in the context of well over 200 cases the picture changes. In this broad, practical sense even the airing of a dispute has a peacemaking function.

More important than a justification of the UN's role is the fact that this approach provides lessons in the success of settlements rather than examples of its failures. Again, as in the case of industrial disputes, it is the settlements that are reached without a strike – or in the case of international disputes without war – from which one can learn the most.

Coverage of the book

This compilation includes virtually all the cases that have gone to the UN over forty years, whether as part of a struggle for independence, an insult to sovereignty or a marauding aeroplane. All these have the seeds of a potential conflict, as the assassination at Sarajevo in 1914 should remind us. However, there are exceptions, falling into three main categories:

(1) The score of incidents between Israelis and Arabs are not given separately; rather, the major conflicts of which they have been a part are covered. (Nothing could settle the septic incident which did not cure the malignant dispute.)

(2) The many complaints to the Secretary-General recording alleged misdemeanours but without a request for action are not covered.

(3) Likewise omitted are the occasions when the UN has, on request, sent

observers to oversee elections in non-self-governing territories achieving independence, provided there has been no particular dispute. (It is, of course, recognised that a struggle for independence may be the prelude to a conflict, such as in the Western Sahara.)

All cases of Trust Territories have been included, because the UN was given a special role in their achievement of self-determination. Ten of the former Trust Territories have completed their right of choice without having to resort to liberation struggles; only Micronesia remains. These are examples of involving the UN early, in a continuing role, when it provided solutions to potentially controversial situations such as Togoland and the Cameroons.

The listing of continuing or current cases has been done alphabetically; past ones are listed in the year with which they are most likely to be associated rather than the year in which they were first brought to the UN. This, of course, is open to question. The reason for a chronological order is twofold. It makes it possible to trace (i) changes in the type of cases which arose, i.e. post-war, cold war, colonial etc., and (ii) changes in the method of treating cases. It is evident that there was, in the early days, imaginative use of commissions, observers, mediators, even constitutional advisers. There followed a period when mediators were superseded by special or personal representatives, after Dr Galo Plaza was charged by Turkey with exceeding his mandate in offering a basis for settlement negotiations in Cyprus. The more informal term allows greater scope and is not subject to legalistic construction.

In the 1970s there was a return to Security Council missions, which the USSR considers a constitutional application of the Charter. In recent years there has also been frequent use of the good offices of the Secretary-General because they are informal, private and not open to great-power involvement. As they are private it is hard to learn how often the Secretary-General has exercised his 'quiet diplomacy' or 'preventive diplomacy' as it is often called. But the instances that have been publicised are included here. This is a most valuable and growing form of peacemaking, although it can be misused by the Security Council to avoid its own responsibilities.

Another development is the willingness of the General Assembly to take up matters of human rights, even if they border on a country's domestic jurisdiction, while the Security Council is reluctant to do so. This reflects the General Assembly's tendency to become a forum for world opinion and a pressure body for a world conscience. But in asking much of nationalistic states General Assembly resolutions sometimes risk being counter-productive.

Since this compilation is aimed at the future as a basis for investigating whether machinery can be devised to improve the effectiveness of the UN, it is necessary to be able to weed out the type of cases which are unlikely to arise again. For this reason, under the column headed *Case*, there sometimes appears the classification post-war, colonial, ex-colonial or semi-colonial. In a largely post-colonial political world, it is not likely that many such cases will recur, which eliminates some of the problems that have arisen in the past. Future disputes will probably concern coups d'état and subversion supported from outside, human rights, religious and political ideologies, sea and fishing boundaries, economic colonialism and environmental problems.

Under the column headed *UN bodies involved* there has been a question of whether to list the different missions, representatives or organisations beside their authorising or administrative body. Here they have been usually listed after the authorising body, although the Secretary-General is often charged with choosing the people to be involved and directing them. Sometimes the Security Council or General

Assembly may give a blanket authorisation leaving it to the Secretary-General to interpret. In such cases a relief organisation or other UN body may appear, associated with the Secretary-General. The positions of personal and special representatives are often blurred and inter-changeable.

Lessons from the past

Many times one hears the assertion: 'There is nothing wrong with the UN, it is the member states which are at fault.' This is frequently true. The UN has often been used for confrontation, not for conciliation. Members have treated the UN as a propaganda platform for nationalistic justification. Rhetorical, counter-productive denunciations came into fashion with the 'cold war' and were adopted periodically by many countries or groups of countries in the following years. Action has been blocked by vetoes, or restricted to humanitarian efforts, because the political problem is claimed to be a domestic one, not subject to UN interference. This compilation reveals such misuse to a considerable degree.

Most of these disputes are political rather than legal, and therefore not appropriate for the International Court of Justice (ICJ). If however, the ICJ should become transformed to deal with elements of 'human rights' this would make a profound difference. African countries know well that none of them would have gained their right to independence on a Court decision, and they are inclined to regard the ICJ as a bulwark of archaic treaties and of the status quo. At present, parties involved in disputes, either international or industrial, prefer negotiations over which they have control to formal methods of arbitration or mediation, rather than although they may be glad of informal conciliation and good offices.

The Security Council has 'the primary responsibility for the maintenance of international peace and security' under the Charter. Yet there is a great dilemma because it is expected to declare guilt in the case of a misdemeanour and then to conciliate. This puts a premium on propaganda and scoring points. Surely, the Council should avoid ascribing guilt if it is to help solve a dispute? If called for, it might establish a breach of the Charter rather than aggression against a member. This would be difficult to introduce in view of past history and expectations. For example, Iran has boycotted the Council because it did not condemn Iraq for aggression and believes it to be biased in Iraq's favour.

As a start the Security Council might ask parties involved in a dispute what they have done to settle it. This should emphasise the aim of conciliation instead of confrontation. True, it might be completely futile to pose this question in long-term, obstinate disputes, but it could be used discreetly at the beginning of and during relatively new ones. It follows that the Council should use sub-committees to consider reports on efforts to resolve disputes and even act as conciliators when possible, as part of crisis management.

The Security Council should seriously attempt some form of early warning or crisis anticipation system. Prime ministers or foreign ministers should take part in Private Council meetings periodically to do this and to identify difficult situations. They should consider whether as a body or as individual states they could forestall a dispute. This would provide an opportunity to review issues and resolve misunderstandings not under conditions of crisis or unwarranted expectations.

The Secretary-General might propose an agenda and submit a report, as an essential component of his responsibilities under Article 99 of the Charter. But for this he would need a special group in the Secretariat to provide information, and UN 'ambassadors' in trouble-spot regions. Such meetings would be far more effective if, or when, East-West relations have matured from confrontation to acceptance of co-existence; but even now they might provide constructive dialogue and encourage detente. The Council surely needs to follow crisis anticipation with more crisis management through possible use of missions, rapporteurs and fact-finding sources for itself, the Secretary-General and the General Assembly.

These are essentially procedural matters not subject to veto. The Council should adhere strictly to Article 27 (3) of the Charter, which provides that 'in decisions under Chapter VI [concerning the pacific settlement of disputes] and under paragraph 3 of Article 52, a party to a dispute shall abstain from voting'. This should prevent permanent members involved from vetoing any resolutions for the settlement of a dispute. A resolution for a ceasefire, based on withdrawal to recognized international boundaries, is a prerequisite to a settlement, provided it is not mandatory under the stringent Chapter VII on acts of aggression. However, a Security Council resolution for a ceasefire is no guarantee of its implementation, as shown in the Lebanon. From the number of cases which refer to past unfulfilled resolutions, it seems that the Council must also devise means for monitoring and increasing the implementation of its policy decisions.

After forty years of ad hoc methods has the time not come for a settlement service within the Secretariat for early, informal use by parties seeking a 'peaceful means of their own choice' (Article 33) to resolve their differences? At present a heavy load rests on the Secretary-General. He could always be called on if others fail. The Security Council has shifted many disputes onto his shoulders using his good offices, and he should be given more institutional support for this work. Often a case seems to smoulder on until the next crisis as he concentrates on a more immediately urgent one, when continuing efforts for a solution during the simmering period would have a greater chance of success than during the ensuing crisis. Is there not a need, and is it not time, for there to be a fully fledged office dealing with negotiations on disputes, which can sustain persuasion at the appropriate time in such problems as Cyprus?

Several of the above suggestions are similar to ones proposed by the Secretary-General and in the Manila Declaration on the Peaceful Settlement of International Disputes adopted by the UN General Assembly in 1982. The Security Council has been considering ways to improve its effectiveness and the General Assembly's 'Special Committee on the Charter of the UN and on the Strengthening of the Role of the Organisation' has discussed many proposals and is initiating a handbook on methods for settlement. Examination of the disputes in this compilation should prompt other suggestions on how to make the UN more effective.

The idealistic aspirations of the UN Charter need to be bolstered by specific procedures, not ones based on traditional theories of settlement methods, but on those currently favoured and the experience of these forty years and over 200 cases.

CASES CONSIDERED BY THE UNITED NATIONS

Note: The first sentence of each case attempts an appraisal, the remainder is a factual account.

Date	*Case*	*Nature*	*UN bodies involved*
1946	Iran, USSR (post-war)	Alleged interference of Russian troops remaining in Iran after war	SC

Pressure in the SC contributed to Russian troop withdrawals from Iran stationed in north during the war to facilitate movement of western supplies to USSR. On 19 Jan. 1946 Iran charged Russians with interfering in Iranian affairs. SC noted parties willing to negotiate and asked to be informed of results. Iran again raised dispute in SC, USSR claimed understanding reached. Russian troop withdrawals completed May 1946.

Date	*Case*	*Nature*	*UN bodies involved*
1946	Syria, Lebanon (post-war)	Call for British and French troop withdrawal	SC

Airing in the SC probably ensured against delay of French and British withdrawal from Syria and Lebanon. Continued presence of their troops following the war, raised in SC 4 Feb. 1946. Resolution expressing confidence troops would be withdrawn vetoed by USSR as not going far enough, but UK and France stated they would comply. Withdrawal completed by end of 1946.

Date	*Case*	*Nature*	*UN bodies involved*
1946	Spanish question	Attempt to outlaw Franco regime	SC (subcommittee) GA

Attempt to use UN to express general political disapproval of a regime. GA resolution 9 Feb. 1946 had the effect of precluding Franco's Spain from admission to UN. In April 1946 Poland asked SC to declare Franco's regime a danger to peace and to call on UN members to break off diplomatic relations. SC subcommittee of five reported 6 June that regime a 'potential' menace to peace. USSR vetoed resolution embodying subcommittee's views that GA recommend severance of diplomatic relations unless regime withdrawn and political freedom assured, because USSR considered regime an 'existing' not 'potential' threat and SC (not GA) should recommend severance of relations. GA recommended 12 Dec. 1946 regime should be barred from UN agencies, UN members should recall their diplomatic representatives, and SC should consider ways of remedying situation. GA considered question several times and on 4 Nov. 1950 revoked its recommendations, deciding exchanges of diplomats did not involve approval, and as UN agencies were largely technical (not political) they should determine whether Spain should join. Spain admitted to UN 14 Dec. 1955.

Date	*Case*	*Nature*	*UN bodies involved*
1947 (1947–49)	Corfu Channel	UK alleged Albania responsible for damaging ships by mines in Corfu Channel	SC (subcommittee), ICJ

SC failed to agree on dispute because of Cold War involvement, ICJ gave judgment, but not implemented. On 10 Jan. 1947 UK brought case to SC of damage to two destroyers with loss of life, by mines in Corfu Channel. SC three-member subcommittee reported findings, but one member – Poland – did not agree Albania responsible. USSR vetoed resolution attributing responsibility to Albania. In April 1947 SC recommended reference to ICJ. Two years later ICJ found Albania responsible for explosions, but that UK had violated Albania's sovereignty by its subsequent mine-sweeping. ICJ assessed compensation due to UK, but not paid.

Date	*Case*	*Nature*	*UN bodies involved*
1947	Egypt, UK (colonial)	Call for withdrawal of British troops and administration from Sudan	SC

Airing in SC, but no action, resolved by Anglo-Egyptian Agreement of 1953 negotiated outside UN. Egypt sought UK troop withdrawals from Egypt and Sudan, and end to UK's administration of Sudan – problem of legal (Treaty of 1936) claims vs. political claims. In August and September 1947 SC considered, but rejected, proposals for negotiations with report to SC.

Date	*Case*	*Nature*	*UN bodies involved*
1947 (1946–49)	Indonesia (post-war and colonial)	Alleged British troop action, followed by hostilities between Netherlands and Indonesia leading to independence	SC (Consular Commission at Batavia, Good Offices Committee later Commission for Indonesia, Military Observers), GA

UN pressed for end to hostilities over Indonesian independence, helped parties to restore peace and arrange transfer of sovereignty.

On 21 Jan. 1946 the Ukrainian SSR alleged in the SC that British and Japanese troops (left over from war) were taking action against Indonesians and proposed investigation commission, but this rejected and matter dropped.

On 30 July 1947 Australia and India brought up fighting between Netherlands and Indonesia in the SC. The SC pressed for a ceasefire between them in August 1947, asked for joint reports from consuls of SC members in Batavia, established a three-member Good Offices Committee of the SC with Frank Graham as chairman, which helped achieve the Renville Agreements as a basis for settlement on 17 and 19 Jan. 1948. The Netherlands repudiated agreements 18 Dec. 1948 and restarted military operations. On 24 December SC urged end to hostilities and release of Indonesian president and other political prisoners by the Dutch, which they did two months later. SC recommended on 28 Jan. 1949 a federal independent state, elections, and transfer of sovereignty. UN Commission for Indonesia (formerly Committee of Good Offices) arranged meetings of two delegations during 14 April – 1 Aug. 1949, helping parties to restore peace, to implement SC resolution, and to agree on Round Table Conference. Dutch troops evacuated in presence of UN military observers. UN Commission for Indonesia assisted preparations for Round Table Conference at the Hague during 23 Aug. – 2 Nov. 1949, at which it was represented. Conference arranged transfer of sovereignty and Indonesia became independent on 27 Dec. 1949. UN Commission for Indonesia observed implementation of Hague agreements until 6 April 1951.

Date	*Case*	*Nature*	*UN bodies involved*
1948 (1947–55)	Palestine (ex-colonial)	Future of Palestine after League mandate administered by Britain	SC (Truce Commission for Palestine, UN Truce Supervision Organisation, Acting Mediator), GA (Special Committee on Palestine, UN Palestine Commission, Conciliation Commission, Mediator, TC, UN Relief for Palestine Refugees, UN Relief and Works Agency, Mixed Armistice Commissions), S-G

UN efforts to solve conflict over birth of Israel failed because of attitude of Arabs and Israelis. UN Acting Mediator assisted negotiations for Armistice Agreements in 1949.

At the UK's request a special session of GA met during 28 April – 15 May 1947 and it set up Special Committee on Palestine which recommended, and on 29 Nov. 1947 GA adopted, majority plan for partition into Arab and Jewish states with international regime in Jerusalem, all three to be part of an economic union. GA established UN Palestine Commission to implement its recommendations and SC asked to assist in this. On 17 April SC called for truce and on 23 April established a Supervisory Truce Commission for Palestine with representatives of SC members having consular services in Jerusalem. A special session of the Assembly approved TC recommendations for Jerusalem and on 14 May decided to appoint a mediator in place of the Palestine Commission – to promote a settlement and to cooperate with the SC's Truce Commission, which was provided with military observers – later known as the UN Truce Supervision Organisation (UNTSO). Count Bernadotte chosen as mediator.

On 14 May 1948 British mandate expired and Israel established. The following day Arabs attacked (the Arab Higher Committee had rejected the partition plan from the start). SC obtained a four-week truce from 11 June 1948, but Arabs would not renew it. SC *ordered* a ceasefire and this was accepted. UN mediator, Count

Bernadotte, assassinated in Israeli sector on 17 Sept. 1948 and succeeded by Ralph Bunche. Large scale fighting renewed in October 1948; SC called repeatedly for ceasefire. On 11 Dec. 1948 GA established a Conciliation Commission to try to achieve final settlement along specified lines. Acting mediator's negotiations resulted in Armistice Agreements between Israel and Egypt, Lebanon, Jordan and Syria separately in 1949, which established Armistice Commissions to see to their implementation. But behaviour of parties caused their break-down. SC resolution 11 Aug. 1949 urged negotiation and relieved mediator of further responsibility. In June 1950 TC reported Israel and Jordan would not cooperate on Statute for Jerusalem. UN Palestine Commission continued efforts to implement GA's resolutions, but parties concerned made this impossible. In following years incidents occurred, too numerous to mention, requiring SC consideration, and work continued for the military observers of the UN Truce Supervision Organisation and for the UN Relief and Works Agency to alleviate the plight of Arab refugees.

Date	*Case*	*Nature*	*UN bodies involved*
1948	Junagadh (ex-colonial)	Dispute with India over annexation	SC (UN Commission for India and Pakistan)

No UN action in case arising from Indian independence and the possibility for Indian state to accede to Pakistan or India, or theoretically to become independent. Muslim ruler announced accession to Pakistan, but Hindu subjects opposed this; India invaded, plebiscite favoured India, which annexed state. SC considered matter January – May 1948; in June SC referred it to UN Commission for India and Pakistan dealing with Kashmir.

Date	*Case*	*Nature*	*UN bodies involved*
1948	Czechoslovakia	Charge that USSR violated Czech independence during coup	SC

Part of Cold War, SC action vetoed. SC considered request from Chile March 1948 on behalf of Czech representative at UN for an investigation into alleged violation of Czechoslovakia's independence, charged USSR with threatening use of force and participating in the coup of 22 Feb. 1948. But Czechoslovakia declined invitation to take part and USSR vetoed proposal for subcommittee to receive evidence.

Date	*Case*	*Nature*	*UN bodies involved*
1948	Hyderabad (ex-colonial)	Dispute with India over independence	SC

No UN action in case arising when India became independent and the state of Hyderabad could choose to accede to India or theoretically be independent. Hyderabad called attention of SC to danger of invasion and blockade from India on 21 Aug. 1948. On 13 September hostilities reported to SC, which met and heard

India's claim that Hyderabad was not a state, therefore could not bring up question, and that it (India) had acted against terror of private armies. Nizam of Hyderabad withdrew case in telegrams of 20 and 22 Sept. 1948, although SC continued to discuss it. State incorporated into India January 1950.

Date	*Case*	*Nature*	*UN bodies involved*
1948–49	Berlin (post-war)	Soviet blockade	SC, SC Pres. (Technical Committee on Berlin Currency and Trade) GA Pres., S-G

Part of Cold War, SC action vetoed. Restrictions on communications with Berlin started March 1948, raised at UN 29 Sept. 1948. SC draft resolution for end to Berlin blockade and meeting on unification of currency vetoed by USSR, despite Art. 27 (3), which would seem to require USSR to abstain. Technical Currency and Trade Committee set up by Pres. of SC, unable to reach an acceptable solution. GA Pres. and S-G appealed to powers to solve question, offer of 'good offices'. Agreeement, to remove all restrictions on 12 May 1949, reached through informal conversations at UN by four occupying powers, S-G was asked to convey this to SC.

Date	*Case*	*Nature*	*UN bodies involved*
1948 (1946–54)	Greece	Communist complaints; external aid to Greek guerrillas	SC (Commission of Investigation), GA (Special Committee on the Balkans – UNSCOB, two conciliation committees, Peace Observation Commission and its Balkan subcommission with Observers), S-G

UN involvement discouraged encroachments and helped preserve Greek territorial integrity.

USSR brought presence of British troops in Greece before SC (21 Jan. 1946), alleging that this was interference in Greece's internal affairs. This was noted and matter considered closed.

In August 1946 Ukrainian SSR complained that Greek policies a threat to peace. Greece denied this and alleged Albania provoked border incidents. In September Albania charged border violations by Greek soldiers.

On 3 Dec. 1946 SC requested by Greece to consider situation on northern borders involving aid to Greek guerrillas. SC established a Committee of Investigation to go into border violations and make proposals to prevent repetition (19 Dec. 1946). Its recommendations failed to be adopted. GA called on Albania, Bulgaria and

Yugoslavia to do nothing to help guerrillas and for them, together with Greece, to cooperate in settling their dispute. It established a UN Special Committe on the Balkans (UNSCOB) to help the governments in carrying through its recommendations. Several GA resolutions in 1948 aimed at persuading parties to settle dispute. GA First Committee appointed two conciliation committees, reported failure. GA resolution 18 Nov. 1949 that the active help to Greek guerrillas was contrary to Charter. UNSCOB recommended UN vigilance over Balkans, so GA established in its place (7 Dec. 1951), a Balkan sub-commission of the Peace Observation Commission to report on Greece's northern frontiers, this continued until 1954 (the only instance when the Peace Observation Commission was used). USSR used veto six times on Greek question.

In 1948 UNSCOB reported that 25 000 Greek children had been taken across the northern borders. GA repeatedly tried to get their return and set up a standing committee. The S-G, on instruction of the GA, elicited help from Red Cross. Yugoslavia repatriated a number of children, but not the other countries.

Date	*Case*	*Nature*	*UN bodies involved*
1948 (1947–64)	India, Pakistan (ex-colonial)	Military dispute over Kashmir	SC (Commission for India and Pakistan – UNCIP, Military Observer Group for India and Pakistan – UNMOGIP, Plebiscite Administrator, two UN Representatives)

UN efforts to settle problem of Kashmir stalled by disputants, observers helped keep the ceasefire.

Kashmir, an Indian princedom, with theoretical choice between independence or to accede to India or Pakistan. Muslim uprising in 1947 supported by tribesmen from Pakistan. Hindu ruler appealed to India and signed accession with understanding to be referred to people when order restored. On 1 Jan. 1948 India alleged that Pakistan was assisting invasion. Pakistan charged India with unlawful occupation of Kashmir. SC established (20 January) a UN Commission for India and Pakistan (UNCIP) to investigate and mediate, and on 21 April SC recommended measures to halt hostilities, to create conditions for a plebiscite and to provide observers. The UNCIP proposed on 13 Aug. 1948 the basis for a truce and plebiscite, which was endorsed by SC. Ceasefire effected only 1 Jan. 1949, supervised by observers of Commission (later the UN Military Observer Group for India and Pakistan – UNMOGIP). Plebiscite Administrator, Admiral Nimitz, appointed. Ceasefire line agreed 27 July 1949.

Despite repeated efforts the UNCIP was unable to get parties to accept its proposals for implementation of truce and conditions for plebiscite. Commission recommended an individual attempt to get agreement. On 17 Dec. 1949 SC asked its Pres., General McNaughton, to hold discussions, his proposals rejected by parties, but SC called on them to implement demilitarisation on basis of those proposals, and appointed UN representative, Sir Owen Dixon (followed by Frank Graham 21 Feb. 1951), to assist.

UN Representative continuously tried to arrange demilitarisation and preparations for a plebiscite under auspices of UN and submitted six reports up to 1958. Bilateral negotiations failed. SC considered problem in January and February 1957 and agreed to have its Pres., Dr. Jarring, explore proposals for settlement. He visited India and Pakistan during 14 March – 11 April, submitting report on 29 April 1957, concluding that despite deadlock parties still wanted peaceful solution. The SC then requested UN representative to make recommendations for method to achieve settlement, which he did in his report of 28 March 1958. These were accepted by Pakistan but rejected by India in 1958. Thereafter periodic discussions in SC were to no avail, but Observers (UNMOGIP) remained on ceasefire line.

Date	*Case*	*Nature*	*UN bodies involved*
1949 (1948–51)	Libya (post-war and ex-colonial)	Future government after liberation from Italy	GA (UN Commissioner, Council for Libya, UN Tribunal)

Leading role of UN in formation of new state. After Italian Peace Treaty France, UK, US and USSR failed to agree on disposition of Libya, so issue referred to GA in 1949. GA decided Libya should become independent by January 1952. UN Commissioner, Adrian Pelt, appointed, aided by a Council of 10, to help formulate constitution and prepare Libya for independence. GA resolution 17 Nov, 1950 outlined programme of political development for Libya and urged UN agencies and S-G to extend assistance. UN Tribunal set up which functioned until 1955 when the Italian-Libyan Mixed Arbitration Commission established. Libya achieved independence on 24 Dec. 1951.

Date	*Case*	*Nature*	*UN bodies involved*
1949 (1948–52)	Eritrea (post-war and ex-colonial)	Future government after liberation from Italy	GA (Commission for Eritrea, UN Commissioner, UN Tribunal)

UN active in determining future of Eritrea. After Italian Peace Treaty France, UK, US and USSR failed to agree on disposition of Eritrea, so issue referred to GA, which sent a Commission to investigate and report. One of the three proposals of the UN Commission for Eritrea adopted by the GA, 2 Dec. 1950, under which Eritrea was to become an autonomous unit federated with Ethiopia. A constitution was prepared by the UN Commissioner, E A Matienzo, and a representative assembly was elected which ratified the Federal Act and Constitution, effective as of 11 Sept. 1952. UN Tribunal was given jurisdiction (September 1952 – April 1954) over disposal of former Italian administration's properties.

Date	*Case*	*Nature*	*UN bodies involved*
1949–50	Bulgaria, Hungary, Romania (post-war)	Alleged violation of human rights and failure to implement Treaty	GA, ICJ

No compliance with UN efforts to defend human rights. Bolivia requested GA (16 March 1949) for study of legal proceedings against Cardinal Mindszenty in relation to human rights and freedoms. Australia added question of observance of religious and civil liberties in Bulgarian trials. GA resolution of concern 30 April 1949 noted efforts of signatories of peace treaties regarding accusations. Australia added Romania to list. Three states would not cooperate in designating representatives for treaty commissions to settle matter. GA asked ICJ for advisory opinion. On 30 March 1950 ICJ held case fell under terms of peace treaties and these states obligated to nominate representatives to treaty commissions for settlement of such disputes, which they would not do. GA condemned three governments (3 Nov. 1950) for refusal to fulfil obligations.

Date	*Case*	*Nature*	*UN bodies involved*
1950 (1949–52)	Taiwan, USSR	USSR charged with violating Sino-Soviet Treaty of Friendship	GA (Interim Committee)

Part of two-China problem; no solution. In September 1949 Nationalist China wanted GA to pass judgment on USSR for allegedly violating the Sino-Soviet Treaty of Friendship and Alliance of 14 Aug. 1945 and the Charter, specifically as regards Manchuria and Chinese Communists. On 8 Dec. 1949 GA called for respect for political independence and existing treaties and referred question to Interim Committee. GA resolution 1 Feb. 1952 that USSR had failed to carry out the Treaty.

Date	*Case*	*Nature*	*UN bodies involved*
1950 (1946–60)	South West Africa (colonial)	Question of international status of South West Africa	GA (Ad Hoc Committee on South West Africa, Good Offices Committee), ICJ

Effort of UN to get South Africa, which had held South West Africa as a mandate since 17 Dec. 1920, to administer it under an international system. The only case when a League Mandate did not become independent or come under the trusteeship system.

GA against South Africa's desire to incorporate South West Africa in 1946, favoured it becoming a trust territory, but South Africa refused and stopped submitting reports after 1949. GA asked ICJ for an advisory opinion on the status of South West Africa. ICJ opinion on 11 July 1950 – South Africa could not modify status without UN's consent and obliged to report and transmit petitions. But Charter did not require South Africa to put South West Africa under trusteeship. South Africa did not accept court's opinion.

GA established ad hoc committee to receive reports and petitions, but South Africa would not accept any UN supervision. In November 1953 GA set up

Committee on South West Africa (1954–61), to exercise former obligations of League of Nations and to negotiate. South Africa refused to cooperate. GA sought ICJ advisory opinions on procedure regarding South West Africa, handed down in 1955 and 1956. Committee on South West Africa has sent annual reports to GA on situation and GA has approved its recommendations. It concluded the administration of South West Africa was based on apartheid, which was contrary to the Mandate, Charter, Declaration of Human Rights, ICJ opinion and GA resolutions.

In 1956 GA asked the Committee to study possible actions of UN organs and states to get South Africa to fulfil obligations. GA established Good Offices Committee to discuss with South Africa way of giving South West Africa an international status. It met (1958) in Pretoria, but its proposals unacceptable to South Africa, and GA rejected consideration for partition of South West Africa.

As a result of views of Committee on South West Africa on legal measures open to states, Ethiopia and Liberia charged South Africa with violating mandate obligations in ICJ case of 1960–66.

Date	*Case*	*Nature*	*UN bodies involved*
1950 (1947–65)	Korea (ex-colonial and post-war)	Conflict over a national government, attack by North on South Korea	SC (Unified Command under US), GA (Temporary Commission on Korea, – Commission on Korea – UNCOK, Commission for Unification and Rehabilitation of Korea – UNCURK, Korean Reconstruction Agency – UNKRA, Cease-fire Group, Repatriation Commission, Good Offices and Additional Measures Committees), S-G

Problem, but not fighting, continued. Full-scale involvement of UN, yet no settlement because of attitude of parties.

Under Moscow Agreement of December 1945 US and USSR established a Joint Commission to set up a Provisional Korean Democratic Government. The Commission failed to agree so US took problem to GA September 1947. GA set up Temporary Commission on Korea (14 Nov. 1947) to help with elections and withdrawal of USSR occupation forces from North Korea and of Americans from South (occupied at time of Japanese surrender). Commission observed elections in South on 10 May 1948. They were not able to do so in North because of USSR's attitude. GA declared (12 Dec. 1948) Government of Republic of Korea established as lawful (and only such) government of Korea, replaced Temporary Commission by UN Commission on Korea (UNCOK) to unify the country and observe. It observed US troops withdrawn June 1949, but not the reported USSR's withdrawals in December 1948.

On 25 June 1950 UNCOK informed S-G of aggression by North Korea. The SC called for a ceasefire and withdrawal of North Korean forces to 38th parallel (USSR absent from SC from 13 Jan. – 1 Aug. 1950, so did not vote). Call unheeded. SC recommended members to assist South Korea (27 June 1950), US had ordered military support a few hours earlier. On 7 July SC asked states providing military forces to make them available for a unified command under US, sixteen countries participated.

In place of UNCOK, GA created (7 Oct. 1950) a Commission for Unification and Rehabilitation of Korea (UNCURK) to bring about an independent, democratic, unified Korea, which functioned until 28 Nov. 1973. In December 1950 GA heard complaint of aggression on UN forces by People's Republic of China, and it set up the Korean Reconstruction Agency for Relief and Rehabilitation (UNKRA) which operated until 1958, and a Ceasefire Group. On 1 Feb. 1951 it established an Additional Measures Committee and a Good Offices Committee. Progress towards settlement was unsatisfactory, GA recommended embargo of goods to mainland China and North Korea on 18 May 1951.

Armistice negotiations during 10 July 1951 – 27 July 1953 which established demarcation line and demilitarised area, set up a Military Armistice Commission and a Neutral Nations Supervisory Commission. The UN Repatriation Commission helped the exchange of prisoners. GA pressed for political conference envisaged by Armistice Agreement, one was held in Geneva from April to June 1954, but did not reach a solution. Spasmodic attempts to press for a settlement.

Date	*Case*	*Nature*	*UN bodies involved*
1950	People's Republic of China, Taiwan	Complaints of US aggression in defending Taiwan	SC

Airing salutary, part of two-China problem and repercussions of Korean war; no action. People's Republic of China cabled to SC on 24 Aug. 1950 that US troops in Taiwan constituted aggression against China. After ineffectual discussions SC decided, 29 September, to defer consideration until after mid-November and to invite representative of People's Republic of China to attend. On 27 Nov. 1950 SC agreed to consider this together with complaints of 'armed invasion of Taiwan' and 'aggression against the Republic of Korea'. It thus became immersed in the moves of the Korean War.

Date	*Case*	*Nature*	*UN bodies involved*
1950	People's Republic of China, US planes	Complaint of US bombing during Korean War	SC

Airing salutary, repercussion of Korean War; no action. Complaint of People's Republic of China in SC 28 Aug. and 24 Sept. 1950 that US planes had flown over Chinese territory and killed people. USSR vetoed US draft resolution for an investigation commission. US willing to pay compensation if impartial investigation substantiated charges.

Date	*Case*	*Nature*	*UN bodies involved*
1951–52	Anglo-Iranian Oil Co.	Iran's nationalisation of oil	SC, ICJ

No UN action, but airing provided essential relief. Iran nationalised oil industry 1 May 1951. Britain took matter to ICJ 26 May, but Iran denied competence of Court, and later of SC, claiming it a domestic matter. In July 1951 ICJ ordered Iran and company to do nothing to aggravate dispute or prejudice each other's rights. Iran seized refinery 27 September, UK took matter to SC. USSR and Yugoslavia opposed consideration. SC adjourned debate 19 October, until ICJ ruled on its competence. ICJ decided the Court had no jurisdiction on 22 July 1952.

Date	*Case*	*Nature*	*UN bodies involved*
1951	Yugoslavia	Claim USSR threatening its independence	GA

Airing of Yugoslavia's complaint (9 Nov. 1951) that USSR and its 'satellites' had been pressurising Yugoslavia for three years – threatening its independence and territorial integrity. USSR and others denied charge, but GA passed Yugoslav resolution 14 December that the eight states should settle their disputes in accordance with the Charter and other principles for international conduct. Relations gradually normalised.

Date	*Case*	*Nature*	*UN bodies involved*
1951–52	Germany (post-war)	Possibility of free elections and reunification	GA (Commission to investigate), S-G

Part of Cold War, effort to ascertain whether free elections in two zones of Germany and unification possible, stalled by East Germany. At request from France, UK and US, the GA decided (20 Dec. 1951) to create a commission to consider the possibilities. East Germany deemed this intervention in its domestic affairs. Commission concluded arrangements in West, but unable to contact authorities in Soviet zone.

Date	*Case*	*Nature*	*UN bodies involved*
1952–53	Korea, 'Germ Warfare'	To clear allegations of use of Germ Warfare by UN and US	SC, GA

Part of the Korean War confrontation, investigation blocked by USSR veto. Effort to clear UN and US of USSR allegations that they were using bacteriological weapons. UN Command had requested investigation by Red Cross Committee. US draft resolution of 25 June 1952 proposed in SC that governments concerned should cooperate with such a committee. USSR vetoed this and the subsequent draft resolution to conclude that, as those making the charges refused an investigation, it was to be presumed the charges were false. GA resolution 23 April 1953 to establish a commission of investigation if governments concerned accepted one. US, Japan and Republic of Korea agreed, but no others; so effort evaporated.

Date	*Case*	*Nature*	*UN bodies involved*
1952 (1946–62)	South Africa, India	Discrimination against people of Indian and Pakistani origin	GA (Good Offices Commission), S-G

Intransigence paralysed UN efforts. Legislative discrimination against people of Indian origin in South Africa (particularly Land Tenure and Representation Act) was raised in the GA 1946.

South Africa claimed it was a domestic matter under Art 2 (7) and proposed seeking advisory opinion from ICJ. GA held (8 Dec. 1946) treatment of Indians should accord with previous agreements between India and South Africa of 1927 and 1932, and with the Charter, asked for reports from both. Parties failed to discuss matter. On 14 May 1949 GA decided to ask India, Pakistan and South Africa to hold round table discussions. But attitude of parties defeated GA's repeated efforts for such a conference, and failing that, for an agreement on a commission to help the parties to negotiate, in 1950 and 1951.

GA established UN Good Offices Commission in December 1952 to assist parties in a solution in accordance with the Charter and Declaration of Human Rights. South Africa considered GA resolution unconstitutional and would not recognise Commission or allow it to visit, so it was unable to operate. As efforts to initiate direct negotiations proved fruitless, following the GA's instructions, the S-G designated a person, Amb. Luis de Faro Jr., to assist in settlement of dispute June 1955. But again South Africa declined to cooperate. GA continued to urge direct negotiations 1955–61, but South Africa disinclined. Case became submerged in apartheid problems after 1962.

Date	*Case*	*Nature*	*UN bodies involved*
1952 (1948–55)	Austrian Peace Treaty (post-war)	Need for Great Powers to establish peace	GA

Airing problem of persuading Great Powers to fulfil their pledges and agree on a peace treaty. GA urgently appealed to the Great Powers for a treaty 20 Dec. 1952, so occupation could be ended. USSR and others of its Block, claimed resolution invalid (Charter Act. 107). Austrian State Treaty signed 15 May 1955.

Date	*Case*	*Nature*	*UN bodies involved*
1953 (1951–55)	Morocco (colonial)	Independence from France	GA

Airing in GA from 1952 onwards may have increased pressure towards independence. GA urged negotiations 19 Dec. 1952. Matter not included on SC agenda in August 1953 despite efforts of Asian and African states. France objected to UN consideration on basis of Art. 2 (7). GA postponed further consideration 3 Dec. 1955 in view of the initiation of negotiations between France and Morocco. Independence achieved 2 March 1956.

Date	*Case*	*Nature*	*UN bodies involved*
1953–54	Burma	Evacuation of Kuomintang troops who fled from Mainland China	GA

Airing of Burmese complaint may have helped to get a large number of Kuomintang troops evacuated, who had crossed into Burma and refused to disarm or be interned. It was alleged they were supported by Taiwan. On 23 April 1953 GA deplored presence of foreign troops and their hostile acts, declared they must be disarmed and insisted on internment or evacuation. GA reaffirmed this view 4 Dec. 1953. On 29 Oct. 1954 GA noted that nearly 7000 troops had been evacuated, expressed its appreciation for the efforts of Thailand and the US in achieving this, and called for any remaining forces to disarm and be interned.

Date	*Case*	*Nature*	*UN bodies involved*
1954 (1946–77)	Trieste (post-war)	Status of Trieste and problem of peace settlement	SC

Sensitive boundary problem inherited from pre-war, and essentially a matter for peace settlement. On 10 Jan. 1947 SC accepted responsibility for ensuring status of Free Territory of Trieste including appointment of govenor. SC asked for permanent members to consult on a governor and later asked Yugoslavia and Italy to do so, but no agreement on candidate. In October 1954 UK, US, Italy and Yugoslavia sent SC a memorandum of understanding of 5 Oct. 1954 for boundary adjustments after which British, American and Yugoslav troops would withdraw from area north of the boundary, leaving it to be administered by Italy: Yugoslavia to keep area south of the boundary; Italy to maintain Trieste as a free port. Differences concerning Free Territory of Trieste settled by Treaty of Osimo. Representatives of Italy and Yugoslavia informed S-G on 27 May 1977 that SC need no longer be seized of the question.

Date	*Case*	*Nature*	*UN bodies involved*
1954	Thailand	To deter spread of Indo-China conflict	SC

SC action vetoed by USSR. Thailand concerned over danger to itself from Viet Minh forces fighting in Laos and Cambodia. USSR opposed SC consideration then, while Conference of Foreign Ministers met in Geneva on Indo-China. Thailand submitted draft resolution to SC (June 1954) requesting Peace Observation Commission to establish subcommission with power to send observers to Thailand, visit it (if necessary) and report with recommendations to SC. USSR vetoed resolution 18 June 1954 (not able to prevent consideration, since that a procedural matter). Geneva agreement of July 1954 relieved situation.

Date	*Case*	*Nature*	*UN bodies involved*
1954	Guatemala	Attacks from Nicaragua and Honduras with US support	SC

Airing drew attention to (but did not prevent) coup in Guatemala by exiles with outside help, which was further complicated by question of whether the matter should be dealt with by the OAS. In June 1954 Guatemalan exiles from Honduras and Nicaragua advanced into Guatemala and conducted bombing raids. Guatemala complained US had been conniving in campaign against it and wanted SC to warn Honduras and Nicaragua and to send SC observation commission. The US, Honduras and Nicaragua (but not Guatemala) wanted matter to go to OAS. The USSR vetoed Brazilian-Colombian draft resolution for reference to OAS, which however took up the matter. SC adopted resolution calling for immediate end to bloodshed. Guatemala complained (22 June) resolution not being observed, but thwarted in attempts to get this on SC agenda. On 9 July 1954 new government of Guatemala informed SC peace and order had been restored.

Date	*Case*	*Nature*	*UN bodies involved*
1954	US, USSR	Alleged attack by Russian planes destroying US aircraft	SC, ICJ

Airing salutary, part of Cold War. US claimed Russian aircraft destroyed American naval plane over international waters of Sea of Japan on 4 Sept. 1954. SC discussed matter but took no action. US referred it to ICJ on 22 Aug. 1958, but USSR would not accept jurisdiction of Court in this case, so removed from Court List 9 Dec. 1958.

Date	*Case*	*Nature*	*UN bodies involved*
1954–55	People's Republic of China	US airmen held after Korean War	GA, S-G

A successful case of 'quiet diplomacy'. On 10 Dec. 1954 GA considered China's detention of American airmen was contrary to the Korean Armistice Agreement and asked S-G to try for their release. China warned UN not entitled to interfere in domestic affairs, but a visit to Peking by S-G and months of tactful negotiation prevailed in 1955.

Date	*Case*	*Nature*	*UN bodies involved*
1955	Chinese Islands	Hostilities between two Chinas	SC

Part of two-China problem, no action, spotlight may have kept hostilities at low key. Hostilities over islands off mainland China in dispute between People's Republic of China and Taiwan. Originally laid before SC by New Zealand 28 Jan. 1955. People's Republic of China claimed 'liberation' of islands a domestic affair, and would not participate in SC (as invited) unless its representative attended in name of China. USSR proposal to recommend US end 'aggression' and withdraw forces from Taiwan not taken up, and SC adjourned consideration of New Zealand item.

Date	*Case*	*Nature*	*UN bodies involved*
1956 (1946–60)	Togoland (colonial)	Future of British and French Trust Territories	TC (Missions), GA (Commission on Togoland, Plebiscite Commissioner, UN Commissioner)

UN and its Trusteeship Council fostered independence of Trust Territories under British and French Administrations.

Trust Territory under British Administration: Question of whether this Territory should join Gold Coast (Ghana) or the Territory under French Administration. In 1954 UK suggested trusteeship be ended and wishes of people be ascertained. GA approved plans for plebiscite on union with Gold Coast or whether to remain under Trusteeship agreement pending ultimate determination of states. It was held 9 May 1956 under Plebiscite Commissioner, Eduardo Espinosa y Prieto, and observers, 58 per cent for union with Gold Coast (northern section strongly in favour, southern section split). GA decided it should join Gold Coast to form Ghana on independence 6 March 1957.

Trust Territory under French Administration: As with British Togoland the GA and TC gave consideration as to whether the two Togolands should join together. GA fact-finding commission gave advice on modification of new French statute in May 1957. GA sent Commissioner, Max H Dorsinville, to supervise elections to Legislative Assembly 27 April 1958. The GA endorsed end to the trusteeship as of 27 April 1960 on date of independence. Togo joined the UN on 20 Sept. 1960.

Date	*Case*	*Nature*	*UN bodies involved*
1956–57	Suez, Israel, Egypt, France, UK	Nationalisation of Canal, military hostilities and peacekeeping	SC, GA (UNEF, UNEF Advisory Committee), S-G (Committee on Financing UNEF, Group for Canal Clearance), ICJ on financing of UNEF

Successful UN action to halt conflict and restore situation, but no settlement, UN peacekeeping force kept clashes to a minimum for 10 years, and the Canal was cleared.

Following the nationalisation of the Canal 26 July 1956 negotiations outside the UN failed. France and UK called for SC meeting (23 Sept. 1956), as did Egypt the next day. Problem discussed at seven open and three closed meetings during 26 September – 13 October. SC adopted on 13 October six principles which a settlement should meet, previously agreed to by UK, France and Egypt in meetings with S-G. But military action by Israel on 29 October supported by France and UK on 31 October ended talks on further arrangements. SC resolution for ceasefire and Israeli withdrawal vetoed by France and UK on 30 October – despite Art. 27 (3). SC called emergency meeting of GA under the 'Uniting for Peace' resolution which voted on 2 November for ceasefire and withdrawal of all forces (Israeli, French and British) and steps to be taken to clear canal.

On 4 Nov. 1956 GA asked S-G for plan to set up UN force, report submitted; then on 5 November GA established the UNEF to supervise the end of hostilities (6073 men at its peak from ten countries). The USSR abstained from voting, because it felt only the SC could set up such a force. On 7 November the GA established an Advisory Committee to help the S-G regarding the force. GA continued pressing for withdrawal, completed by French and British 22 December, and by Israeli 8 March 1957. Canal clearance started 27 Dec. 1956 and was completed 10 April 1957.

The GA asked S-G in 1962 to request ICJ for advisory opinion on whether the expenditures for UNEF were part of the expenses of the UN under Art. 17 (2). The ICJ decided this was so 20 July 1962.

Date	*Case*	*Nature*	*UN bodies involved*
1956 (1956–62)	Hungary, USSR	Revolution and Russian intervention	SC, GA (Special Committee, Special Representatives, S-G (three-man investigating body), UNHCR

Censure by UN, but action blocked by USSR except in humanitarian field. Intervention of Russian troops 22 Oct. 1956, Hungary opposed consideration by SC 28 October, claiming it a domestic matter Art. 2 (7). But on 2 November, Imre Nagy asked SC to instruct his government and USSR to negotiate for withdrawal of Russian troops. SC resolution for withdrawal of Soviet troops vetoed by USSR 4 November despite Art. 27 (3). SC called for emergency meeting of GA (4–10 November), which voted for Soviet withdrawal, access for UN observers, free elections and asked S-G to investigate situation and the needs of the people. Hungary refused entry to S-G's three-man investigating team. GA established Special Committee 10 Jan. 1957 to observe, collect evidence and report to GA, which it did in 1957. GA appointed Prince Wan (GA Pres.) as its Special Representative September 1957–58, followed by Sir Leslie Munro 1958–62.

S-G agreed (November 1956) that International Committee of Red Cross should carry out relief programme on behalf of UN. Needs assessed by UN-FAO mission January 1957. UNHCR coordinated measures for refugees.

Date	*Case*	*Nature*	*UN bodies involved*
1956 (1951–57)	Eastern Europe, US	Complaints of US interventions in Eastern Europe	GA

Part of Cold War claims and counter-claims propaganda. Complaint by USSR to GA against US interference by recruiting people in Eastern Europe rejected by GA in January 1952 and similar one by Czechoslavakia, rejected in autumn 1952. Also complaint in December 1956 by USSR of US hostile acts with broadcasts, subversive literature, political agitators and saboteurs, rejected by GA Committee 27 Feb. 1957.

Date	*Case*	*Nature*	*UN bodies involved*
1957 (1954–59)	Cyprus (colonial)	Independence and future of Cyprus	GA

Prolonged discussion at UN may have furthered independence of Cyprus. Greece asked for consideration by GA of self-determination for Cyprus. GA considered matter in 1954 but no resolution. On 26 Feb. 1957 GA passed resolution expressing desire for peaceful and just solution in accordance with Charter, and hope for resumption of negotiations. Lengthy discussions later that year, but resolution failed in plenary meeting of GA; and in 1958 GA expressed confidence in effort to reach peaceful just solution (the Iranian draft resolution was not adopted, but envisaged conference between three governments and Cypriots for interim administrative arrangements and final solution). London Agreement reached outside UN, between UK, Greece, Turkey and Cypriot representatives 19 Feb. 1959.

Date	*Case*	*Nature*	*UN bodies involved*
1957	Syria, Turkey	Turkish troop manoeuvres considered a threat	GA

Time and airing in UN helped dispel dispute. Syria asked for consideration by GA, six meetings held 22 Oct. – 1 Nov. 1957. Syria feared Turkish manoeuvres were a threat and asked for commission of investigation. Turkey willing for King Saud to mediate. Problem evaporated while sponsors of GA resolutions agreed not to press for a vote.

Date	*Case*	*Nature*	*UN bodies involved*
1958	Sudan, Egyptian border	Fear of Egyptian troop concentrations and border dispute	SC

Airing helped to reach an understanding for delay in negotiations. On 20 Feb. 1958 Sudan called for SC meeting because of Egyptian concentration of troops. Sudan stated Egypt demanded two areas of border, Sudan willing to negotiate after its elections on 27 February. Egypt agreed to postpone question until after Sudanese elections. SC noted these assurances.

Date	*Case*	*Nature*	*UN bodies involved*
1958	Lebanon, Jordan	Alleged infiltration from from Syria into Lebanon: US and UK sent forces	SC (UN Observation Group in Lebanon – UNOGIL), GA, S-G (Special Representative in Jordan)

UN success in helping to quieten a threatening situation and facilitating troop withdrawals, although Great Powers involved.

Lebanese complaint to SC of intervention by United Arab Republic (Syria and Egypt) 22 May 1958, with infiltration of men and arms from Syria and violent UAR media campaign. SC decided to send UN Observation Group (UNOGIL) on 11 June. US informed SC 15 July, that it had sent forces at request of Lebanon. On 17 July Jordan complained of UAR intervention and informed SC it had asked for British troops. Several resolutions submitted and vetoed. On 7 August SC called for an emergency session of GA which considered a number of resolutions 8–21 August and agreed to one on 21 August from 10 Arab states – welcoming assurances by Arab states of respect for system of governments of other states and calling on S-G to facilitate withdrawal of foreign troops and to continue studies on Arab development institution. S-G appointed P P Spinelli as Special Representative in Jordan to implement GA resolution.

US withdrawal completed 25 Oct. 1958, British on 2 November, and relations between Lebanon and UAR resumed. UN Observation Group ended operation 9 Dec. 1958.

Date	*Case*	*Nature*	*UN bodies involved*
1959 (1959–61)	Laos	Request for UN force to stop aggression by North Vietnam	SC (subcommittee), S-G (Special Representative, Special Consultant)

UN efforts to alleviate problem which was involved in the troubles of all Indo-China, particularly Vietnam – a conflict generally kept out of the hands of the UN. In September 1959 Laos asked S-G for a UN emergency force to halt alleged aggression from North Vietnam. S-G asked for SC meeting. SC resolution for fact-finding subcommittee to report to SC (adopted as a procedural matter against USSR's objection). Subcommittee visited Laos 15 Sept. – 13 Oct. 1959, reported actions of 'guerrilla character' although they appeared to have 'centralised coordination'. Any SC action on report would have been susceptible to USSR veto. S-G visited Laos and sent Special Representative, Mr Tuomioja, to review economic needs and appointed Special Consultant to implement recommendations. At beginning of January 1961 Laos complained Soviet planes parachuting material to rebels and North Vietnam had attacked 'several important points'.

Date	*Case*	*Nature*	*UN bodies involved*
1959 (1959–65)	Tibet	China's intervention in Tibet, Freedom and Human Rights	GA

Problem involving human rights and Art. 2 (7), moral pressure of little effect in such circumstances with the People's Republic of China not a member of UN, so UN's activity limited to humanitarian. Malaya and Ireland brought the actions of the People's Republic of China in Tibet before the GA in 1959. Several states, including the USSR, claimed this was a domestic matter under Art. 2(7). But on 21 Oct. 1959 GA resolution affirmed respect for Charter and Declaration of Human Rights as essential, and called for respect of Tibetans' human rights. These views were re-affirmed by GA 20 Dec. 1961 and 18 Dec. 1965. UNHCR concerned with some 50 000 Tibetan refugees in India and Nepal.

Date	Case	Nature	UN bodies involved
1960 (1947–61)	Cameroons (colonial)	Future of French and British Trust Territories	TC (Missions), GA (Plebiscite Commissioner for two plebiscites)

The UN helped to foster the independence of the French and British Trusteeships and to solve the problems of their future, which involved two major powers and two African states.

French Trusteeship: GA pressed for target date for independence. The TC, on the basis of findings of its visiting mission, recommended to GA – the latter agreed in March 1959 – to end trusteeship on independence day 1 Jan. 1960. Cameroon joined the UN 20 Sept. 1960.

British Trusteeship: The northern section was administered by Northern Region of Nigeria, the southern as part of the Eastern Region, and from 1954 as a political unit in the Nigerian Federation. The TC visiting mission recommended separate votes on their respective futures; this was endorsed by GA 13 March 1959. The northern area in November 1959 favoured deciding its future later. Plebiscites for both North and South were held in February 1961 under UN Plebiscite Commissioner, Djalal Abdoh, on whether to join independent Nigeria or the Republic of Cameroons (formerly French Cameroons). The North decided in favour of Nigeria, the South for the Republic of Cameroons. The GA ended the trusteeship agreement for the North as of 1 June 1961, and for the South of 1 Oct. 1961.

Date	Case	Nature	UN bodies involved
1960 (1952–65)	Apartheid	South African racial discrimination	SC (Committee of Experts), GA (Commission on Racial Situation in South Africa, Special Committee on the Policies of Apartheid), S-G (Group of Experts, Training Programme for Africans Abroad)

UN efforts against apartheid for causing racial conflict and a dangerous situation, blocked by South Africa.

GA on 5 Dec. 1952 established three-man Commission for study of situation and adopted resolution laying down basic principles for equality in a multi-racial society, affirming discriminatory policies as inconsistent with Charter. South Africa claimed resolutions contrary to Art. 2(7) regarding domestic jurisdiction and would not recognise Commission, which continued to report to GA. From 1953–59 GA repeatedly urged South Africa to change its policy.

After Sharpeville shootings 21 March 1960, SC met and appealed to South Africa to abandon its apartheid policy and asked S-G to consult with South Africa on measures to uphold Charter. On government's invitation S-G visited South Africa 6–12 Jan. 1961, but no agreement. As South Africa disregarded UN's resolutions, GA, on 2 Nov. 1962, called states to break off diplomatic relations, impose economic boycott, close ports and airports to South Africa and keep ships from South African harbours. It asked SC to take action (including sanctions) to get compliance of South Africa. It also established a Special Committee on the Policies of Apartheid, which has reported on events and made recommendations.

In 1963 SC kept apartheid under review, its resolutions of 7 August and 4 December called for voluntary arms embargo and freedom for those imprisoned under apartheid. SC asked S-G to provide expert group to examine ways to deal with situation, which on 20 April 1964 recommended a national convention representing all people in South Africa for consultation on country's future, and an amnesty for opponents of apartheid. This was endorsed by SC in June and referred to South Africa, which rejected it, again claiming the matter a domestic one. On 9 June 1964 SC urged South Africa to stop executions for acts against apartheid and to end Rivonia trials. South Africa claimed this illegal. SC asked S-G to set up training programme for South Africans abroad, and itself established a Committee of Experts of all its members to study measures it could take. The Committee reported February 1965 that South Africa not easily affected by economic sanctions and their effectiveness would depend on whether they were universal and were enforced.

Date	*Case*	*Nature*	*UN bodies involved*
1960 (1958–60)	US Military flights	Russian complaints, including U-2	SC

Cold War manoeuvring which appears to have eased during the considerations.

SC met in April 1958 on request of USSR complaining that US military aircraft, armed with nuclear bombs, had been flying towards USSR. US countered with request for a northern zone of international inspection to prevent surprise attack. Resolutions from both sides failed because of veto by other, despite Art. 27(3).

In May 1960 USSR complained re U2 incident, when American plane was brought down by Russian rocket, while flying over USSR. US announced flights over USSR not to be resumed. SC adopted resolution recommending negotiations between parties, the pursuit of disarmament and prevention of surprise attack.

In July 1960 USSR informed SC it had shot down a US bomber coming from Barents Sea into its airspace. US proposed investigation, claiming flight was over international waters. SC members could not agree on any of three resolutions. USSR submitted complaint to GA, but did not press discussion.

Date	*Case*	*Nature*	*UN bodies involved*
1960	Adolf Eichmann	Israeli kidnapping from Argentina violated its sovereignty	SC

Airing salutary. SC met at Argentina's request 22–23 June 1960. Israel apologised for kidnappers breaking laws of Argentina in taking Eichmann to Israel for trial as a Nazi criminal. SC adopted resolution on need to safeguard sovereign rights and requesting 'appropriate reparation'. Israel considered statement of regret sufficient reparation.

Date	*Case*	*Nature*	*UN bodies involved*
1960 (1949–60)	Somaliland (post-war colonial)	Future of Trust territory; border problem with Ethiopia	TC (Committee for Italian Somaliland), GA (Advisory Council, GA authorised choice by King of Norway of independent person for delimiting frontier – Trygve Lie)

The UN helped prepare Somaliland for independence. France, UK, US and USSR failed to agree on disposition of territory, so referred matter to GA which decided for a trusteeship agreement with Italy. GA and TC followed closely progress in self-government, financing and development until it joined with British Protectorate of Somaliland to form Republic of Somalia 1 July 1960 (five months before date Trusteeship Agreement had set for independence). It joined the UN on 20 Sept. 1960.

The frontiers between Somalia and Ethiopia were undefined. In 1950 GA recommended bilateral negotiations to settle borders, but these failed so in 1957 GA recommended arbitration tribunal. Delay in agreeing on choice of independent person so GA suggested King of Norway be invited to nominate one. He chose Trygve Lie.

Date	*Case*	*Nature*	*UN bodies involved*
1960 (1952–63)	Bureimi Oasis	Ownership of oasis disputed between Saudi Arabia and UK	S-G (Special Diplomatic Representative)

Border problem lingered on. Oasis claimed by Saudi Arabia and Sheikh of Abu Dhabi and Sultan of Muscat and Oman (then under British protection). S-G's good offices sought. He (then occupied with Congo) appointed Herbert de Ribbing his representative July 1960, to study problem, Little progress for three years, but diplomatic relations re-established between Saudi Arabia and Britain.

Date	*Case*	*Nature*	*UN bodies involved*
1960 (1960–64)	Congo (ex-colonial)	To re-establish Congo after its independence and subsequent hostilities	SC (Opération des Nations Unies au Congo – ONUC, Special Representatives), GA (Conciliation Commission, Commission of Investigation), S-G (Consultative Group, Chief of Civilian Operations, constitutional law experts), UN Fund for the Congo, ICJ on financing ONUC

A noteworthy UN effort to stabilise a new government, to achieve conciliation, to provide expertise including a constitutional plan in order to normalise the situation.

On 12 July 1960, 12 days after independence, Congo asked for UN military assistance against external aggression and to end secession of Katanga allegedly fostered by Belgium. S-G (acting under Art. 99) brought this to SC 13 July which called on Belgium to withdraw troops and authorised S-G to provide military and technical assistance on 14 July. S-G set up Opération des Nations Unies au Congo (ONUC) comprising civilian operations and peace force (later 21 Feb. 1961 authorised by SC to use force to prevent civil war, and on 24 Nov. 1961 to eliminate mercenaries). Special Representative Ralph Bunche negotiated withdrawal of Belgian troops, who left by September 1960. UN force at its height numbered 20 000. Congolese PM Lumumba wanted ONUC to help against secession of Katanga. S-G said this was against its mandate, which SC confirmed 9 August, but S-G negotiated, and led, UN entry into Katanga 12 Aug. 1960. Trial of strength between Pres. and PM of Congo, Chief of Staff Col. Mobutu seized power 13 Sept. 1960; crisis for 11 months. ONUC tried to protect the many political leaders and foster conciliation. Congo referred to special session of the GA under 'Uniting for Peace' resolution 17–20 Sept. 1960. It appealed to Congolese to seek peaceful solution and established Conciliation Commission, called on members to refrain from military assistance in Congo except on request of S-G. Amb. Rajeshwar Dayal succeeded R Bunche as Special Representative.

Lumumba left his residence 27–28 November, where he had been guarded by the UN, and was arrested by Congolese, transferred to Katanga and murdered in January 1961. UN Commission of Investigation into death indicated he was probably killed by mercenaries in presence of Katangese officials. Conciliation Commission (established by GA 20 Sept. 1960) reported opposing groups intransigent, considered parliament should be reconvened and approve a national unity government. SC in February 1961 urged reconvening of Parliament, and, at request of Pres. Kasa-Vubu, ONUC helped to reopen it 22 June 1961. National unity government formed 2 August under Adoula. Stanleyville and Katanga would not participate.

Foreign interference, military personnel and mercenaries in Katanga, SC on 21 Feb. 1961 urged withdrawal of such foreign personnel. S-G's efforts hampered by Katangese. National government ordered expulsion of mercenaries from Katanga (24 Aug. 1961), and asked for ONUC's assistance to do so. ONUC started rounding them up for deportation, consular corps promised to repatriate them, but did not do so fully. ONUC prepared to repeat operation when attacked by Katangese September 1961. ONUC sought ceasefire. S-G killed in air crash on way to meet Tshombe 18 September. Ceasefire concluded 21 September but flouted by Tshombe. SC resolution opposed secessionist moves in Katanga and authorised use of force to remove mercenaries 24 Nov. 1961. Katanga launched campaign against ONUC, which removed roadblocks, fighting followed. ONUC re-established its security and freedom of movement, helped arrange meeting of Tshombe with PM Adoula, at which he signed declaration recognising central government (21 Dec. 1961), but negotiations under UN auspices from March to June 1962 broke down.

Acting S-G proposed in August 1962 'Plan of National Reconciliation', a constitutional outline as a basis to settle differences between central government and Katanga, accepted by both. Constitution drafted by UN experts. Katanga did not implement it. In December 1962 police fired on ONUC, which moved to demolish roadblocks. Tshombe agreed to end Katangese secession 14 Jan. 1963. S-G reported on 4 Feb. 1963 that secession had ended. But GA extended stay of UN force to 30 June 1964 to assist in maintaining order at request of Congolese government.

ONUC also undertook relief operations, particularly for famine victims in South Kasai (autumn 1960). UN experts helped with programmes to reorganise every field of government service, develop economy, improve monetary and budgetary position, also in field of training.

In 1962 GA asked S-G to request ICJ for advisory opinion on whether expenditures for Congo were rightly an expense of UN under Art. 17 (2), ICJ decided this was so, 20 July 1962.

Stanleyville area: Insurgents took control in Stanleyville area. In November 1964 US and Belgium drew SC's attention to danger to a thousand foreigners held as hostages there. Combined rescue operation by two countries. Congo informed SC it had authorised rescue, but many UN states thought this intervention. SC met seventeen times on matter 9–30 December, called for end to foreign intervention, ceasefire and withdrawal of mercenaries, and supported efforts of OAU to help Congo to achieve national reconciliation.

Date	*Case*	*Nature*	*UN bodies involved*
1960 (1960–62)	Dominican Republic, Venezuela	Alleged aggression against Venezuela	SC

No UN action required. OAS informed UN August 1960 of intention to take diplomatic and economic sanctions against Dominican Republic for its 'acts of intervention and aggression against the Republic of Venezuela'. SC decided its approval not necessary, as these sanctions did not constitute enforcement action under Art. 53. OAS cancelled measures 4 Jan. 1962 as Dominican Republic no longer a danger to the peace.

Date	*Case*	*Nature*	*UN bodies involved*
1960 (1960–71)	South Tyrol, Italy, Austria	Human Rights problem of German-speaking minority in Italy	GA

UN may have helped to keep negotiations going between Italy and Austria, but did not hasten them or provide a solution. Austria contended Italy had misapplied provisions of Paris Agreement of 5 Sept. 1946 on autonomy of South Tyrol, asked GA to consider dispute. On 31 Oct. 1960 GA recommended resumption of negotiations and, if these failed, recourse to ICJ or other peaceful means of settlement. Agreement signed 1971.

Date	*Case*	*Nature*	*UN bodies involved*
1960–61	Mauritania (colonial)	Moroccan claim to Mauritania	SC, GA

Question of Morocco's claim to Mauritania probably needed airing. In 1960 GA's First Committee dismissed this claim which France refuted. SC and GA heard same claim in October 1961, when Mauritania, which had achieved independence from France (28 Nov. 1960) applied for UN membership. Matter settled by its admission to UN on 27 Oct. 1961.

Date	*Case*	*Nature*	*UN bodies involved*
1960 (1955–62)	Algeria (colonial)	Campaign for independence	GA

Little evidence that the UN influenced granting of independence, apart from increasing pressure in favour of it. French operations in Algeria before GA from 1955 to 1961, which expressed its concern and hope for solution conforming with Charter. France claimed Algeria a domestic matter Art. 2(7). SC would not consider Algeria in June 1956. In 1957 GA again declared its concern and noted offer of good offices by King of Morocco and Pres. of Tunisia, hoping a solution would be found in accordance with Charter. In 1960 GA, for the first time, passed resolution recognising right of Algerians to self-determination. Negotiations suspended in 1961, GA called for their resumption aimed at independence, which Algeria achieved July 1962.

Date	*Case*	*Nature*	*UN bodies involved*
1960 (1960–62)	Cuba	Alleged US aggression in aiding counter-revolutionaries	SC, GA

UN airing of Cuba's complaint against US aid to counter-revolutionaries, but little more. Cuba brought matter to SC in July 1960, SC noted 19 July it was being considered by OAS and asked OAS members to help towards a peaceful solution. On 31 Dec. 1960 Cuba alleged US preparing armed aggression. In March 1962 Cuba wanted ICJ advisory opinion on points of OAS decision January 1962, excluding Cuba from Inter-American system, but rejected by SC.

Bay of Pigs 'invasion' by Cuban exiles with US support, occurred 17 April 1961. Cuba took matter up in GA which was then meeting. GA called on all members to act peacefully to ease tensions.

Date	*Case*	*Nature*	*UN bodies involved*
1961 (1961–66)	South West Africa (colonial)	Future of South West Africa, aim of eliminating apartheid and achieving independence	GA (Committee on South West Africa, Special Committee for South West Africa, Special Committee of 24, UN Technical Assistance Resident Representative for South West Africa), S-G, ICJ

UN's effort to promote steps towards independence, rejected by South Africa.

GA proclaimed in 1961 the right of South West Africa to independence, called for repeal of apartheid there, elections under UN supervision, the assistance of specialised agencies, and asked S-G to set up special education and training programme. These goals were to be achieved (in consultation with South Africa) by Special Committee for South West Africa, which replaced Committee on South West Africa (1961). Two members of the Special Committee for South West Africa visited it in 1962 at invitation of South Africa and reported that population desired UN administration and independence. The functions of this committee were taken over in 1962 by the overall Special Committee of 24.

The GA asked the S-G (December 1962) to appoint a Technical Assistance Resident Representative for South West Africa to try to establish an effective UN presence there, but not accepted by South Africa. The GA, from 1963, has urged South Africa to remove military installations in South West Africa and refrain from using it as a base. In 1964 South Africa approved, in principle, the establishment of separate 'homelands' in South West Africa, but deferred action until after ICJ opinion (1966). Concerned by this the GA, in 1965, held any partition would violate mandate and any annexation would constitute aggression, it condemned apartheid and large-scale settlement of immigrants, and appealed to members to give help to legitimate struggle for independence. It also endorsed the conclusions of Special Committee of 24, on activities of international companies in South West Africa, and condemned policies which exploited material or human resources and impeded independence.

On 18 July 1966 ICJ gave its judgment on case brought in 1960, rejecting by one vote claims of Ethiopia and Liberia because these countries had not established their right of interest in charging South Africa with violating its mandate obligations.

Date	*Case*	*Nature*	*UN bodies involved*
1961 (1947–62)	Western Samoa (colonial)	Independence for Trust Territory of New Zealand	TC (Special Visiting Missions), GA (Plebiscite Commissioner)

UN fostered self-government and independence of Trust Territory administered by New Zealand. In 1960 GA established basis for plebiscite under UN supervision, to ask voters whether they agreed with the constitution and whether they wanted independence on 1 Jan. 1962 on basis of that constitution. Voting held under UN Plebiscite Commissioner 9 May 1961, large majority for both. GA endorsed results 18 Oct. 1961 decided trusteeship should end on day of independence 1 Jan. 1962. Became a member of the UN as Samoa 15 Dec. 1976.

Date	*Case*	*Nature*	*UN bodies involved*
1961 (1952–63)	Tunisia (colonial)	Independence and French occupation of Bizerta	SC, GA, S-G

UN pressure for self-government and thereafter to discourage encroachments during French-Algerian hostilities.

Question of Tunisia's self-government before GA 1952–54. France claimed it a domestic matter under Art 2(7). In 1954 the GA encouraged negotiations with a view to self-government. Independence achieved on 20 March 1956.

In February 1958 Tunisia complained to SC of French border violation. France lodged counter-claim of Tunisian aid to Algerian rebels. SC adjourned discussion 18 Feb. 1958 pending efforts of US and UK towards conciliation. On 18 June 1958 France and Tunisia informed SC of agreement that all French forces to be evacuated from Tunisia except those in Bizerta. Several complaints by Tunisia to Pres. of SC 1959–60. In July 1961 Tunisia asked SC to end alleged French naval and air aggression against Bizerta (started on 19 July). SC called for ceasefire and return of forces to original positions 22 July. Tunisia complained France did not comply. SC convened again but rejected three resolutions. S-G visited Tunisia attempting to reach a settlement, but France would not receive him. Call for special session of GA, which met 21–25 Aug. 1961. GA reaffirmed SC resolution of 22 July and urged France to carry it out, and to enter negotiations for full withdrawal of French troops. Negotiations lasted two years and withdrawal completed 15 Oct. 1963.

Date	*Case*	*Nature*	*UN bodies involved*
1961 (1956–65)	Portuguese Territories (colonial)	Pressure for independence	SC, GA (Sub-committee on Angola, Committee on Territories under Portuguese Administration, Special Committee of 17 – later of 24, special fund for training), S-G

Repeated UN pressure contributed to reforms in African territories and encouragement of liberation movements, but little effect in short run.

When Portugal joined the UN in 1955 it claimed these territories were overseas provinces. In 1960 GA held they were non-self-governing territories and Portugal was obliged to transmit information on them to the S-G, but Portugal would not.

SC met over Luanda riots February 1961, but because of Art. 2 (7) rejected resolution calling for reforms in Angola. GA adopted similar resolution 20 April 1961 and established five-member subcommittee on Angola. Repressive measures and disturbances later led many to flee to Congo. On 9 June 1961 SC resolution called for end to repression, as did GA resolution 30 Jan. 1962. GA established Special Committee on Territories under Portuguese Administration December 1961. Reports and recommendations made in 1961 and 1962 by Subcommittee on Angola, Committee on Territories under Portuguese Administration and by Special Committee of 17; this last committee became Special Committee of 24 and took over the functions of the Committee on the Territories under Portuguese Administration in December 1962. On the basis of these recommendations the GA affirmed, 18 December 1962 the right of territories to self-government and independence, urged an end to repression, withdrawal of military, amnesty and negotiations with view to transfer of power. It requested states to deny help for suppression and to end supply of arms. GA asked S-G to set up special fund for training people from these territories in administration etc. Another GA resolution on Angola condemned 'colonial war' and called on SC to take appropriate measures (including sanctions) to get Portuguese compliance.

In July 1963 SC endorsed GA's general recommendations on Portuguese territories of 1962. Then in 1965 SC demanded Portugal carry out recommended measures and requested states to stop shipment of, and material for, arms (reaffirmed by GA). In 1965 GA condemned Portugal's policy and its refusal to implement recommendations and urged states to boycott Portugal.

Date	*Case*	*Nature*	*UN bodies involved*
1961	Kuwait, Iraq (ex-colonial)	Kuwait alleged Iraq threat, Iraq alleged UK threat	SC

UN airing probably facilitated Arab pressure on Iraq. In June 1961 Kuwait became independent (formerly British Protectorate). Iraq claimed it as part of a province. Kuwait appealed to Britain which sent a small force. On 1 July Kuwait complained to SC against Iraq's threat. Iraq countered, charging UK threatening its independence. No resolution agreed. On 19 Oct. 1961 Kuwait stated British troops had withdrawn and Arab League forces were safeguarding its independence.

Date	*Case*	*Nature*	*UN bodies involved*
1961 (1946–64)	Ruanda-Urundi (colonial)	Independence for Trust Territory of Belgium and strife	TC (visiting missions), GA (two Commissions for Ruanda-Urundi to supervise elections and re-establish order, Special Commission on Amnesty), S-G

UN fostered self-government and independence of Trust Territory administered by Belgium. In early days TC mission felt first consideration given to social, economic and educational advances and not enough to political, but development in this field reported in 1957. GA invited to send mission to observe elections for national assemblies. GA recommended (December 1960) conference of political parties should be held before national elections, it established three-member commission to attend conference and supervise elections. Commission attended conference January 1961, but coup d'état in Ruanda complicated matter. In April 1961 GA reaffirmed resolutions, decided elections and referendum should be under UN supervision, established three-member Special Amnesty Commission.

Burundi (Urundi): Elections under UN supervision held 18 Sept. 1961, government formed, but PM assassinated 13 October. UN Commission asked to investigate.

Rwanda (Ruanda): Election and referendum held 25 Sept. 1961 under UN supervision. Referendum favoured Republic against Mwami – Kingdom.

After elections GA (February 1962) established five-man commission to ensure objectives necessary for independence. On 27 June 1962 GA asked S-G to report on needs of Burundi and Rwanda in the technical and economic fields; he did so in November 1962, and GA subsequently encouraged the provision of aid. GA decided to end trusteeship on independence day 1 July 1962. Both joined the UN on 18 Sept. 1962.

Date	*Case*	*Nature*	*UN bodies involved*
1961 (1949–61)	Tanganyika (colonial)	Future status of Trust Territory administered by UK	TC (missions), GA

UN fostered self-government and independence of Trust Territory administered by Britain. Visiting TC Mission in 1954 estimated 10–15 years for independence. TC anxious for gradual transformation of land tenure system and for advancement in social fields. It was also concerned that the voting, on a basis of three racial communities with a system of separate representation, should evolve into an integrated system of elected representatives. The GA expressed same concern in its resolution of 26 Feb. 1957. GA agreed trusteeship to end on independence 9 Dec. 1961. It joined the UN as Tanzania 14 Dec. 1961.

Date	*Case*	*Nature*	*UN bodies involved*
1961	Goa, Damao, Diu (colonial)	Portuguese enclaves attacked by India	SC, S-G

SC failed to act, members divided and India's annexation speedy. Letters from Portugal and India to Pres. of SC December 1961. The former alleged military build-up and violation of Portuguese frontier and airspace, and the latter alleged attacks on Indian villages. S-G cabled both 14 December urging restraint and negotiations. India attacked. Despite opposition of USSR, SC decided to consider dispute. Resolution calling for end to hostilities, Indian withdrawal and peaceful settlement, vetoed by USSR 19 December. Ex-colonies and USSR supported India.

Date	*Case*	*Nature*	*UN bodies involved*
1962 (1958–68)	Cambodia, Thailand	Border dispute over Temple of Preah Vihear	S-G (three-Special Representatives), ICJ

Example of S-G's 'quiet diplomacy' effort to solve border dispute. Cambodia informed S-G Thailand had occupied Temple of Preah Vihear 29 November 1958. Two governments invited S-G to send Special Representative, he sent Johan Bech-Friis who visited area 20 Jan. – 23 Feb. 1959. While he was there the two countries re-established normal relations (6 February). On 6 October Cambodia asked ICJ to judge on ownership of temple, and it decided on 15 June 1962 that temple belonged to Cambodia and Thailand should withdraw.

S-G informed SC 19 October 1962 that two states had charged each other with aggression and had asked him to send a representative, he chose Nils Gussing, whose appointment was prolonged until mission withdrew end of 1964. Border encroachements broke out again in 1966 with charges from both Cambodia and Thailand. After consulting with them the S-G chose Herbert de Ribbing as a Special Representative (16 Aug. 1966) to explore ways of resolving differences. His appointment continued until 16 Feb. 1968.

Date	*Case*	*Nature*	*UN bodies involved*
1962 (1954–69)	West Irian (colonial)	Dispute over status between Indonesia and the Netherlands	GA, S-G (Mediator, UN Temporary Executive Authority – UNTEA, UN Administrator, military observers and UN Security Force, Special Representative for 'Act of Free Choice')

After failing to act over several years, when fighting broke out UN mediated in conflict between Indonesia and the Netherlands over West Irian. UN administered area for a transitional period and supervised an act of free choice.

Negotiations between Indonesia and the Netherlands over West Irian failed, Indonesia took problem to GA 1954, but no action. It claimed West Irian, while the Netherlands insisted it was administering the area in a way to lead to self-determination. GA resolution of 1955 encouraged negotiations. No agreement in 1961 on several alternative GA draft resolutions for good offices of S-G or five-member commission etc.

Fighting started end 1961. S-G sent appeals to both countries in December and January, urging peaceful solution, and on 17 Jan. 1962 requesting them to instruct their representatives to discuss possibilities for peace with him. Consultations followed, S-G appealed to Netherlands to release Indonesian prisoners, repatriation completed 11 March 1962. Amb. Ellsworth Bunker acted as mediator for S-G, offering proposals for negotiations. Agreement reached and signed at UN 15 August for eventual self-determination of West Irian, and for UN Temporary Executive Authority (UNTEA) to administer area from 1 Oct. 1962 to 1 May 1963, after which Indonesia to administer territory and arrange for self-determination by 1969, supervised by UN. GA approved agreement 21 Sept. 1962 and S-G's role. Dutch troops withdrawn November 1962. UNTEA administered area from October 1962 to following May under S-G's jurisdiction. Pakistan supplied security force of 1500 during UN administration until Indonesia took over.

'Act of free choice' took place 14 July – 2 Aug. 1969, observed by UN Representative Fernando Ortiz-Sanz. It decided in favour of remaining with Indonesia.

Date	*Case*	*Nature*	*UN bodies involved*
1962	Cuban Missiles (US, USSR)	Russian missiles in Cuba and US naval blockade	SC, S-G

S-G's good offices effort was a contribution to resolving a very serious threat to peace. On requests of US, Cuba and USSR , SC met 23–25 Oct. 1962. US called for withdrawal of Russian ballistic missiles. Cuba claimed US naval blockade an act of war. USSR stated weapons sent to Cuba for defence, asked SC to condemn US and to insist US cease inspecting ships bound for Cuba. On 24 October S-G told SC he had, at request of many delegations, appealed to Kennedy and Krushchev to suspend arms shipment and quarantine for 2–3 weeks and to negotiate. He also appealed to

Castro to halt work on installations and offered his good offices. Favourable replies from Kennedy and Krushchev, implementation led to settlement. S-G visited Cuba 30–31 October and was informed missiles being dismantled. On 7 Jan. 1963 S-G received joint letter of appreciation from US and USSR.

Date	*Case*	*Nature*	*UN bodies involved*
1963 (1962–65)	Yemen	Civil war supported by the United Arab Republic and Saudi Arabia	SC (UN Yemen Observation Mission – UNYOM), S-G (fact-finding mission, Special Representatives)

UN Mission possibly had a restraining influence during civil hostilities which were supported by the UAR and Saudi Arabia, but it laboured under difficulties – a limited mandate and number of observers, a wild terrain, and the failure of the parties to disengage. Problem first posed at UN when two delegations claimed to represent Yemen at GA December 1962. GA accepted credentials from the Yemen Arab Republic as opposed to those from the Iman of Yemen. On his own initiative and interpretation of Art. 99, the S-G sent Ralph Bunche on a fact-finding mission February – March 1963, and US sent Ellsworth Bunker on similar mission, resulting in UAR and Saudi Arabia agreeing to end support of republicans and royalists respectively, zone between Saudi Arabia and Yemen to be demilitarised with UN observers (nearly 200 reduced to about 25), financed by two parties. USSR requested SC meeting, on 11 June 1963 it confirmed S-G's arrangements (with USSR abstaining). UNYOM established 4 July 1963 limited to observation. Special Representative P P Spinelli appointed to encourage disengagement. UNYOM extended several times and ended 4 Sept. 1964 on request of parties. Peace agreement signed 24 Aug. 1965, although many Egyptian forces still in Yemen at time of war with Israel 1967.

Date	*Case*	*Nature*	*UN bodies involved*
1963	Haiti, Dominican Republic	Alleged Dominican aggression	SC

UN left dispute to OAS peace mission. Haiti complained 8 May 1963 to SC that Dominican Republic threatening invasion. Dominican Republic counter-charged Haiti with provocation and an attack on its Embassy. OAS committee already studying situation. Parties and SC decided to await results from OAS.

Date	*Case*	*Nature*	*UN bodies involved*
1963	Malaysian Federation (colonial)	Whether Sabah and Sarawak were to join the Federation	S-G (mission to ascertain wishes of people)

Case of S-G diplomacy in sending mission which ascertained the wishes of people of Sabah and Sarawak to join the Malayasian Federation. In 1961 Malaya proposed the formation of a Federation of Malaysia to include Sabah and Sarawak (then administered by the UK). On 1 Aug. 1962 the UK and Malaya agreed to the establishment of a federation on 31 August 1963. Following a meeting in Manila, between Malaya, Indonesia and the Philippines they asked the S-G on 5 Aug. 1963 to send a mission to ascertain the wishes of Sabah and Sarawak. With the consent of the UK, the S-G sent a mission of members of the secretariat (16 August – 5 September). On the basis of its report he concluded, on 14 September 1965, that the majority of people wanted to belong to the Federation, which was then proclaimed on 16 Sept. 1963; but Indonesia and the Philippines were not satisfied.

Date	*Case*	*Nature*	*UN bodies involved*
1963	South Vietnam	Charge of violation of human rights, particularly those of Buddhists	GA Pres. (fact-finding mission), S-G

Airing of charges that South Vietnam violating human rights, especially of Buddhists. Even before the memorandum of 13 Sept. 1963 by 14 UN states with an account of deaths, injuries and arrests after celebration of Buddha's birthday, the S-G had written to Pres. Diem of members' 'grave concern' and their request to his government to ensure human rights. On 4 October South Vietnam invited a UN mission to see for itself. GA agreed 8 Oct. 1963 and its President named seven-member fact-finding mission, which visited South Vietnam during 24 October and 3 November. Pres. Diem assassinated 2 Nov. 1963 and regime overthrown, so no further action.

Date	*Case*	*Nature*	*UN bodies involved*
1963 (1957–71)	Oman (colonial)	Alleged UK domination; tribal conflicts	SC, GA (Ad Hoc Committee, Special Committee of 24), S-G (Special Representative)

GA pressure for self-determination of Oman had little effect against feudal and colonial interests. Historical territorial claims to Oman by Imam of Oman with Arab support and by Sultan of Muscat and Oman with UK support and protection. In August 1957 11 Arab states asked (without success) SC to consider alleged UK aggression on Imamate of Oman; Sultan of Muscat and Oman protested. From 1960–62 matter on GA agenda, but draft resolutions failed. UK, in name of Sultan of Muscat and Oman, invited a representative (to be named by S-G) to visit area. Herbert de Ribbing named and went to area in June 1963. He reported he could not evaluate all the issues involved. GA established five-member Ad Hoc Committee December 1963 to examine question and report, but Sultan refused it admission to Oman. On basis of Committee's report the GA, in December 1965, recognised right of people to self-determination and independence, and considered the UK presence prevented this. It called on UK to withdraw troops, release prisoners, allow exiles to return and end its domination.

During 1966 and following years GA deplored UK's policies and its refusal to implement GA's resolutions and called on it to fulfil them while UK claimed

Sultanate of Muscat and Oman already independent. Coup of July 1970 deposed feudal Sultan, replaced by his son. Oman admitted to UN 7 Oct. 1971. British officers continued to train Omanis to fight against revolutionary guerrillas in the Dhofar mountains.

Date	*Case*	*Nature*	*UN bodies involved*
1964 (1963–73)	Cyprus (ex-colonial)	Inter-communal tensions and problems, threats of intervention	SC (UNFICYP, two Mediators) GA, S-G (Personal Representative, four Special Representatives)

UN effort to keep peace between Greek and Turkish communities, while constitutional settlement considered, generally successful in keeping peace but not in getting a solution owing to the intransigence of parties and their supporting states.

Treaty of Alliance and Treaty of Guarantee drafted at Zurich 1959, included the right of UK, Greece and Turkey to intervene jointly or separately to maintain the state of affairs established by the basic articles of the constitution, the prohibition of union with another state or of partition, and the right to station certain national contingents from Greece and Turkey on the Island. The Constitution of 1960 gave the Turkish community (18 per cent of the population) a veto on a number of government decisions like income tax, which resulted in a deadlock. The Pres. of Cyprus suggested amendments to constitution on 30 Nov. 1963; the Turkish Cypriots refused to consider any. Violent disturbances broke out 21 Dec. 1963. On 26 December Cyprus accepted offer of UK, Greece and Turkey for joint peacekeeping force (necessarily largely a British responsibility as others parties to dispute). The SC met 27 Dec. 1963 to hear Cyprus charge Turkey had violated its airspace and territorial waters and threatening use of force. S-G informed SC 13 Jan. 1964 that Cyprus (together with UK, Greece and Turkey) had asked him to send a personal representative to observe situation, he appointed Lt.-Gen. Gyani on 16 January to observe peacekeeping efforts of three states. London Conference January 1964 of four states reached no agreement. The SC met 17 February – 4 March. Resolution of 4 March for a peacekeeping force – UN force in Cyprus (UNFICYP) – and a mediator. On 13 March SC met again on allegation that Turks about to invade; it reaffirmed call to states not to worsen the situation. Lt.-Gen. Gyani became Commander of the quickly formed UNFICYP, which reached 6411 by June 1964. It was extended, at first for three-month periods, then six-month ones, each time SC received reports by S-G and reviewed situation. Force reduced when possible.

S S Tuomioja appointed mediator until his death in September 1964, just after another crisis, for fighting broke out August 1964 between the communities, with Turkey giving air and naval support in Tylliria area. SC called for ceasefire 9 August, reaffirmed 11 Aug. 1964. Galo Plaza, who had replaced Lt.-Gen. Gyani as Special Representative in May 1964, became new Mediator in Sept. 1964. In long report to S-G 30 March 1965 he suggested certain bases for reaching settlement. Turkey charged he had gone beyond his mandate and rejected the report. Finding he could not get cooperation from Turkish Cypriots, Galo Plaza resigned 22 Dec. 1965, five days after the GA had adopted resolution calling for continuation of mediation efforts and recognising right of Cyprus to full sovereignty and complete independence without foreign intervention. From March 1966 S-G extended the duties of his Special Respresentative, C A Bernardes (September 1964 – January 1967 and Orsorio-Tafall January 1967 – July 1974), so that he could exercise good offices. No mediator has since been appointed.

Several clashes, the most serious was in Ayios Theodhoros-Kophinou area 15 Nov. 1967 between National Guard and Turkish Cypriots, resulted in a number of casualties (particularly Turkish villagers). S-G and UNFICYP achieved ceasefire, but incident caused international crisis. S-G appealed on 22 Nov. 1967 to all three for restraint, sent Personal Representative, José Rolz-Bennett, to three capitals. On 24 November Cyprus called for SC meeting charging 'threat of invasion' by Turkey. SC approved S-G's efforts and called on all parties to refrain from actions that might aggravate situation. S-G on 3 December requested Greece and Turkey to withdraw forces in excess of permitted contingents.

S-G and his Special Representative, Orsorio-Tafall, exercised good offices for normalisation, including freedom of movement for Turkish Cypriots through Greek areas (but Turks would not allow Greeks in their areas). Orsorio-Tafall got inter-communal talks on constitution started Beirut 2–5 June 1968, then in Cyprus 24 June 1968 onwards. These went on spasmodically, dormant September 1971 – June 1972, during which time there was trouble about import of arms by Cyprus February 1972. The S-G expressed concern, UNFICYP was allowed to inspect them 15 March 1972, then they were stored subject to inspection without warning. On 18 Oct. 1971 S-G suggested that Orsorio-Tafall should attend inter-communal talks to exercise good offices (not mediation) and that Greece and Turkey each provide a constitutional expert to advise. Talks had bogged down on problem of local government and guarantees for independence, they were reactivated 8 June 1972 with S-G present and the constitutional experts.

Date	*Case*	*Nature*	*UN bodies involved*
1964	Panama, US	Clashes in the Canal zone	SC Pres.

Canal zone incident eased but problem not resolved. Complaint to SC 10 Jan. 1964 by Panama of US firing over hoisting of flags in Canal zone, which developed into serious clashes and loss of life. Panama and US asked OAS Inter-American Peace Committee to investigate, and Panama also requested meeting of SC. In a consensus statement SC Pres. appealed to US and Panama to end firing and restrain military forces and civilians.

Date	*Case*	*Nature*	*UN bodies involved*
1964–66	UK, United Arab Republic, Yemen and Federation of South Arabia	Border incidents	SC, S-G

Airing of border incidents important. On 1 April 1964 Yemen asked for SC meeting to consider alleged British aggression. UK charged Yemen with air raids against

Federation of South Arabia and reported it had counter-attacked near Harib on 28 March. SC resolution condemned reprisals, deplored all attacks and asked for restraint.

In 1966 the Amirate of Beihan was part of Federation of South Arabia – a British Protectorate. On 30 July 1966 UK charged that two planes, believed to be UAR from an airfield in Yemen, had strafed town of Nuqub in Beihan; both denied operation. SC Pres. issued consensus statement 16 Aug. 1966 noting complaint and denial, and asked for lessening of tension and for S-G to continue his good offices. Border closed August 1966 but reopened December 1966.

Date	*Case*	*Nature*	*UN bodies involved*
1964	Cambodia	Alleged US and South Vietnamese aggression, ill-defined borders	SC (three-member mission for fact-finding)

Airing of over-spill from Vietnam war and problem of undefined border. Cambodia complained to SC May 1964 of repeated acts by South Vietnam and US, denied its territory used by Vietcong and offered to accept a UN commission of inquiry. US and South Vietnam regretted any incidents, blaming ill-defined borders, urged a UN commission of experts to mark them and institute joint patrols. SC asked that compensation be paid to Cambodia and efforts be made to avoid border violations, sent mission of three SC members, which recommended formation of Group of UN Observers and that SC should appoint a person to help Cambodia and South Vietnam to re-establish relations and resume talks on marking frontiers and other matters in dispute. Cambodia asked that proposals be 'placed on file', so no action.

Date	*Case*	*Nature*	*UN bodies involved*
1964	Gulf of Tonkin, US, North Vietnam	US complaint of attack on naval vessels	SC

Incident of Vietnam war. US requested (4 Aug. 1964) SC to consider situation due to North Vietnamese attacks on 'US naval vessels in international waters'; US claimed it then attacked torpedo boats in self defence. North Vietnam charged US with violating its waters and air space, and with acts of war. It considered this a matter for the Geneva Conference of 1954 and not the SC and would view any decision by SC as null and void.

Date	*Case*	*Nature*	*UN bodies involved*
1964–66	Malaysia, Indonesia	Complaint of Indonesian aggression	SC

Airing may have discouraged further encroachments, but SC efforts to encourage negotiations vetoed. Clashes across Borneo border, talks between parties failed. In September 1964 SC met over Malaysian charge that Indonesian paratroops had been dropped in South Malaya. Indonesia claimed Malaysia being used by British to subvert Indonesian government. SC draft resolution calling on parties to respect territorial integrity, to refrain from force and to resume talks, vetoed by USSR. Indonesia withdrew from UN when Malaysia became member of SC January 1965. It resumed participation in UN 19 Sept. 1966, a month after Malaysia and Indonesia had agreed to restore relations.

Date	*Case*	*Nature*	*UN bodies involved*
1965–66	Dominican Republic	US intervention during civil strife	SC, S-G (Special Representative)

UN participated, with OAS, in restoration of peace after civil disturbances and intervention by US. Letter of US to SC 29 April 1965 reported American troops had landed in Dominican Republic to protect American lives during fighting between political factions, and the US had asked the OAS to consider matter. Protection became intervention. USSR requested SC meeting: on 14 May SC called for ceasefire and asked S-G to send a representative to the Dominican Republic. Representative, J A Mayobre, reported 21 May 1965 that both factions ready for truce. SC resolution 22 May for ceasefire to be permanent and S-G to report on its implementation. The OAS Ad Hoc Committee was negotiating for a political settlement. UN Representative continued to work for lasting ceasefire and settlement. S-G concerned over violation of human rights and economic situation. SC kept informed of developments. New government installed 1 July 1966, OAS Inter-American Peace Force withdrawn 21 Sept. 1966 and S-G Representative 22 Oct. 1966.

Date	*Case*	*Nature*	*UN bodies involved*
1965 (1965–68)	Rann of Kutch (ex-colonial)	Problem of boundary	S-G nominated neutral chairman for independent Award Tribunal

Boundary dispute between India and Pakistan resolved by Tribunal award, UN only marginally involved. Hostilities early in 1965, written complaints to SC, agreement between parties on 20 June 1965 constituting Tribunal. S-G nominated neutral Chairman, Gunnar Lagergren, 14 Dec. 1965. Award rendered 19 Feb. 1968.

Date	*Case*	*Nature*	*UN bodies involved*
1965–66	India, Pakistan (ex-colonial)	Violation of 1949 ceasefire, hostilities	SC (UNMOGIP), S-G (India-Pakistan Observation Mission – UNIPOM, Representative)

Another episode in the Indian-Pakistan dispute, mitigated by UN efforts and Tashkent Declaration, which achieved a ceasefire and withdrawal of troops.

Late in 1963 there were complaints by both sides regarding events in Kashmir. SC considered problem February – May 1964 with Pakistan complaining at integration of Kashmir into India, and India refusing a plebiscite and insisting Kashmir now a part of India. Trouble complicated by hostilities over Rann of Kutch.

On 3 Sept. 1965 S-G reported to SC, on basis of UNMOGIP information, that ceasefire of 1949 had collapsed, especially since 5 August. S-G had met with and appealed to both parties. On 4 September SC called for ceasefire and withdrawal to previous ceasefire line, but fighting extended. SC again called for ceasefire (6 September) and withdrawal to 5 August positions, and asked S-G to try to get this implemented and to strengthen the UNMOGIP. S-G visited India and Pakistan 7–15 September; both parties agreed. On 20 September SC demanded ceasefire and withdrawal starting 22 September and asked S-G to provide assistance for supervision and to seek a peaceful solution. Parties again agreed. S-G organised UNIPOM, UN India-Pakistan Observation Mission, to observe ceasefire and withdrawals outside Kashmir (UNMOGIP already covered Kashmir).

Numerous violations of ceasefire. SC called on parties to fulfil ceasefire and withdrawals 27 September and 5 November. S-G appointed Representative, Brig. Gen. Tulio Marambio, 25 November to talks with India and Pakistan on schedule for withdrawals. Talks began 3 Jan. 1966 and reached agreement on disengagement 29 January, following Declaration of Tashkent (10 Jan. 1966) when PM of India and Pres. of Pakistan met under USSR aegis and stated withdrawal to 5 Aug. positions should take place by February – which they did. Tasks of UN Representative and UNIPOM ended in February and March 1966 respectively.

Date	*Case*	*Nature*	*UN bodies involved*
1965 (1962–71)	Southern Rhodesia (colonial)	Status and future of Southern Rhodesia	SC (Committee on Sanctions) GA (Special Committee of 17 – later of 24), S-G, Commission on Human Rights (Special Rapporteur)

UN effort to bring about a regime based on adult suffrage leading to independence, blocked by Southern Rhodesia with support from South Africa and Portugal.

Shortly after 1961 Constitution of Southern Rhodesia adopted, GA asked Special Committee of 17 whether it had attained full self-government, as UK claimed since 1923, or was a non-self-governing territory within the provisions of the Charter. Southern Rhodesia was still a part of the Central African Federation (1953–63). On basis of Committee's findings, GA affirmed 28 June 1962 that Southern Rhodesia was a non-self-governing territory, for which UK had the responsibility to lead to independence.

GA then called for end to 1961 Constitution, the holding of a constitutional conference, release of political prisoners and extension of political rights. This was the gist of many subsequent resolutions both of the GA and SC. In September 1963 UK vetoed – despite Art. 27 (3) – SC resolution calling on it not to transfer sovereignty or military forces to Southern Rhodesia, but GA passed the resolution in November 1963 and called on UK not to grant independence without majority rule. S-G consulted OAU in accordance with a GA resolution asking him to lend his good offices to get conciliation. On 27 Oct. 1964 UK PM made clear UK would not accept unilateral declaration of independence. In anticipation of a possible UDI the

SC urged all states not to accept a UDI and UK to prevent it. The GA condemned it in advance and echoed views expressed by SC. The UK declared its five principles for independence. GA opposed independence not based on adult suffrage and asked UK to use all means (including military force) to implement resolutions.

UDI proclaimed 11 Nov. 1965, on same day GA asked SC to consider situation, as did UK and 35 African states. SC met 12 Nov. 1965 , condemned UDI, called on states not to recognise it and refrain from assisting it. UK claimed it was the only legal government, it then imposed its own economic and financial restrictions.

On 20 November SC called on UK to end the rebellion, on states to stop arms to Rhodesia and to do their best to break off economic relations (including an embargo on oil), and asked OAU to help implement resolutions. The UK added its sixth principle – January 1966. In April 1966 a British frigate stopped a tanker going to Beira and thought to be carrying oil for Rhodesia. The Captain would not alter course, so UK asked SC to meet. On 9 April SC approved UK resolution calling on British government to prevent the arrival at Beira of ships carrying oil for Rhodesia.

After failure of HMS Tiger talks (December 1966) between UK and Rhodesia, SC, for first time, imposed selective mandatory sanctions on the basis of a UK draft 16 Dec. 1966. These were extended to all exports and imports May 1968, except medical, educational supplies and food in special circumstances. It also established a Sanctions Committee to examine reports. From 1968 the GA and Special Committee of 24 drew the SC's attention to the need to impose sanctions also on two governments which refused to carry them out – South Africa and Portugal – and to get the scope of sanctions widened to include communications etc.

On 20 June 1969 Rhodesians (who had the vote) approved a new constitution and the country proclaimed itself a Republic 1 March 1970. On 18 March 1970 SC condemned proclamation of Republic, called on states not to recognise it or give assistance, but to sever diplomatic relations. It condemned South Africa and Portugal for continuing their relations with Rhodesia, demanded withdrawal of South African police, called on states to see that sanctions observed and to interrupt transport, and urged moral and material help to those struggling for independence. These were the points frequently covered in resolutions, together with a call for the UK to use force. There was also frequent consideration of sanctions because of the laxity shown. In October 1971 the US Senate (against its international obligations and the protest of the State Dept.) removed chrome from its sanction list.

Date	*Case*	*Nature*	*UN bodies involved*
1965 (1947–68)	Nauru (colonial)	Future independence of Trust Territory administered by Australia	TC, GA (Special Committee of 24)

UN concerned with Trust Territory 1947–68 attaining independence, and question of resettlement or rehabilitation, because of gradual exhaustion of phosphate deposits. Nauru administered by Australia on behalf of joint authority of UK, New Zealand and Australia. Six TC missions visited island and TC endorsed efforts to find another island for resettlement, but in 1965 people of Nauru rejected an offer of one off Australia as it did not include sovereignty. In December 1965 GA urged rehabilitation of island, reaffirmed Nauru's right to independence, pressed for implementation of a legislative council by 31 Jan. 1966 and requested a date for independence not later than 31 Jan. 1968, when it was achieved.

Date	Case	Nature	UN bodies involved
1966 (1965–73)	Vietnam (ex-colonial)	Hostilities in Vietnam	SC, S-G (personal capacity)

A conflict with intense ideological Cold War currents, further complicated because North Vietnam, South Vietnam and Communist China were not members of UN. A veto would be likely in SC, and most parties involved opposed UN consideration.

S-G continually kept problem before the public and tried personal diplomacy to get talks started. In his Annual Report of 1965 he stated that some parties to conflict considered UN had no place in seeking a solution, but he had personally tried to get parties to end fighting and talk and had advocated reconvening the Geneva Conference. On 7 July 1965 he again asked for revival of the Geneva Conference. During the 37-day suspension of bombing on North Vietnam in January 1966 the S-G asked parties for proposals on the type of government for South Vietnam. While it suspended bombing, US claimed it consulted with over 115 governments to get negotiations going. On 29 January Hanoi publicised three pre-conditions for negotiation.

On 31 Jan. 1966, US requested meeting of SC to call for discussions to arrange conference (without pre-conditions) on application of Geneva agreements of 1954 and 1962 and establishment of peace in South East Asia. SC seriously split, although it voted to include matter on agenda. USSR opposed, and several members felt that because US only principal party to be a UN member and quite a few members against discussion in SC, there was little they could do. In February Pres. of SC decided to summarise common feeling of members rather than hold a formal meeting with such serious differences of opinion.

In February 1966 S-G suggested three steps to help open negotiations, which he reiterated on several occasions. He continued his efforts, particularly during February 1968. After a meeting with the Consul-General of North Vietnam while at an UNCTAD conference in India, he saw leaders in Delhi, Moscow, London, Paris and Washington on the need for talks. A month later the US and North Vietnam agreed to prelimiary negotiations and in April S-G appealed twice for parties to decide on a venue. Talks opened in Paris early May 1968. After Cambodia involved, in May 1970, S-G put forward ideas for a Geneva-type conference on Indo-China and in June visited UK and USSR for discussions. The S-G, in April 1972, offered his good offices – no response. On 9 May he made a statement that all UN machinery should be used to end hostilities and assist settlement. On 11 May his memorandum to Pres. of SC suggested its members should consult on how to stop the fighting.

Four-party agreement to end war reached 27 Jan. 1973. Peace conference 26 Feb. – 2 March 1973 with S-G present. Fighting continued but the UN was not involved in arrangements for stopping it, which was achieved in the spring of 1975. The UN became active in the humanitarian field through UNICEF, UNHCR and FAO.

Date	Case	Nature	UN bodies involved
1966–67	Congo (Zaire), Portugal	Complaint of threat from mercenaries allegedly based in Angola, Portuguese complaint of firing its Embassy in Congo	SC

Airing may have discouraged mercenary attacks. SC met 30 Sept. 1966 on complaint of Congo (Zaire) that Portugal allowing use of Angola and Cabinda as bases for attacks on the Congo by mercenaries recruited by Tshombe, and complaint of Portugal that its Embassy in the Congo had been set on fire and its Chargé d'Affaires wounded and abducted, because of a hate campaign. SC resolution 14 Oct. 1966 urged Portugal not to allow its territory to be used as a base for mercenaries and called upon States to refrain from interfering in the Congo.

In July 1967 Congo complained to SC of mercenaries being parachuted in by unknown aircraft and of attacks – including ones by Belgian, French and Spanish mercenaries together with a former Katangese police. On 10 July 1967 SC reaffirmed previous resolution of 14 Ocot. 1966 and condemned States permitting recruitment of mercenaries and urged States not to allow training or transit for such mercenaries. Congo complained that on 1 November mercenary bands had invaded Kisenge and asked SC to stop the aggression. SC resolution of 15 November again condemned any interference in the Congo and particularly Portugal's failure to prevent use of its territory by mercenaries, and called on countries to which they had gone to prevent them from carrying on such activities.

Date	*Case*	*Nature*	*UN bodies involved*
1966 (1963–67)	Aden and Federation of South Arabia (colonial)	Future independence	GA (Committee of 24 and sub-committees), S-G (Special Representative, Special Mission on Aden)

UN efforts to foster independence of British Protectorate. GA and its Special Committee of 24 considered Aden from 1963 onwards. UK did not cooperate with sub-committee of the Special Committee of 24 and would not allow it to visit. UK established state of emergency December 1963. GA pressed UK for constitutional changes to establish representative government for whole area and to hold elections with UN presence for independence, it also called for repeal of repressive acts and removal of military base.

In 1964 UK announced territory would have independence by 1968. UK suspended Aden's constitution, followed by general strike, September–October 1965. S-G appointed Special Representative on Aden, O A H Adeel, June 1966. GA asked S-G in December 1966 to appoint Mission to Aden to consider ways of implementing its resolutions and urged UK to end state of emergency (since 1963) and repressive acts. Report of Mission that conditions prevented it meeting representatives of all opinion, but the UK had announced territory would be independent in November 1967 and troops then withdrawn. Aden and Federation of South Arabia became independent 30 Nov. 1967, combining in the People's Democratic Republic of Yemen.

Date	*Case*	*Nature*	*UN bodies involved*
1967	Six-day War	Part of Middle East conflict between Israel, Egypt, Jordan and Syria	SC (UNTSO, Special Representatives), GA (UNRWA, Personal Representative), S-G

UN effort to halt hostilities partially successful, but settlement of dispute blocked by intransigence of parties.

Deterioration in relations between Israel and Syria, then a partner with Egypt in United Arab Republic. Egypt requested recall of UNEF from Sinai and Gaza 16 May 1967 (Israel had not allowed, and would not allow, any UNEF on its territory). UN Advisory Committee undecided on what could be done in view of withdrawal of consent by host country. S-G reluctantly complied 19 May. UAR blockaded Straits of Tiran 22 May, S-G visited Cairo in peace effort 23 May. SC met 24 May onwards. Israel attacked 5 June, occupied Sinai, Gaza, Western Jordan and Golan Heights. SC called for ceasefire 6 June, demanded it the following day, accepted on 7th by Israel, Jordan and UAR, although fighting continued between Israel and Syria for some days. UN observers deployed in Israel-Syria sector.

On 14 June SC called on Israel to secure safety, welfare and return of people where military operations had taken place. GA convened a special session 17 June – 21 July, no two-thirds majority on basis for agreement, but debate helped formulate SC resolution of November. GA concerned with humanitarian aid and called on Israel to rescind its alteration of the status of Jerusalem 4 July. SC asked S-G (9 July) to arrange for military observers in Suez Canal area, they began observing the ceasefire 17 July. S-G appointed Special Representative, N Gussing, to obtain information on prisoners of war and civilians, and Personal Representative, E Thalmann, for information on Jerusalem.

In October SC condemned violations of ceasefire and adopted resolution 242 on 22 November 1967 as a basis for peace, that acquisition of territory by war is inadmissible, Israel to withdraw from occupied territories, belligerency to end, there must be respect for territorial integrity and right to live in peace within secure boundaries, guarantee of free navigation and a just settlement of refugee problem. SC also asked S-G to designate a Special Representative to promote agreement, S-G appointed Dr Jarring, who continued efforts for agreement until 1973. In 1969 French suggested four-power discussions (France, UK, USA, USSR), these were held outside the UN for two years (April 1969–70), but in contact with it. Very uneasy situation as occupation continued, with sporadic ceasefire violations.

Date	*Case*	*Nature*	*UN bodies involved*
1967	Guinea, Ivory Coast	Seizure of Guinean statesmen, as against Ivory Coast fishing boat	S-G (Personal Representative)

S-G diplomacy and OAU efforts fostered settlement. Guinea protested, June 1967, to S-G that Ivory Coast detaining its foreign minister, Representative to UN and others. OAU and a number of African states asked S-G to help. Ivory Coast claimed these people held, because Guinea had seized one of its fishing trawlers and detained some of its nationals. S-G refused to link the two problems, appointed his Personal Representative, José Rolz-Bennett, to discuss matters with the governments. S-G suggested procedures to resolve dispute, but not accepted. S-G asked for matter to be put on GA agenda on Guinea's request; OAU encouraged settlement. Both countries released nationals of each other end of Sept. 1967.

Date	*Case*	*Nature*	*UN bodies involved*
1967 (1963–69)	Ifni (colonial)	Cession of Spanish enclave to Morocco	GA (Special Committee of 24)

UN pressure on Spain to decolonise territory of 50 000 people and transfer it to Morocco, in which it formed an enclave. Special Committee of 24 and GA considered this problem from 1963. In 1965 GA urged Spain to decolonise and from 1967–69 GA pressed Spain to hasten decolonisation with arrangements for transfer. Treaty of Fez Jan. 1969 retroceded Ifni to Morocco on 30 June 1969.

Date	*Case*	*Nature*	*UN bodies involved*
1968	USS Pueblo	US complaint of seizure of ship by North Korea	SC

Part of larger Korean problem, airing of incident may have helped momentarily, but no solution. SC meetings 26 and 27 January 1968 on complaint by US of North Korean violation of Armistice Agreement, and specifically of seizure in international waters and detention of USS Pueblo and crew on 23 January. USSR opposed it coming before SC and charged vessel with espionage for CIA; it could not prevent discussion but could prevent action. None taken.

Date	*Case*	*Nature*	*UN bodies involved*
1968	Haiti	Bombing by private plane, origin in doubt	SC

Airing of bombing salutary. Haiti complained to S-G that on 20 May 1968 a plane had bombed Port-au-Prince and later Cap Haitien, alleged to be done by Haitian exiles. On 27 May 1968 SC met on request from Haiti to prevent further acts. US ready to investigate, Jamaica and Dominican Republic disclaimed use of their territory and UK reported no real evidence of flight from Bahamas. No action as insufficient information.

Date	*Case*	*Nature*	*UN bodies involved*
1968–69	Hijackings to Algeria and to Syria	Release of hijacked El Al plane, passengers and crew, and of TWA plane	S-G

S-G's good offices contributed to release of passengers, crew and plane in two instances.

To Algeria: El Al plane hijacked to Algiers 23 July 1968. S-G tried for weeks to get release of plane and occupants, to which Algeria finally agreed.

To Syria: TWA plane hijacked to Damascus 28 Aug. 1969. S-G in contact with Syrian government and with IFALPA (International Federation of Air Line Pilots), advising them against 24-hour plane strike or series of stoppages. Aircraft and occupants released.

Date	*Case*	*Nature*	*UN bodies involved*
1968	Czechoslovakia	USSR intervention	SC

SC action blocked by parties. In August 1968 six members requested SC to consider situation. USSR opposed discussion, claimed it and four allied countries acted in collective self-defence. SC meetings 21–24 August. Draft resolution condemning intervention and calling for withdrawal of USSR and other Warsaw Pact members, vetoed by USSR. Second draft resolution for S-G to send special representative to Prague to ensure safety and seek release of detained Czechoslovak leaders not put to vote. On 27 August acting Czechoslovak Representative asked matter be withdrawn from SC agenda in view of talks held in Moscow 23–26 August.

Date	*Case*	*Nature*	*UN bodies involved*
1968 (1967–70)	Nigeria	Civil War	S-G (Representatives for Human Activities)

Government of Nigeria claimed Biafran action a rebellion and an internal matter on which UN could not act under Art. 2 (7). S-G explored possibility of good offices and decided to encourage OAU to seek settlement. S-G concentrated on humanitarian help. OAU active in trying to get peaceful solution.

Fighting between federal troops and Biafrans from 6 July 1967 to January 1970. With agreement of Nigeria on 1 Aug. 1968 S-G appointed his Representative, N Gussing, for humanitarian activities. On the basis of his reports UN bodies, particularly UNICEF and the World Food Programme (WFP) encouraged to mobilise relief in conjunction with Red Cross. At invitation of Nigeria S-G Representative accompanied International Observer Team and reported to S-G no evidence of genocide, with possibly one exception Okigwi incident. This team observed conduct of Nigerian troops advancing into Biafra, October – November 1968. S-G appealed to Nigeria 11 Jan. 1970 to show humaneness and instruct forces to exercise restraint. S-G invited to Nigeria 18-19 January and consulted on humanitarian help as result of which UN operations intensified. S-G's Representative, Said-Uddin Khan (from April 1969), withdrawn 30 May 1970.

Date	*Case*	*Nature*	*UN bodies involved*
1969 (1963–69)	Equatorial Guinea (colonial and ex-colonial)	Independence from Spain. Charge that Spanish forces violating sovereignty	GA (Special Committee of 24 and sub-committee, Mission for Supervision of the Referendum and Elections in Equatorial Guinea), S-G (Personal Representative)

UN encouraged independence and supervised elections. S-G's quiet diplomacy solved dispute between Equatorial Guinea and Spain over charge that Spanish forces were violating sovereignty of Equatorial Guinea.

Equatorial Guinea administered by Spain, granted own legislature and executive under constitution of 1963 with Spain responsible for foreign relations and defence. Special Committee of 24 and GA considered territory from 1963, urging independence and UN supervision of elections. Special Committee of 24 sent subcommittee to study conditions in June 1966 at invitation of Spain. On basis of its recommendations GA asked Spain to hold elections, to convene constitutional conference and to set date for independence. S-G appointed UN Mission for Supervision of Referendum and Elections August 1968, which reported favourably on elections. Independence 12 Oct. 1968, admission to UN 12 November 1968.

In February 1969 Pres. of Equatorial Guinea telegraphed S-G for UN peace force, charging Spain violating its sovereignty with forces stationed there. Spain claimed its police there, on invitation of country, to protect Spaniards. S-G appointed Personal Representative, M Tamayo, to lend good offices, early March 1969 to 21 April 1969. Spanish forces withdrawn by 5 April and any Spaniards, who wished, left through help of S-G Representative. Equatorial Guinea also appealed to OAU but S-G thought, and the Emperor of Ethiopia agreed, that UN should deal with the matter as Spain not in OAU.

Date	*Case*	*Nature*	*UN bodies involved*
1969	Zambia, Portugal	Complaint of bombing of Zambian village	SC

Airing and censuring of border attacks. On 18 July 1969 SC considered Zambian complaint of Portuguese attacks and particularly of bombing of Zambian village of Lote on 30 June from Mozambique. Portugal claimed it had to engage in clean-up operation after Zambian encroachments. SC resolution 28 July 1969 censured Portuguese attack on village and called on Portugal to desist from territorial violations and to release Zambian civilians.

Date	*Case*	*Nature*	*UN bodies involved*
1969	Northern Ireland	Communal dispute	SC, S-G

SC provided safety-valve, but no action, as UK claimed matter domestic, Art.(2)7. SC met 20 Aug. 1969 on request from Ireland for UN peacekeeping force in Northern Ireland. It had already put proposals for a UN or a British-Irish peacekeeping force to the UK and had them rejected. SC heard statement of Irish Foreign Minister, but did not put matter on agenda because domestic. S-G repeated offer of his good offices. UK held to Art.2(7) and would not request them.

Date	*Case*	*Nature*	*UN bodies involved*
1970 (1968–70)	Bahrain (colonial)	Future of Bahrain after UK evacuation; claimed by Iran	SC, S-G (Personal Representative)

S-G preventive diplomacy solved dispute between UK and Iran over future status of Bahrain. UK had treaty of protection with Bahrain, but was about to leave the Gulf, Iran had long-standing claim to Bahrain. S-G held exploratory talks with UK and Iran 1968–69, willing to exercise good offices if requested. Iran made request 9 March 1970, UK concurred. S-G sent Personal Representative, Winspeare Guicciardi, to Bahrain to ascertain wishes of people 30 March – 18 April 1970. Report to S-G transmitted to SC 30 April 1970, that overwhelming majority wanted independence, endorsed by SC on 11 May 1970, and parties accepted conclusions.

Date	*Case*	*Nature*	*UN bodies involved*
1970 (1962–70)	Guyana, Venezuela	Boundary dispute and Tribunal Award of 1899	GA (Special Political Committee)

UN played little or no part, although prospects of agreed obligation to submit dispute to UN procedure appears to have hastened Protocol Moratorium on Venezuelan claims to Guyanese territory.

Venezuela claimed large area of British Guiana (colony of UK), against Arbitral Award of 1899. GA's Special Political Committee considered problem November 1963, no recommendation to GA in view of possibility of negotiations between parties. Geneva Agreement February 1966, by which UK and Venezuela established Mixed Commission to seek solution, and if not found by February 1970 to resort to procedures under UN Charter Art. 33. British Guiana achieved independence 26 May 1966 as Guyana, and became party to Geneva Agreement. Incidents and strained relations 1966 onwards, but border conferences continued. In June 1970 Port of Spain Protocol for 12 year moratorium on Venezuelan claims.

Date	*Case*	*Nature*	*UN bodies involved*
1970 (1969–71)	Guinea, Portuguese Guinea (semi-colonial)	Complaints of attacks by Portuguese troops and mercenaries etc.	SC (fact-finding mission, special mission)

SC attempts to discourage Portuguese attacks on Guinea from Guinea-Bissau, part of colonial problems of Africa.

15 Dec. 1969: SC considered complaints by Guinea against Portuguese attacks on Guinean frontier villages, motor barge, and detention of aircraft and crew. Portugal prepared to release plane, barge and occupants if Guinea released 24 of Portuguese forces, and charged Guineans with border attacks. SC resolution 22 Dec. 1969 deplored damage to Guinean villages and called on Portugal to desist and release plane, barge and occupants.

22–23 Nov. 1970: SC met on Guinea's claim that Portuguese forces and mercenaries had landed in its capital from Guinea-Bissau, denied by Portugal. Guinea asked for assistance by UN airborne troops. SC demanded withdrawal of external forces, sent five-member mission 24 November. It reported 3 December that in its judgment attack had been by Portuguese units with Guinean dissidents. On 8 December SC condemned Portugal, demanded compensation and requested S-G to help in assessment, but Guinea declined S-G's offer and the monetary reparation.

3 Aug. 1971: Guinea's complaint to SC, based on intelligence reports, that Portuguese preparing attack, presumably to liberate mercenaries implicated in November 1970. SC sent mission, which reported 15 September, but no recommendations. SC consensus took note of report and reiterated that Guinea's territorial integrity and independence must be respected.

Date	*Case*	*Nature*	*UN bodies involved*
1970 (1966–71)	South West Africa – Namibia, South Africa (colonial)	Efforts to end mandate of South Africa and establish interim UN Administration	SC (Ad Hoc sub-committee of SC), GA (Ad Hoc Committee for South West Africa, UN Council for South West Africa), S-G (UN Commissioner for Namibia), ICJ

UN effort to take over administration of Namibia in preparation for independence, blocked by South Africa and its homelands policy.

After the ICJ opinion GA voted, 27 Oct. 1966, to end mandate and place South West Africa under UN. It established Ad Hoc Committee for South West Africa to recommend means for administering it in preparation for independence. Acting on Ad Hoc Committee's recommendations the GA special session in 1967 established UN Council for South West Africa to administer territory, hold elections, help draw up constitution and transfer power with aim of independence by June 1968. But South Africa would not comply with GA resolutions. On 16 Dec. 1967 GA called on South Africa to withdraw, and to release and repatriate 37 SWAPO freedom fighters, and requested SC to take steps so Council for South West Africa could discharge its responsibilities.

The SC considered the problem of South West Africa and on 25 Jan. 1968 it called for release of SWAPO members on trial, which it reiterated on 14 March 1968. After the UN Council for South West Africa reported South Africa had prevented it entering South West Africa the GA proclaimed, on 12 June 1968, that South West Africa would be known as Namibia, and then, and on several occasions in 1968–69, recommended that SC should ensure withdrawal of South Africa. But South African Parliament passed the Development of Native Nations in South West Africa Act, providing for six 'homelands'.

On 20 March 1969 SC called for withdrawal of South Africa, which it rejected on 12 Aug. 1969. The SC, on 30 Jan. 1970, declared all acts of South Africa in Namibia after end of mandate invalid. It set up Ad Hoc Subcommittee of SC members on ways to implement its resolutions. On basis of its reports the SC (29 July 1970) asked states to do nothing that would imply recognition of South Africa's authority over Namibia, to stop commercial or financial dealings with Namibia and discourage investment in, or tourism and emigration to, Namibia. It asked the GA to set up the UN Fund for Namibia to finance education and training and to aid persecuted Namibians, it also requested the ICJ for an advisory opinion on the legal consequences for states of the continued presence of South Africa in Namibia. The ICJ judgment on 21 June 1971 was that the presence of South Africa in Namibia was illegal and South Africa should withdraw, and that states should refrain from any acts implying recognition of South Africa's authority there.

Meanwhile the GA repeated its condemnation of South Africa and of the allies and trading partners giving support to South Africa, it appealed to SC for measures (including ones under Chap. VII). It endorsed action of UN Council of Namibia on identity documents, set up the UN Fund for Namibia requested by the SC and called on South Africa to treat Namibians fighting for freedom as prisoners of war under 1949 Geneva Convention. In December 1971 GA urged S-G to nominate UN Commissioner for Namibia; Agha Abdul Hamid chosen.

Date	*Case*	*Nature*	*UN bodies involved*
1971 (1961–72)	Senegal, Portuguese Guinea (semi-colonial)	Complaints of attacks from Portuguese Guinea-Bissau	SC (fact-finding mission)

Part of colonial problems of Africa, beyond powers of UN to settle, but publicity important.

April 1963: SC discussed complaints of Portuguese violation of Senegal's territory from Guinea-Bissau, in particular of grenades dropped on Bougniack. It recalled previous violations in 1961. Charges denied by Portugal. SC deplored incursions on 24 April 1963 and asked Portugal to prevent territorial violations.

May 1965: SC meeting on complaint of Senegal that Portugal had violated its air-space and territory 16 times since April 1963. Portugal denied charges, alleged Senegal had helped attackers against Portuguese Guinea and suggested a three-man team of investigation, but Senegal did not agree. On 19 May 1965 SC again deplored incursions and asked Portugal to prevent any violation of Senegal's territory.

4 Dec. 1969: SC considered Senegal's complaint alleging shelling by Portuguese of Samine village, and past violations of its territory. Portugal claimed self-defence against anti-Portuguese organisations and attacks. SC resolution 9 Dec. 1969 condemning Portugal for shelling, called on it to stop violations.

July 1971: SC considered complaint by Senegal of several incidents, in particular the laying of mines by Portuguese on Senegalese territory. Portugal suggested that as mines were Russian this might have been a PAIGC manoeuvre.

SC resolution 15 July 1971 condemned mine-laying and demanded end to acts of violence against population and villages of Senegal by Portuguese armed forces since 1963. It requested Pres. of SC and S-G to send fact-finding mission of SC members (assisted by military experts) to border, in order to report to SC 'making any recommendation aimed at guaranteeing peace and security in this region'. Mission in Senegal 25 July – 1 August, refused access to Guinea-Bissau, reported 16 September and recommended SC to call for immediate end to acts of violence. As it was not allowed in Guinea-Bissau it lacked additional information to carry out its mandate, but on the evidence it considered the attack on Kandjenou could have only been conducted with a trained and fully equipped force.

23 Oct. 1972: SC resolution condemned attack of Portuguese on Senegalese post of Nianao (12 October), and demanded respect of Senegal's territory. Portugal stated apologies had been expressed with offer of compensation. Senegal rejected compensation.

Date	*Case*	*Nature*	*UN bodies involved*
1971	Zambia, South Africa (semi-colonial)	Complaint of attacks from Namibia	SC

Part of strains of decolonisation in southern Africa; airing may have discouraged incidents. On 12 Oct. 1971 SC unanimously called on South Africa to respect territorial integrity of Zambia, and if it did not, SC would examine the situation further. Complaint by Zambia against South Africa listing two dozen incidents of incursions and airspace violations since 1968 across Namibian-Zambian border.

South Africa alleged attacks by armed bands from Zambia and violation of its airspace.

Date	*Case*	*Nature*	*UN bodies involved*
1971	Gulf Islands, Iran (ex-colonial)	Iran seized three Gulf islands after evacuation by UK	SC

Airing may have eased a clash of claims. SC held discussions 9 Dec. 1971, but adjourned in view of third-party efforts to resolve problem. On 30 Nov. 1971, the day before the UK's protection treaty expired, Iran occupied three islands – Abu Musa, Greater and Lesser Tumbs, sparsely inhabited, but strategically located and of particular concern to the United Arab Emirates whose federation was formed on 2 Dec. 1971 (including Gulf state of Sharjah). It was alleged this occupation was done with the connivance of the UK, but the UK claimed an agreement had been reached beforehand between Iran and the ruler of Sharjah over Abu Musa, but not with the ruler of Ras al Khaima over the two Tumbs. Libya nationalised British oil interests in retaliation.

Date	*Case*	*Nature*	*UN bodies involved*
1971 (1971–73)	Bangladesh, Pakistan, India	Struggle for autonomy; then independence, involving hostilities between India and Pakistan	SC (UN Military Observer Group, Special Representative), GA, S-G (Personal Representative, UN East Pakistan Relief Operation, UN Relief Operation in Bangladesh, UN Relief Operation in Dacca, group of consultants to review needs, consortium to clear Chalna Port), UNHCR

UN mobilised humanitarian help, but members reluctant to tackle dispute and only took political action to stop hostilities after outbreak of war between India and Pakistan.

East Pakistan's aim for autonomy within a federal government, thwarted in March 1971, followed by demand for independence and civil war in April. Refugees from East Pakistan fled into India, estimated at seven million by October. Because of Art. 2 (7), ruling out UN action in domestic matters, S-G concentrated on humanitarian help. On 22 April 1971 he offered relief assistance for people of East Pakistan. To help refugees in India he designated UNHCR as coordinator, and made an international appeal.

On 20 July the S-G reported on the problem in a memorandum to the Pres. of the

SC, drawing attention to its responsibility for the maintenance of peace, but members reluctant to take up dispute for fear nothing would be achieved. On 20 October S-G offered his good offices to India and Pakistan.

Full-scale war started 3 Dec. 1971. SC met on 4th, USSR vetoed resolutions for ceasefire and withdrawal of forces, dispute referred to GA under 'Uniting for Peace' resolution. On 7 December GA called for ceasefire and withdrawal. Pakistan capitulated 16 December. SC demanded on 21 December end to hostilities and withdrawal of troops to previous lines (including Kashmir line of 1949), called for relief assistance and authorised S-G to appoint Special Representative for good offices regarding humanitarian problems. Winspeare Guicciaridi chosen and went to area immediately. UN organised large amounts of aid for Bangladesh and consortium of firms to clear approaches of Chalna Port (completed May 1973). UNHCR repatriated by air nearly a quarter of a million people between Bangladesh and Pakistan.

Date	*Case*	*Nature*	*UN bodies involved*
1972 (1963–72)	Burundi, Rwanda	Inter-tribal civil strife	S-G (Special Representative, Special Mission to assess humanitarian needs), UNHCR

Tribal strife and subversive activities involving Rwanda and Burundi. UN concentrated on humanitarian help, problem of Art.2(7).

In December 1963 troubles started in Rwanda which alleged guerrilla Batutsis had infiltrated from Burundi: the latter counter-charged Rwanda with killing Batutsis in Rwanda and appealed to S-G and OAU. S-G called on both countries to do everything possible to establish peaceful relations. He sent a Special Representative from the Congo to assess situation and make recommendations which the governments used as a basis for agreement, and S-G arranged for humanitarian help of UNHCR for refugees. OAU took an increasingly active part in recurring troubles.

In April 1972, there was serious tribal strife in Burundi with 80 000 reported dead; allegations of connivance of Rwanda. On 26 May 1972 S-G sent message to Pres. of Burundi offering humanitarian assistance, while assuring him of the S-G's commitment to Art. 2 (7). With agreement of Burundi S-G sent special three-member team to assess needs 22–28 June, which reported on 24 July. Special Mission informed about 40 000 had taken refuge in Rwanda, Tanzania and Zaire. It discussed conditions for assistance by UN system. S-G sent technical mission 1 Aug. 1972.

Date	*Case*	*Nature*	*UN bodies involved*
1972 (1972–74)	Guinea-Bissau (colonial)	Struggle for independence	GA (Special Committee of 24 – Special Mission of three-members)

UN efforts to foster independence. Despite Portuguese opposition, Special Committee of 24 sent a special mission of three members, which visited the area controlled by PAIGC 2–8 April 1972, to report on situation and ascertain where effective control of areas lay. Guinea-Bissau proclaimed itself an independent state. GA resolution 2 Nov. 1973 welcomed Guinea-Bissau's 'recent accession to independence' (24 Sept. 1973) and called on Portugal to withdraw. Coup in Portugal 25 April 1974 made negotiations possible between PAIGC and Portuguese government, which agreed in August for independence on 10 Sept. 1974, whereupon Guinea-Bissau became a member of the UN on 17 Sept. 1974.

Date	*Case*	*Nature*	*UN bodies involved*
1972–73	Uganda	Expulsion of Asians	S-G (two Special Representatives), UNHCR

UN was restricted to humanitarian help in the case of the expulsion of Asians from Uganda, because of Art. 2(7). The S-G sent two Special Respresentatives to give humanitarian assistance and the UN then helped 3300 stateless Asians to leave from 28 Oct.–9 Nov. 1972. The UNHCR arranged for their temporary settlement and then undertook their permanent settlement.

Date	*Case*	*Nature*	*UN bodies involved*
1973	Zambia, Southern Rhodesia	Economic blockade of Zambia, reversed into Zambian boycott of Southern Rhodesia	SC (Special Mission and Group of Experts), GA (Consultative Group on Aid to Zambia), S-G (Coordinator of Aid)

Airing and support; part of confrontation with Southern Rhodesia over its treatment of African majority: UN efforts to give Zambia economic support in applying sanctions.

SC met at end of January 1973 on complaint of Zambia against closing of border by Southern Rhodesia on 9 Jan. 1973, imposing an economic blockade and demanding Zambia stop supporting and harbouring freedom fighters. On 2 February SC condemned economic blockade and military threats of Southern Rhodesia in collusion with South Africa, and decided to send Special Mission of four SC members with six UN experts to assess needs for other systems of transport. It commended Zambia for severing all economic and trade relations with Southern Rhodesia, in compliance with SC decisions (sanctions).

The Special Mission reported to SC in March on tensions heightened by acts of Southern Rhodesia and deployment of South African forces and claimed key to situation in application of majority rule in Southern Rhodesia. It reported on feasibility of alternative trade routes. On 10 March SC appealed to all states for assistance to Zambia to maintain its normal flow of traffic. S-G announced, 26 April 1973, Sir Robert Jackson would coordinate UN aid to Zambia. On 15 November GA Consultation Group on aid to Zambia discussed assistance.

Date	*Case*	*Nature*	*UN bodies involved*
1973	Cuba, Chile	Complaint of attack on Cuban Embassy and ship	SC

Airing possibly helpful. Complaint in September 1973 before SC that Chilean forces had attacked Cuba's embassy and one of its merchant ships while in international waters. Chile rejected charge and said it 'did not constitute a situation capable of threatening peace'. No resolution.

Date	*Case*	*Nature*	*UN bodies involved*
1973–74	October War	Part of Middle East conflict between Israel, Egypt and Syria	SC (UNTSO, UNEF, UNDOF), GA (Continuing activity of UNRWA and Special Committee to Investigate Israeli Practices affecting the Human Rights of the Populations of the Occupied Territories), S-G (Personal Representative)

Efforts of UN to get a ceasefire and to provide a buffer force, between Egyptians-Israelis and Israelis-Syrians, played an essential part in disengagement.

Arab attack on 6 Oct. 1973 to regain territories occupied by Israel in Six-day War of 1967. Outbreak discussed in SC and GA then in session. SC held three inconclusive meetings 8 and 9 October. Members divided on when to call a ceasefire and to what line; complicated because neither Arabs nor Israelis wanted a ceasefire. S-G waited for SC action, but on 11 October appealed especially to its members to 're-double their efforts' and himself continued intensive consultations with all concerned. At SC meeting on 12 October no agreement on whether to give priority to ceasefire or whether this should be linked with Israeli withdrawal from occupied territories. European Community conveyed to S-G its appeal for a ceasefire and a settlement on basis of SC resolution 242 (1967). US airlifted arms to Israel, and Arab states imposed oil weapon.

Consultations between Kissinger and Brezhnev in Moscow; US and USSR then urgently requested SC meeting, held 21 October, to consider a draft they co-sponsored. This resolution 338 was adopted at 4.50 am 22 October unanimously (with China not participating). It called for ceasefire within 12 hours in present positions, an immediate start to implementing SC resolution 242 (1967) and negotiations 'under appropriate auspices aimed at establishing a just and durable peace'. SC confirmed its resolution 338 on 23 October and urged return to positions at the time of its effect (22 October). It called on S-G for UN observers to supervise ceasefire, for which S-G had already made preparations, and he informed SC that number of observers might have to be increased. The night of 24 October at 11.35, US issued its precautionary military alert in fear that USSR intended sending troops to Middle East.

Violations of ceasefire continued. SC adopted resolution 340 of non-aligned states on 25 October demanding a complete ceasefire and return to position of 22 October at 16.50 hours; it requested increase in UN observers, set up UN Emergency Force (UNEF) from UN members. No permanent members allowed to provide personnel to UNEF, although UK, US and USSR did provide transport. In observer group (UNTSO) 36 Americans and 36 Russians allowed to serve.

S-G reported on 26 October to SC on guidelines for the force, providing that the command be vested in the S-G under authority of SC and further that 'all matters which may affect the nature of the continued effective functioning of the force will be referred to the Council for its decision'. It outlined the rights and privileges of the force – freedom of movement etc., and provided the composition should be selected in consultation with the SC, the weapons to be defensive and 'it shall not use force except in self-defence' which would include resistance to any hindrance of its duties. S-G recommended a total stength of 7000 for six months, and he appointed Maj.-Gen Siilasvuo of UNTSO as Interim Commander and was arranging for the transfer of some forces from Cyprus as an interim measure. (first elements arrived within 30 hours). S-G's report adopted by SC 27 October, but his proposal that the force should be financed as an expense of the UN apportioned by GA was not accepted and the GA later made other arrangements. China said it would not contribute, USSR prepared to take part in financing if it continued to function lawfully under SC authority, and France had no objection to financing the force.

Limited breaches of ceasefire and no withdrawal. An agreement devised by Kissinger was signed at Kilometre 101 on Cairo-Suez road, 11 November, providing for strict observance of ceasefire, non-military supplies for town of Suez, evacuation of civilian wounded, replacement of Israeli checkpoints by UN ones, exchange of prisoners of war and wounded and immediate discussions 'to settle the question of the return to the 22 October positions in the framework of agreement on the disengagement and separation of forces under the auspices of the UN'. The UN checkpoints established 15 November and the exchange of wounded and prisoners of war took place, but the talks at Kilometre 101 floundered, Israel would not contemplate return to 22 October positions.

On 11 December GA approved the method of financing for the UNEF. It appropriated $30 million from 25 Oct. 1973 to 24 April 1974, and apportioned the assessment, which on a percentage basis amounted to:

5	SC permanent members	63.15%
25	Other developed countries (specified)	34.78%
	Less developed countries	2.02%
25	Even less developed countries (specified)	.05%

On 21 December S-G opened Geneva Conference, arranged by US and USSR, with Egypt, Israel, Jordan also present (but not Syria). He recalled the SC resolution 338 and the fact that the return to the 22 October position had not been implemented. He hoped the conference would progress on that as well as negotiations for a settlement; R Guyer was his Personal Representative at the Conference. After ministerial meetings the working group of Egypt and Israel met on 26 December, with Gen. Siilasvuo of UNEF as chairman, to discuss principles of disengagement. Israeli elections 31 December.

After Kissinger's visit to Middle East, the Disengagement Agreement was reached and signed at Kilometre 101 on 18 Jan. 1974 with the UNEF commander acting as witness. It provided for Israeli withdrawal across the Canal and three parallel strips of six miles each on the east bank, with Egyptians nearest the Canal, a UNEF buffer in the middle zone, and Israelis in the eastern strip. The arms and forces in the Egyptian and Israeli strips were to be limited and subject to inspection by UNEF. The Agreement was specifically recognised as a first step towards a durable peace. The plan detailing disengagements was signed 24 January and the exercise was to be completed within 40 days. As the disengagement phases progressed UNEF took over each area for a short interim period. It proceeded smoothly and was completed 4 March. UNEF numbered 6973 men by 21 February (nearly the 7000 planned), coming from Austria, Canada (logistics), Finland, Ghana (evaluation team), Indonesia, Ireland (withdrawn in May as needed at home), Panama, Peru, Poland (logistics), Senegal (advance party), Sweden. SC extended UNEF repeatedly until July 1979 when it lapsed as a result of Camp David.

Kissinger's shuttle negotiations between Israel and Syria ended in the Disengagement Agreement signed in Geneva 31 May 1974 providing for ceasefire, repatriation of all wounded and prisoners of war, the establishment of a UN buffer zone in part of the Golan Heights, and for a working group (presided over by Gen. Siilasvuo) to detail disengagement. Under a protocol the two parties agreed to support a SC resolution establishing a UN Disengagement Observer Force (UNDOF) of 1250 men for six months (but none from SC permanent members). SC met 31 May to approve accord and establish UNDOF. Initially S-G provided for force from Austrians and Peruvians (serving in Canal area) under Brig.-Gen Gonzalo Briceno of Peru. The S-G visited the Middle East early in June seeing UN contingents and meeting government leaders. Disengagement put into effect smoothly, completed by 25 June, UNDOF acting as buffer. The situation was calm, 1218 officers and men on inspection activities. (UNEF reduced to 5079 men in order to establish UNDOF).

Date	*Case*	*Nature*	*UN bodies involved*
1974	Guinea, West Germany	Three West Germans held in Guinea for subversive activities	S-G

Successful quiet diplomacy of S-G. Relations broken between Guinea and West Germany because three West Germans held in Guinea charged with participation in plot against Pres. Sekou Toure. S-G secured statement from Pres. Scheel of West Germany (22 July 1974) condemning any intervention or use of violence and referring to German nationals 'who it has been established have regrettably contravened' these principles in Guinea. The three Germans released at end of July 1974.

Date	*Case*	*Nature*	*UN bodies involved*
1974 (1966–75)	Portuguese territories in Africa (colonial)	Pressure for independence	GA (Special Committee of 24), SC, S-G, UN missions

UN pressure for decolonisation of Portuguese territories in Africa continued. In 1966 the GA appealed to all states to support the peoples of the territories and condemned financial interest that obstructed their struggle. In 1969 it called on specialised agencies to increase their assistance to the people, and leaders in East and Central Africa adopted a Lusaka Manifesto which the GA commended on 20 November. This urged independence for the territories preferably by peaceful change. In 1970 the GA called on states particularly NATO ones to desist from collaboration with Portugal that might hamper decolonisation. It asked Portugal to treat freedom fighters as prisoners of war under the 1949 Geneva Convention, and states to end any exploitation of the territories and to discourage their nationals from activities that impeded their independence. The SC held that Portuguese colonialism in Africa was a threat to peace and security of independent states there.

In 1972 the GA held that the liberation movements of Angola, Guinea-Bissau, Caper Verde and Mozambique were representatives of the peoples of those territories, while the SC reaffirmed their right to independence and called on Portugal to cease all repression of them.

Following a change of government (April 1974) Portugal approved a constitutional law 24 July 1974 acknowledging the right of self-determination including independence for these territories and on 3 August it advised the S-G it would cooperate with the UN in decolonisation. In January 1975 a special UN mission visited Cape Verde on food needs, followed the next month by a mission of the Special Committee of 24 on financial requirements, whereupon the S-G appealed for two types of international aid for the emerging state and made emergency arrangements. In April a joint UN and OAU mission visited Angola to assess future needs.

The territories became independent in 1975, Mozambique on 25 June, Cape Verde on 5 July, Sao Tome and Principe on 12 July, and Angola on 11 November. Three of them became members of the UN on 16 Sept. 1975, but Angola on 1 Dec. 1976.

Date	*Case*	*Nature*	*UN bodies involved*
1974 (1969–75)	Iran, Iraq	Boundary and navigation dispute	SC, S-G (Special Representative)

Boundary disputes aired, UN helped stop border fighting pending agreement. Iran and Iraq were in dispute for some years about the navigation of the Shatt al-Arab river (one of the borders between these countries for 80 miles). This came to a head in 1969. Iran abrogated, in April 1969, so-called colonial Boundary Treaty of 1937, but recognised right of free navigation. Iraq charged massing of troops. Iran claimed Iraq was hampering free navigation and had therefore not carried out its commitments under the treaty, so Iran had the right to declare it null and void. From 1969 to 1973 parties aired their dispute in annual speeches to the GA, they suggested various methods for a settlement – direct negotiations, ICJ, fact-finding mission, informal conversations with S-G to get a 'good officer', a Special Representative of S-G; but they never agreed on what measure to take. Thousands of Iranians summarily expelled from Iraq in 1971. But tension eased so that relations restored in October 1973.

On 10 Feb. 1974 armed clash occurred far north of river border dispute, in Badra-Mehra area, with some 100 troops killed. This followed previous clashes in December 1973 connected with the delineation of the border and road-building. Boundary Treaty of 1937 again in dispute. Each party blamed the other. Iraq asked for SC meeting, held 15 and 20 February. SC consensus of 28 February deplored loss of life, appealed to parties to refrain from all military action, requested S-G to appoint Special Representative to investigate events. China dissociated itself as it did not favour UN involvement in any form of boundary dispute. S-G appointed Amb. Luis Weckmann-Munoz, the S-G reported to SC in May 1974 that Iran and Iraq had agreed to simultaneous withdrawal and to observe ceasefire. According to Weckmann-Munoz Iran and Iraq also intended to stand by the findings of a joint delimitation commission which would settle sharing of the waters that flowed from one to the other country, and that they were prepared to negotiate an agreement for unhampered navigation of the Shatt al-Arab. This was welcomed by a SC resolution of 28 May.

Spasmodic border troubles continued despite negotiations in Istanbul. Kurds revolting in Iraq received some support from Iran. At Algiers summit meeting of OPEC early in March 1975, Iran and Iraq reached an agreement which legalised Iran's claim to part of Shatt al-Arab estuary in return for an end to Iran's help for Kurdish rebels. A ceasefire was announced 13 March and a reconciliation treaty between Iran and Iraq was signed 13 June 1975.

Date	*Case*	*Nature*	*UN bodies involved*
1974	Cyprus, Turkey	Short-lived coup, Turkish intervention, followed by occupation of over a third of the island	SC (UNFICYP), GA, S-G (Special Representative), UNHCR

UN efforts to minimise communal hostilities, arrange military ceasefire, assure independence and territorial integrity of Cyprus and provide relief.

On 2 April 1974 communal talks between Greek and Turkish Cypriots suspended by Pres. Makarios because Turkish PM favoured federation for Cyprus. Talks resumed 11 June. On 11 July Luis Weckmann-Munoz became S-G's Special Representative.

EOKA-B guerrillas caused trouble in June, allegedly directed from Athens through 650 Greek officers staffing Cypriot National Guard. Pres. Makarios, on 2 July, demanded the Greek government withdraw officers. Coup against Pres. Makarios believed to be engineered from Athens 15 July, EOKA backer – N Sampson assumed Presidency.

S-G appealed to Greece and Turkey for restraint. Makarios government representative at UN called for SC meeting 16 July. Makarios escaped, attended SC on 19th. Turkey intervened in Cyprus 20 July, claiming this as its right under 1960 Treaty of Guarantee. UNFICYP repeatedly tried to get ceasefire in Nicosia and prevent spread of hostilities (not its mandate to oppose military forces of two sides). SC meeting 20 July adopted resolution 353 for respect of independence and territorial integrity of Cyprus, a ceasefire, withdrawal of foreign military personnel not authorised there by international agreement, negotiations by Greece, Turkey and UK for peace and constitutional government.

On 23 July Clerides became acting Pres. (as Speaker of National Assembly this was constitutional) and coup in Athens made Karamanlis PM displacing the Junta. SC reaffirmed ceasefire call. On 25 July foreign ministers of UK, Greece and Turkey met in Geneva, with R Guyer as UN observer, and agreed on 30 July that SC resolution 353 should be implemented, areas held by each side should not be extended beyond those controlled on 30 July and that a security zone under

UNFICYP should be established between areas to be determined by their representatives and UNFICYP, with subsidiary provisions, and agreement to meet 8 August. UNFICYP enlarged on 31 July to 3484 but Turks resented presence in any area they controlled. On 1 August SC authorised S-G to carry out function ascribed to UN by Geneva Agreement.

At 8 August meeting Greek and Turkish Cypriots also represented, and S-G on two day visit. Talks collapsed 14 August, and Turks attacked in force immediately. SC met 14 August and adopted UK draft, which reaffirmed resolution 353, demanded ceasefire and called for resumption of negotiations. On 15th SC deplored UNFICYP casualties, demanded cooperation for force in carrying out its tasks including humanitarian ones. On 16th it disapproved of 'unilateral military actions' against Cyprus, urged withdrawals and compliance with SC resolutions and resumption of negotiations in accordance with resolution 353. Turkey announced ceasefire for 16 August.

On 21 August the UNHCR was in Cyprus to examine humanitarian needs. The Red Cross had asked UNIFICYP to assume responsibility for relief convoys. S-G visited Greece, Cyprus and Turkey, 25–26 August, and arranged meeting of Clerides and Denktash (Turkish-Cypriot leader) on relief matters, agreed to be held weekly. On 30 August SC called for relief to refugees, believed to number 200 000 in same proportion as Greek and Turkish Cypriots (4:1), formerly spread throughout the island.

On 1 November the GA unanimously called for respect of the sovereignty, territorial integrity, independence and non-alignment of Cyprus, and an end to foreign interference, withdrawal of foreign forces and return of refugees. It left constitutional matters for the Cypriots to settle but urged their continuing contacts with the help of the S-G. On 13 Dec. 1974 the SC endorsed and urged implementation of the resolution.

Date	*Case*	*Nature*	*UN bodies involved*
1975 (1946–75)	Papua New Guinea, Australia	Future status of Trust Territory, administered by Australia	TC (Visiting Missions), GA (Special Committee of 24, Special Mission to observe elections)

UN fostered self-government and independence of Trust Territory of New Guinea, administered by Australia jointly with territory of Papua. TC concerned with social, educational, economic and political development of the territories and made recommendations accordingly. It received and considered regular reports and sent missions. After a House of Assembly was established in 1964, the TC urged greater effort to promote people for executive authority and to extend functions and responsibilities of local government councils, as well as planning for economic development.

GA affirmed people's right to self-government and independence, and called for target date; it was anxious for Australia to discourage separatist movement. Two members of Special Committee of 24 joined two members of TC on visiting mission 24 Jan. – 6 March 1971, and again when Special Mission sent, on invitation of Australia, to observe elections to House of Assembly 19 Feb. – 11 March 1972. Self-government achieved December 1973 and independence on 16 Sept. 1975. Papua New Guinea became a UN member on 10 Oct. 1975.

Date	*Case*	*Nature*	*UN bodies involved*
1975	Iceland, UK	Fishery claims and ramming of vessels	SC

Airing but no action. Iceland extended its fishing limits to 200 miles on 15 Oct. 1975, claiming extensive catches were endangering its stocks, disregarded by UK trawlers. Negotiations with UK for agreement on catches failed. British support ships accompanying trawlers collided with Icelandic coast guard vessel. SC met 16 Dec. 1975 and Iceland complained of British naval deployment in three subsequent letters.

Date	*Case*	*Nature*	*UN bodies involved*
1976	France, Somalia, French Somaliland	Border clash during rescue of school children from terrorists	SC

Necessary airing. France and Somalia requested meeting of SC over an incident of 3–4 February 1976 in vicinity of Loyada. France alleged its soldiers were fired on from Somali territory when rescuing 30 Djibouti school children in a bus seized by terrorists, and had to respond. Somalia charged France with unprovoked aggression. France expressed regret if any Somali civilians were killed or wounded. No resolution was tabled.

Date	*Case*	*Nature*	*UN bodies involved*
1976	Mozambique, Southern Rhodesia	Aggressive acts by Southern Rhodesia and UN sanctions	SC, S-G (team of experts)

Airing and support. In March 1976 Mozambique severed all economic relations with Southern Rhodesia to implement UN sanctions. On 17 March SC commended it for this action, condemned Southern Rhodesia for incursion into Mozambique, called on states to provide assistance and for S-G to organise material help for Mozambique. In April a UN team visited Mozambique to assess its needs.

Date	*Case*	*Nature*	*UN bodies involved*
1976	Angola, South Africa	South African troops in Angola	SC

In March 1976 South Africa affirmed withdrawal of its troops from Angola during course of seven SC meetings. They had entered Angola on 9 Aug. 1975 allegedly to protect workers on Calueque dam. SC met at request of Kenya at Angola did not become a member until the following December. On 31 March the Council condemned South African aggression, demanded respect for Angola's sovereignty and called for compensation.

Date	*Case*	*Nature*	*UN bodies involved*
1976	Israel, Uganda, OAU	Entebbe raid to free hostages from hijackers	SC, S-G

Airing but no action. An Air France plane was hijacked 27–28 June 1976 to Uganda by pro-Palestinian terrorists. The S-G took a number of steps to get the hostages released. He met Amin for this purpose on 2 and 3 July at an OAU meeting in Mauritius. On 3–4 July Israeli commandos, after a skirmish at the airport, freed the hostages and flew them back. The OAU complained of 'an act of aggression'. The SC met five times during 9–14 July but failed to adopt a resolution, lacking a majority.

Date	*Case*	*Nature*	*UN bodies involved*
1976	Zambia, South Africa	Raid on Zambian village	SC

Airing and condemnation. Zambia complained that South Africa had inflicted casualties in its village of Sialola on 11 July 1976 aiming at the SWAPO freedom fighter transit camp. South Africa claimed no knowledge of the action. The SC met five times. South Africa was willing for an investigation, but the SC opposed this lest it confer legitimacy on South African activities in Namibia. On 30 July 1976 the SC condemned the armed attack, demanded South Africa respect Zambian territory, not use Namibia as a launching base and commended 'front line' states for their support of Namibia.

Date	*Case*	*Nature*	*UN bodies involved*
1976	Greece, Turkey	Continental Shelf	SC, ICJ

Dispute over Aegean continental shelf not resolved by SC or ICJ. On 10 Aug. 1976 Greece complained to the Pres. of SC of violations of its sovereignty on its continental shelf, which arose from seismological explorations by Turkey; and at same time Greece asked ICJ to indicate interim measures of protection. Turkey denounced 'unfounded claims'. On 25 August SC adopted consensus resolution appealing to both parties to exercise restraint, resume direct negotiations and to take account of the contribution of the ICJ.

Date	*Case*	*Nature*	*UN bodies involved*
1976	Lesotho, South Africa	Closing of Transkei border posts	SC, S-G (mission)

Airing, condemnation of disguised South African effort to get Lesotho to recognise Transkei, and supportive assistance. Transkei independence declared 26 Oct. 1976, GA then called on all governments not to recognise it. Three border posts with Lesotho closed and travel documents required. SC adopted resolutions by consensus on 22 December, endorsing the GA's resolution, condemning South Africa for trying to coerce Lesotho into recognising Transkei, calling on it to take steps to open the posts and on all states and UN agencies to help Lesotho and for S-G to organise such help. S-G then sent a mission to assess Lesotho's needs, which recommended $66 million was required for emergency programme and $47 million for a development programme, which was endorsed by the SC 25 May 1977.

Date	*Case*	*Nature*	*UN bodies involved*
1976	Bangladesh, India	Division of waters of Ganges	GA

Airing of a long-standing dispute and call for negotiations. Complaint of Bangladesh over India's unilateral withdrawal of water from Ganges at Farakka. GA consensus of 26 Nov. 1976, in which parties concerned concurred, that a solution was urgent and they were to meet for negotiations. Agreement on Ganges issue initialled 30 Sept. 1977.

Date	*Case*	*Nature*	*UN bodies involved*
1976–77	Botswana, Southern Rhodesia	Hostile acts	SC, S-G (mission)

Airing and assistance. On 14 Jan. 1977 the SC strongly condemned hostile acts by Southern Rhodesia against Botswana and demanded their cessation. Recent ones had been between 17 and 19 Dec. 1976. The resolution accepted Botswana's invitation to send a mission to assess its needs, as security could only be strengthened at expense of development. The SC asked the S-G to arrange assistance. On 25 May 1977 the SC unanimously endorsed the mission's assessment, that $53.5 million would be needed over three years for normal development, of which $28 million would cover diversions for security needs. The SC requested UN members and organisations to assist Botswana.

Date	*Case*	*Nature*	*UN bodies involved*
1977	Benin	Attack by mercenaries	SC (mission) S-G (team of experts)

Airing and assistance. Mercenaries landed at Cotonou on 16 Jan. 1977, but were beaten back. The SC decided on 8 February to send a mission of its members to investigate and affirmed the territorial integrity of Benin. The mission reported Benin had been subjected to aggression by mercenaries (non-nationals of Benin), but it had not the time to verify responsibility for the attack. On 14 April the SC condemned the aggression, appealed for measures to outlaw mercenaries and asked the S-G to help Benin assess the damage. A team of experts evaluated Benin's losses at $28 million and on 24 Nov. 1977 the SC appealed to international organisations and states to assist Benin to repair the damage.

Date	*Case*	*Nature*	*UN bodies involved*
1977 (1966–77)	France, French Somaliland (Djibouti) (colonial)	Independence	GA (Special Committee of 24), UN mission

UN pressed for the independence of this French territory. The GA and Special Committee of 24 first considered it in 1966. The GA urged that the referendum to be held before July 1967 be conducted on a democratic basis, and that a UN presence supervise and observe it. In March 1967 the Special Committee of 24 regretted that the GA's resolution had not been complied with. No UN presence was permitted before or at the referendum on 19 March 1967, which gave a majority vote for association with France.

On 1 Dec. 1976 the GA called on France to implement the independence of French Somaliland by the summer of 1977. It urged political groups to resolve their differences and welcomed the declarations of Ethiopia and Somalia to respect the independence and territorial integrity of French Somaliland. A UN mission observed the election of 8 May 1977 with more than 90 per cent favouring independence, which was attained on 27 June 1977. Djibouti became a member of the UN on 20 Sept. 1977.

Date	*Case*	*Nature*	*UN bodies involved*
1977	Mozambique, Southern Rhodesia	Aggressive acts by Southern Rhodesia	SC, S-G

Airing and assistance. SC considered Mozambique's complaint of frequent aggressive acts by Southern Rhodesia and on 30 June 1977 unanimously condemned such acts, calling on states to assist Mozambique to strengthen its defence and overcome its losses. It asked the S-G to coordinate assistance efforts of the UN system and to organise a programme of international help. UN mission then left for Mozambique to assess needs.

Date	*Case*	*Nature*	*UN bodies involved*
1977 (1964–79)	Panama Canal	New agreement between Panama and US	SC, S-G (Special Representative)

UN pressure for a new agreement between Panama and the US on future status of the Canal. On the basis of the Joint Declaration of Panama and the US (13 April 1964) the two parties started negotiations about the canal, which resulted in three draft treaties (1967), that were rejected by Panama. Negotiations were broken off until resumed 29 June 1971.

SC held its meeting in Panama City 15–21 March 1973. UC vetoed a resolution on the Canal claiming is was unbalanced, over-simplified and subject to misinterpretation, but it had recognised that the Treaty of 1903 should be replaced.

On 7 Sept. 1977 the US and Panama signed two treaties which provided that the US would gradually hand over control of the Canal and Canal Zone to Panama to be completed by 2000, and guaranteed its neutrality with a provision that American warships had permanent right of passage. A plebiscite was held in Panama on 23 Oct. 1977, witnessed by the S-G's Special Representative. Ratification documents were exchanged on 16 June 1978 and sovereignty of the zone was formally restored to Panama on 1 Oct. 1979.

Date	*Case*	*Nature*	*UN bodies involved*
1978	Chad, Libya	Alleged foreign intervention	SC

Airing. Chad complained at a SC meeting 17 Feb. 1978 that Libya was occupying part of its territory and asked for the withdrawal of Libyan troops and an end to its interference in Chad. On 21 February Chad informed the SC it was withdrawing its complaint according to a Chad-Libyan-Sudanese communique on an agreement of the three delegations for steps to solve their dispute.

Date	*Case*	*Nature*	*UN bodies involved*
1978 (1968–78)	Israel, Lebanon	Part of Palestinian Middle East problem, Israeli attacks on Lebanon	SC (UNIFIL, UNTSO), GA, S-G

UN efforts to control the spasm of attacks, which could only be cured by solving the Palestinian problem.

Tensions built up on the Israeli-Lebanese border with Israel complaining of terrorist attacks and Lebanon of military retaliation. In December 1968 the Israelis bombed Beirut airport as a reprisal for an attack by fedayeens. From then to the severe attack of 1972 the SC adopted five resolutions against Israeli military intervention.

On 28 Feb. 1972 the SC demanded Israel withdraw and refrain from ground and air action. In April, at the request of Lebanon the SC increased the UN observers on its side of the border and set up three observation posts.

In the period that followed the SC adopted several resolutions against subsequent Israeli interventions. Tension culminated in 1978, after a PLO attack against buses on the Tel-Aviv road causing a number of casualities on 11 March 1978. The Israelis advanced into South Lebanon 14–15 March. On 19 March the SC called on Israel to withdraw and established a UN Interim Force in Lebanon (UNIFIL) to confirm the withdrawal and to ensure return of the area to Lebanon. An advance party of UNIFIL arrived three days later.

In April the GA authorised the necessary funds for UNIFIL until 18 Sept. 1978. After a visit of the S-G to Lebanon the SC approved an increase in the force from 4000 to 6000 (3 May 1978). The Israelis confirmed their withdrawal on 13 June, but handed over a border zone to a Christian irregular faction with its backing.

Date	*Case*	*Nature*	*UN bodies involved*
1978 (1972–78)	Namibia, South Africa, SWAPO, (colonial)	Effort to achieve independence for Namibia	SC (Group of three, Western Contact Group), GA (Special Committee of 24, UN Council for Namibia, UN Commissioner for Namibia), S-G (Representative and Special Representative for Namibia)

UN efforts to prepare for, and promote, independence in face of South Africa's intransigence.

The SC meeting in Addis Ababa January – February 1972 condemned South Africa for its policies, requested its withdrawal from Namibia and called for an end to any form of labour system or hiring that conflicted with human rights. The SC also invited the S-G, in close cooperation with a group of three of its members, to initiate contacts with South Africa. The S-G visited South Africa and Namibia in March 1972 and reported to SC 17 July 1972. The SC then asked him to continue his efforts and approved his appointing a representative. He chose Amb. Escher of Switzerland, who visited South Africa 8 October – 3 November.

In December 1972 the SC asked S-G to continue contacts, but South Africa's clarification of its position considered unsatisfactory, particularly when South Africa established two 'Bantustans' in Namibia February 1973. The UN Council for Namibia, Special Committee of 24 and OAU were all against continuing contacts. The SC decided to discontinue them on 11 Dec. 1973. The next day the GA recognised the liberation movement of Namibia, SWAPO, as the authentic representative of Namibian people. It also called for moral and material support for the Namibian people in their struggle for independence. Sean MacBride became UN Commissioner for Namibia 1 Jan. 1974.

UN Council for Namibia (27 Sept. 1974) approved plan for creating an Institute for Namibia to train administrators, and enacted a decree that natural resources not to be exploited without Council's consent, punishable by forfeiture.

GA resolution 13 Dec. 1974 urged SC to consider measures to end South Africa's illegal occupation of Namibia. SC demanded (17 December) South Africa recognise territorial integrity and unity of Namibia, take steps to transfer power to people with UN help, comply with the Declaration of Human Rights, release political prisoners, abolish discriminatory practices and allow safe return to political exiles.

South African letter to S-G 27 May 1975 stated that it did not claim Namibia, would administer it as long as the people wished and was prepared to negotiate with S-G's Special Representative to hold discussions with the Council for Namibia and the Special Committee of OAU. SC met 30 May to review South Africa's compliance with its resolution of 17 Dec. 1974. Non-aligned countries for mandatory arms embargo, vetoed by France, UK and US (6 June 1975) on grounds that South Africa's role in Namibia was not a threat to peace. In November the GA condemned South Africa for not withdrawing from Namibia and for consolidating its illegal occupation through a so-called constitutional conference. It called for free national elections under UN supervision and for protection of its natural resources.

On 30 Jan. 1976 the SC resolution 385 unanimously demanded the transfer of power to the people of Namibia and elections under UN control. It condemned South Africa's repressive practices and use of Namibia to attack neighbouring countries. In August South Africa sent proposals to the S-G for the future of Namibia, issued by the 'Constitutional Committee of the South West African Constitutional Conference'. The Council for Namibia rejected them as lacking in legitimacy and recalled the conference had excluded SWAPO.

Again (19 Oct. 1976) France, the UK and US vetoed a SC draft resolution, which would have declared South African occupation of Namibia a threat to international peace and instituted a mandatory arms embargo. It also would have denounced the so-called Turnhalle constitutional conference as a device to avoid compliance with SC resolutions.

On December 20 the GA adopted eight resolutions on Namibia, supporting the armed struggle led by SWAPO, granting SWAPO observer status, condemning the Windhoek constitutional talks and urging SC to impose a mandatory arms embargo.

Martti Ahtisaari of Finland was appointed UN Commissioner for Namibia replacing Sean MacBride 1 Jan. 1977.

From mid-1976 the then SC members – Canada, France, UK, US and West Germany (Western Contact Group) – tried to reach a settlement on Namibia. In 1977 they held talks with African representatives, South Africa and SWAPO. On 4 Nov. 1977 the SC voted unanimously for a mandatory arms embargo against South Africa. The same day the GA held that independence talks must be between South Africa and SWAPO, that South Africa was liable for reparations for damage caused by its occupation, and condemned South Africa for its annexation of Walvis Bay as illegal.

Proposals of the Western Contact Group were submitted to the SC 10 April 1978 providing for free elections under the UN, a UN representative as interim administrator, the reduction of South African troops and a sizeable UN force, which were accepted by South Africa. The GA held a special session on Namibia 24 April – 3 May which took no account of the Western plan, but declared SWAPO must be involved in negotiations, reiterated Walvis Bay was part of Namibia and urged the SC to adopt measures, like sanctions, against South Africa.

On 27 July 1978 the SC took note of the Western proposals and asked the S-G for recommendations on their implementation, to appoint a Special Representative for Namibia and for the reintegration of Walvis Bay. The S-G appointed Martti Ahtisaari as Special Representative, who prepared a report of 29 August submitted by the S-G to the SC, which envisaged a UN Transition Assistance Group (UNTAG) with military and civilian components for about a year and independence in approximately seven months. SWAPO accepted the proposals. On 29 September the SC approved the recommendations in resolution 435.

South Africa objected to certain elements of the plan and held elections in Namibia 4–8 December, although the SC had declared on 13 November that they would be a clear defiance of the UN. The GA, on 21 December, condemned South Africa for holding the elections and called on the SC for economic measures against South Africa. In a letter next day to the S-G, South Africa agreed to cooperate in implementing the UN plan.

Date	*Case*	*Nature*	*UN bodies involved*
1978–79	Zambia, Southern Rhodesia	Armed invasion	SC (Ad Hoc Committee)

Airing and condemnation. Zambia asked for an urgent meeting of the SC following attacks by Southern Rhodesia, particularly the air and ground ones of 6–8 March 1978 which resulted in a number of casualties. The SC held three meetings and on 17 March unanimously 'strongly condemned' the armed invasion, called on the UK to end the illegal regime and decided to consider more effective measures, including ones under Chap. VII if further violations occurred.

On 22 Nov. 1979 Zambia complained to the SC of further attacks by Southern Rhodesia, particularly the bombing of bridges. The next day the SC strongly condemned such attacks and called on the UK to insure that Southern Rhodesia desisted from aggression and provocation against Zambia. The SC established an Ad Hoc Committee to help implement its decision and its call for compensation.

Date	*Case*	*Nature*	*UN bodies involved*
1978	Angola, South Africa	Armed invasion	SC

Airing and condemnation. On 5–6 May 1978 the SC considered a complaint from Angola that South African troops had parachuted in and its planes had attacked the Kassinga area in order to intimidate Namibian refugees and destabilise Angola.

The SC's unanimous resolution of 6 May 'strongly condemned the latest armed invasion' and the use of Namibia as a springboard. It demanded respect for Angola's territorial integrity, South Africa's immediate withdrawal and an end to its illegal occupation of Namibia. In the event of further such acts it was to consider more effective measures including those under Chap. VII.

Date	*Case*	*Nature*	*UN bodies involved*
1978–79	Uganda, Tanzania, OAU	Border clashes, Tanzanian incursion into Uganda against Amin	SC (not formally involved), S-G

African members wanted the UN to leave this conflict to OAU, which it finally did.

Border clashes in the autumn of 1978, in which Uganda occupied an area of Tanzania, were followed by a Tanzanian incursion into Uganda against the Amin regime. Twice in November the S-G appealed for an end to the fighting. In January 1979 Pres. Amin sent messages to the S-G which were passed to the SC, but he did not request a meeting. In March Amin asked the S-G for his good offices and later requested a SC meeting to consider Tanzania's aggression, which was to take place on 30 March. But in accordance with the wishes of the Africa Group, representing the OAU, the SC decided against action. Kampala fell to the Tanzanians in April.

Date	*Case*	*Nature*	*UN bodies involved*
1978–79	Nicaragua, Costa Rica, OAS	Civil war threatening neighbouring area	GA, S-G

Airing, left largely to OAS. GA resolution of 15 Dec. 1978 called on Nicaragua to stop activities that endangered security and threatened neighbouring countries, particularly Costa Rica. It censured repression in Nicaragua, urged respect for human rights and the continuation of efforts towards a peaceful solution of its internal conflict. Nicaragua wanted the matter left to the OAS which was considering it, but Costa Rica welcomed GA action.

On 21 June 1979 S-G regretted the loss of life in Nicaragua and reported he was in touch with OAS members and hoped that current efforts would lead to a settlement. Pres. Samoza fell in July 1979.

Date	*Case*	*Nature*	*UN bodies involved*
1979	Angola, South Africa (decolonisation)	Attacks on Angola connected with Namibian problem	SC

Airing and condemnation. In March 1979 Angola complained to the SC of South

African air attacks, including the bombing of a SWAPO refugee centre and a ground attack. The SC condemned South Africa on 28 March 1979 for 'premeditated, persistent and sustained armed invasions' of Angola, and for using Namibia as a springboard for invasions. It demanded that these cease and urged states to help Angola and front line states to strengthen their defence capacities.

Date	*Case*	*Nature*	*UN bodies involved*
1979 (1979–80)	Iran, US	Seizure of US Embassy and American hostages in Teheran	SC, GA, S-G (UN Commission of Inquiry), ICJ

Failure of UN efforts to secure the release of American hostages held by Iranian students.

On 4 Nov. 1979 a group of demonstrators seized the US Embassy in Teheran and held a number of its personnel hostage. Twice in November the Pres. of the SC (in its name) called for the release and protection of the personnel, supported by the Pres. of the GA.

On 25 November following efforts to resolve the dispute, the S-G called for a SC meeting because the situation posed a threat to international peace. After five meetings the SC unanimously called for the release of the personnel and on Iran and the US to resolve the remaining issues peacefully. It asked the S-G to use his good offices to implement the resolution. On 31 Dec. 1979 the SC deplored the continuing detention, against the Order of the ICJ (15 December) for the release of the personnel and restoration of the premises. It decided to consider measures under Chap. VII in the event of further non-compliance. The S-G visited Iran 1–4 Jan. 1980. A USSR veto of 13 January blocked a US resolution for economic sanctions against Iran.

Consultations led the S-G, on 20 February, to appoint a UN Commission of Inquiry as a fact-finding mission to Iran to hear its grievances in order to facilitate a solution of the crisis with the US. The Commission of five members visited Iran 23 February – 10 March. It then suspended its activities to confer with the S-G as it had not been able to see the hostages. After the abortive US military attempt to release the hostages (24–25 April) the S-G sent the Syrian member of the Commission to Iran (24 May – 15 June) to discuss resumption of the Commission's work and completion of its report, to no avail.

On 20 Jan. 1981 the hostages were released as the result of Algerian negotiations. Pres. Carter acknowledged appreciation of the efforts of the S-G, SC and the Commission to secure their release. The Pres. of GA paid tribute to the mediation of Algeria.

Date	*Case*	*Nature*	*UN bodies involved*
1979 (1971–80)	Southern Rhodesia (Zimbabwe), UK (colonial)	Achievement of independence and majority rule	SC (Sanctions Committee, Special Representative), GA, S-G (inter-agency mission), UNHCR

The UN role in moves for the independence of Zimbabwe was largely supportive – to see that it was achieved through genuine majority rule by full participation of its political leaders.

In November 1971 the UK informed the SC that it and Southern Rhodesia had agreed to proposals for a settlement. On 20 December the GA rejected the proposals as violating the people's right of self-determination. Owing to a UK veto the SC did not reject them (30 December) but the UK found they were not acceptable to the Africans themselves.

In the following years the UN continued on two courses – trying to tighten sanctions and ensure majority rule. In April 1976 the SC expanded mandatory sanctions to insurance and trade names. In 1977 the US returned chrome to its sanction list and on 27 May the SC banned the transfer of funds to Southern Rhodesian agents abroad.

The GA was particularly active in pressing for majority rule with the participation of representatives of its people's leaders. It did so in resolutions of November 1975 and December 1977.

In August 1977 an Anglo-American plan was worked out which, if implemented, would have involved a UN presence and force in Southern Rhodesia. On 29 September the SC approved sending a UN Special Representative to consider, with Field Marshal Lord Carver (British Resident Commissioner designate), security arrangements for transition to majority rule. The S-G chose Maj.-Gen D Prem Chand. Meanwhile Ian Smith was working on an internal settlement and the Patriotic Front leaders while agreeing to a UN presence, opposed a UN force, so the Anglo-American plan was soon left in abeyance.

On 3 March 1978 Ian Smith and three black leaders (but not the Patriotic Front) signed an internal settlement pact for majority rule by 31 Dec. 1978. On 14 March the SC declared this settlement illegal since made under an illegal regime. It called for a democratic transition to independence in 1978. The GA also declared the settlement null and void on 13 December. Before and after the elections in April 1979 the SC declared them null and void and continued to condemn Southern Rhodesia for attacks on its neighbours.

In September 1979 the Lancaster House negotiations started, which agreed on a constitution and ceasefire. Lord Soames was named Governor and reached Salisbury on 12 December when the rebellion ended. Six days later the GA again reaffirmed no independence without majority rule and commended the Patriotic Front for its contribution to the Lancaster House negotiations. On 21 December the SC ended sanctions. The UK then asked the UNHCR for help with the repatriation of Zimbabwean refugees.

On 2 Feb. 1980 the SC adopted a resolution for full implementation of the Lancaster House agreements and the rescinding of emergency measures. The S-G sent UN officials to observe the elections that month, and later, in agreement with Mr Mugabe he sent an inter-agency mission to assess Zimbabwe's needs.

Date	*Case*	*Nature*	*UN bodies involved*
1981 (1981–84)	Iraq, Israel	Israeli bombing of Iraq nuclear plant	SC, GA (experts study), S-G, IAEA

Airing and UN effort to prevent any further bombing, but Israel would not make such a commitment.

On 7 June 1981 Israel bombed the nuclear plant near Baghdad, which it alleged was to produce bombs. The UN International Atomic Energy Agency (IAEA) inspectors had examined the plant in January and found nothing contrary to the non-proliferation treaty Iraq had signed.

On 19 June the SC strongly condemned the attack and called on Israel to desist from such acts and held Iraq was entitled to redress. It urged Israel, which was not a party to the non-proliferation treaty, to 'place its nuclear facilities under IAEA safeguards', and held the attack was a 'serious threat to the entire IAEA safeguards regime'. In September the IAEA suspended aid to Israel under its technical assistance programme and called on states not to transfer fissionable material or technology to Israel that might be used for nuclear arms.

A GA resolution of 11 November considered Israel's attack as a threat to IAEA safeguards and appealed to members to refrain from the use of force particularly armed attack on a nuclear plant. On 13 November a GA resolution strongly condemned Israel's action, called on states not to provide Israel with arms, and on Israel for compensation. It requested the SC for enforcement action.

In 1982 the General Conference of the IAEA would not accept Israel's credentials, whereupon the US suspended its payments and curtailed its participation, which it resumed in February 1983. On 16 Nov. 1982, the GA demanded Israel withdraw its threat to attack nuclear facilities, and called on the SC to consider measures to deter Israel. It asked the S-G for a study of the consequences of Israel's attack which was undertaken in 1983 and submitted to the GA.

On 10 Nov. 1983 the GA again demanded Israel withdraw its threat to attack nuclear facilities in Iraq and elsewhere and asked the SC to consider deterring Israel. A GA resolution of 16 Nov, 1984 repeated its demand to Israel not to attack nuclear facilities and asked the SC to ensure Israel's compliance with its resolution of 19 June 1981.

Date	*Case*	*Nature*	*UN bodies involved*
1981 (1980–85)	Malta. Libya	Competing claims to Continental Shelf	SC, S-G (Special Representative), ICJ

The UN was called on to facilitate the submission to the ICJ of competing claims to the continental shelf.

On 4 Sept. 1980 the SC met at Malta's request because Libyan warships had stopped an oil rig drilling under licence from Malta. An agreement between Malta and Libya had been signed 23 May 1976 to submit the delimitation of the continental shelf to the ICJ. In April 1980 Malta understood the Libyan People's Congresses would ratify it by June. Failing that Malta went ahead with its postponed drilling. Libya asked that consideration be delayed.

After sending his Special Representative to discuss the problem, the S-G reported on 13 Nov. 1980 to the SC that the parties had agreed to submit it to the ICJ, with Libya pledging to put it to the People's Congresses for ratification within a month. Libya's ratification was conditional on 'decisions and recommendations' of the People's Congresses (i.e. that no drilling should take place pending a decision). Malta insisted it should be unconditional.

During the spring of 1981 the S-G and his Special Representative tried to help the parties remove the obstacles to the exchange of ratification. On 30 July 1981 the SC again considered the issue. Its Pres. called for moderation and the S-G agreed to continue his efforts at reconciliation. On 26 July 1982 Libya and Malta notified the

ICJ of their agreement to submit the case, and the court gave judgment on 3 June 1985.

Date	*Case*	*Nature*	*UN bodies involved*
1981 (1981–82)	Seychelles, South Africa	Unsuccessful coup of mercenaries from South Africa	SC (Commission of Inquiry, Ad Hoc Committee for Special Fund for Seychelles), S-G

An unsuccessful mercenary attack against the government of Seychelles which was aired, condemned and recompense provided.

On 25 Nov. 1981 the attack on Seychelles International airport was repulsed and 44 of the mercenaries then hijacked an Air India plane to escape to South Africa. The Seychelles asked the S-G to issue an official condemnation, he then described the act as 'a flagrant violation of fundamental principles of international law'. On 15 December the SC unanimously condemned the attack and established a Commission of Inquiry of three of its members to investigate and assess damage. It reported on 15 March 1982 that it was difficult to believe the South African authorities did not have knowledge of the preparations for the attack. The South African government denied knowledge, but after the trial and conviction of all but one of the mercenaries for hijacking, it conceded the involvement of some of its defence force and national intelligence service without the government's prior knowledge.

The Commission of Inquiry reported a preliminary assessment of damages which it later increased to include economic consequences, to a total of $18 million. On 28 May 1982 the SC established a Special Fund for the Seychelles of voluntary contributions and an ad hoc committee of four of its members to mobilise the fund.

Date	*Case*	*Nature*	*UN bodies involved*
1982 (1982–83)	Lesotho, South Africa	South African raid into Lesotho allegedly against ANC	SC, GA, S-G (mission), UNHCR

Airing, condemnation and assistance. On 9 Dec. 1982 South Africa attacked targets in Maseru killing some 42 people of whom a number were refugees. Its declared aim was to pre-empt operations by the ANC refugees. The UNHCR sent a special mission to Lesotho to consult with the government. On 15 December the SC unanimously condemned the aggressive act, called on South Africa to declare it would not commit such aggression again and demanded compensation. It requested the S-G to consult with Lesotho to ensure the welfare of the refugees 'in a manner consistent with their security', and asked member states to provide economic assistance.

The S-G sent a mission to Lesotho in January 1983 to investigate ensuring the welfare of the refugees and to assess Lesotho's needs. The SC considered its report on 29 June 1983 and requested member states and international institutions to assist Lesotho accordingly, to an estimated cost of $46 million. This was endorsed by the GA on 20 Dec. 1983.

Date	*Case*	*Nature*	*UN bodies involved*
1983	Libya, US	Alleged provocative military actions by US	SC

Airing, no action. On two occasions Libya complained to the SC against actions by the US that it considered provocative. The first in February concerned the stationing nearby of the aircraft carrier Nimitz and the sending of AWACs aircraft to a neighbouring country, which the US claimed was to discourage Libyan designs on the Sudan. The SC met four times on 22 and 23 Feb. 1983.

It considered a further Libyan complaint on 11, 12 and 16 August against US military rapid deployment manoeuvres with its allies in the African/Middle East region, the sending of military advisers and equipment to Chad and of two AWACs to a neighboring country. The US rejected charges of provoking tension and countercharged on Libya's role in Chad.

Date	*Case*	*Nature*	*UN bodies involved*
1983 (1983–85)	Chad, Libya	Alleged aggression by Libya and intervention in civil war	SC

Airing and UN request that parties settle the dispute peacefully and use the OAU. Chad complained to the SC 22 and 31 March 1983 that Libya had occupied a part of its territory, the Aouzou strip, since 1973 and had been intervening in its internal affairs. Libya claimed the strip as its territory. On 6 April the Pres. (in the name of the SC) called on the parties to settle their differences peacefully and to make use of their regional organisation, the OAU, to this end. Chad again complained to the SC, which met 3, 11, 12, 16 and 31 Aug. 1983 on Libyan aggression and bombing, denied by Libya.

On 30 Jan. 1985, in a statement to the SC, Chad charged Libya with meddling in its internal affairs, occupying its territory and failed plans to attack members of its government. Libya denied the allegations and claimed legitimacy for the Goukouni Oueddei regime.

Date	*Case*	*Nature*	*UN bodies involved*
1983 (1983–84)	South Korea, USSR	South Korean civilian aircraft shot down by USSR near Sakhalin	SC, ICAO (inquiry team and special assembly)

Airing, inquiry and banning of use of weapons against civilian aircraft. On 1 Sept. 1983 a Russian aircraft shot down a South Korean civilian plane off-course over Soviet air space by Sakhalin on its trip from Alaska to Seoul, with the loss of 269 people. The Russians claimed it was mistaken for a spy plane. On 12 September the USSR vetoed a SC draft resolution for an investigation by the S-G which also deplored the destruction and loss of life.

The International Civil Aviation Organisation (ICAO) held an inquiry, which reported that a navigational error was probably to blame, that the USSR had not tried hard enough to identify the plane and that the team had found no evidence of intelligence gathering. At its extraordinary session in May 1984 the ICAO unanimously agreed to a ban on using weapons against civilian aircraft as an amendment to its Convention on International Civil Aviation of 1944.

Date	*Case*	*Nature*	*UN bodies involved*
1983	Grenada, OECS, US	Coup, intervention by US, OECS and others	SC, GA, S-G (team)

Airing and condemnation. Following a local coup the US, with the understanding of the Organisation of the Eastern Caribbean States (OECS), Barbados and Jamaica, invaded Grenada on 25 Oct. 1983. The SC met from 25–28 October. Its draft resolution deplored the armed intervention as violating international law and called for the withdrawal of foreign troops, but was vetoed by the US early on 28 October.

On 2 November the GA adopted a similar resolution, it also called for free elections and a report by the S-G. Diego Cordovez headed a team to Grenada and the S-G reported its findings on 6 Nov. 1983, which included a survey of the situation, concluded that governmental machinery did not then exist and the Governor-General expected elections for a constitutional government would require six to 12 months.

Date	*Case*	*Nature*	*UN bodies involved*
1984	Sudan, Libya	Alleged Libyan plane attack	SC
	Libya, US	Alleged provocation of US spy planes	SC

Airing, no action. On 18 March 1984 Sudan called for SC meeting alleging a Libyan plane had bombed Omdurman on 16 March as part of 'an uninterrupted series of aggressive acts'. The SC met on 27 March, Libya rejected the charges and claimed Sudan had invented the incident to get the dispatch of American espionage AWAC planes.

On 22 March Libya requested a SC meeting to consider 'the deteriorating situation as a result of hostile and provocative American acts', specifically the sending of two AWAC planes on 18 March. The SC met on 28 March and 2 April.

Date	*Case*	*Nature*	*UN bodies involved*
1984	Laos, Thailand	Dispute over three border villages	SC

Airing, no action. On 9 Oct. 1984 the SC met on a Laos complaint that Thai troops had attacked three border villages on 6 June 1984. Thailand reported it had removed its military presence and was ready to accept a fact-finding mission, but warned Laos against harassment of Thai workers.

Date	*Case*	*Nature*	*UN bodies involved*
1985	Botswana, South Africa	South African raid on Botswana's capital	SC (mission)

Airing and mission. On 14 June 1985 South Africa raided Gaborone, capital of Botswana, allegedly against Africa National Congress bases. In a resultion of 21 June the SC unanimously condemned the attack, denounced South African 'hot pursuit' which terrorised countries in Southern Africa and demanded compensation for damage to life and property. A UN mission was sent to Botswana in July and recommended assistance of about $14 million to improve its security and facilities for refugees. On 30 September the SC endorsed their report unanimously and demanded South Africa pay in full for the loss of life and property. It commended Botswana's humanitarian policies towards refugees.

CASES CURRENT IN 1985

When disputes are treated as current cases, incidents before the UN which were involved in them (apartheid, Middle East, Namibia, etc) appear as part of those cases rather than separate. Hence the attacks of South Africa on Angola are referred to under Namibia after March 1979. In the following section the Special Committee of 24 will be referred to by its other name The Special Committee on Decolonisation as it was enlarged in 1979.

Note: All the cases in this section appear in alphabetical order.

Date	*Case*	*Nature*	*UN bodies involved*
1979–	Afghanistan, USSR, Pakistan, Iran	Military intervention by USSR in Afghanistan	SC, GA (Special Representative), S-G, UNHCR, HR Commission

Repeated UN efforts to achieve a settlement for the withdrawal of foreign troops, the independence of Afghanistan free from intervention, its non-alignment and the return of refugees.

On 24–26 Dec. 1979 the USSR airlifted troops into Kabul; Pres. Amin was killed and replaced by Babrak Karmal on 27 December. The SC met on 5 Jan. 1980, but the USSR vetoed (7 January) the resolution deploring the intervention, calling for an immediate withdrawal and non-interference in Afghanistan. Under the 'Uniting for Peace' resolution the Council called for an emergency GA session. On 14 January the GA adopted a resolution similar to the SC one. On 20 Nov. 1980 it again called for withdrawal of troops, reaffirmed the right of the Afghans to choose their own system of government and asked the S-G to appoint a special representative to promote a solution and explore the possibility of guarantees. The S-G appointed Perez de Cuellar who visited Pakistan and Kabul in April and July/August 1981. On 18 Nov. 1981 the GA called for troop withdrawal, respect for Afghan independence and non-alignment.

When Perez de Cuellar became S-G in January 1982 he appointed Diego Cordovez as his Special Representative for Afghanistan. After visits to the area in April, Cordovez held separate talks in June with the foreign ministers of Afghanistan and Pakistan, keeping the Iranians informed. In September he accompanied the S-G to talks with Pres. Brezhnev. On 29 Nov. 1982 the GA reaffirmed its policy.

Diego Cordovez visited Afghanistan, Iran and Pakistan January – February 1983. The S-G received Russian support for UN efforts when he visited Yuri Andropov on 27 March. Cordovez had further separate talks with the foreign ministers of Afghanistan and Pakistan in April, which were continued on 16 June 1983, but negotiations slowed with the worsening of international relations. On 23 November the GA reiterated its policy.

Cordovez visited the two countries and Iran in April 1984 and the S-G discussed Afghanistan with Pres. Chernenko on his trip to Moscow in July. 'Proximity talks' were held at the end of August with the two foreign ministers on the basis of a 'set of understandings' worked out in April dealing with the four issues – withdrawal of foreign troops, non-interference, international guarantees and voluntary return of refugees. Progress was claimed despite serious obstacles. The GA repeated its policy on 15 Nov. 1984.

In May 1985 Cordovez visited Afghanistan and Pakistan in preparation for 'proximity talks' in June, when he presented their foreign ministers with detailed 'instruments' for a package agreement. Apparently differences were tentatively worked out on three of the four issues i.e. non-interference and non-intervention, international guarantees with Moscow and the US showing interest, and the return of some 4.5 million refugees from Iran and Pakistan. The crucial remaining one was the timing for withdrawal of some 115 000 Russian troops. The 'proximity talks' of 27–30 August stalled over this problem and the desire of Afghanistan for direct negotiations (see S-G's report of 7 Oct. 1985 to GA). Further talks were scheduled for December 1985.

The UNHCR was very involved in the care of Afghan refugees in Pakistan, helping some 2.3 million of the three million or so. The GA repeatedly asked member states to provide relief in coordination with UNHCR. Other UN agencies also helped.

Date	*Case*	*Nature*	*UN bodies involved*
1965–	Apartheid South Africa	Pressure against apartheid and for means to alleviate it	SC (watchdog committee on arms), GA (Special Committee on Decolonisation, Special Committee on Apartheid, UN Trust Fund for South Africa, UN Educational and Training Programme for Southern Africa), S-G, ECOSOC (HR Commission, Commission on Transnational Corps)

Pressure to eliminate apartheid hindered by South Africa and others. In December 1965 the GA considered economic sanctions the only means to solve the problem peacefully and SC action under Chap. VII essential. It appealed to major trading countries to stop economic cooperation with South Africa, to specialised agencies to deny assistance, and requested the S-G to set up the UN Trust Fund for South Africa to provide legal help and relief to families of those charged under discriminatory laws.

During 1966–70 opposition to South African apartheid policies strengthened in the GA with resolutions repeating the essence of the resolution of December 1965. The SC (July 1970) considered violations of the voluntary arms embargo and spelt out provisions for strengthening it, but members continued to disregard them.

GA resolutions of 8 Dec. 1970 dealt particularly with ways of affecting the situation by promoting economic, social and humanitarian aid to those struggling against apartheid, publicising evils of it by broadcasts to South Africa and by enlisting the action of trade unions. The SC resolution of 4 Feb. 1972 again condemned apartheid and called once more for observance of arms embargo and release of those imprisoned or restricted under apartheid laws. Meanwhile the GA continued its pressure with resolutions of 1971–73 covering previous grounds but emphasising concern over maltreatment of opponents of apartheid, and the Special Committee on Apartheid was active hearing petitions, reporting and making recommendations.

On 30 Nov. 1973 the GA passed the Draft Convention on Suppression and Punishment of the Crime of Apartheid recommended by ECOSOC. GA resolution 14 Dec. 1973 commended resolutions of the International Conference of Trade Unions against apartheid, and requested the Special Committee on Apartheid to liaise with the organisation in action against apartheid.

In December of each year the GA adopted omnibus resolutions against apartheid and the racist regime of South Africa, pressing for SC action under Chap. VII for mandatory arms embargo, and comprehensive economic sanctions. It repeatedly called for an end to apartheid and collaboration with South Africa – military, nuclear, economic, financial, cultural, sport etc. – condemning, sometimes by name, specific countries which collaborated. It upheld the right of self-determination and the legitimacy of the struggle against apartheid, and called for assistance to liberation movements recognised by the OAU and for contributions to the UN Trust Fund for South Africa. The GA condemned South Africa for repressive measures, and called for the release of political prisoners. The UN also organised numerous conferences and seminars to inform the world of the character of apartheid.

Apart from the yearly resolutions there were many specific efforts. An attempt to oust South Africa from the UN failed on 30 Oct. 1974 because of the veto of France, UK and US. But on 12 Nov. 1974 South Africa was suspended from participation in the GA, its credentials had been refused since 1970. The HR Commission in a resolution of February 1975, declared apartheid incompatible with the Charter.

On 19 June 1976 the SC condemned South Africa for the killings at Soweto, and called on it to eliminate apartheid and recognise the legitimacy of the struggle against it. The Convention on the Crime of Apartheid came into force on 18 July 1976. The day that South Africa declared the independence of Transkei (26 Oct. 1976) the GA rejected it as invalid and called on states not to recognise it. This was repeated as the independence of other bantustans was declared.

The year 1977 saw mounting activity against South Africa. The SC met nine times 21–31 March 1977 on four draft resolutions to halt investments and strengthen the voluntary arms embargo, but no action was taken. A world Conference for Action against Apartheid was held in Lagos 22–26 August which called for the dismantling of apartheid and asked the SC for a mandatory arms embargo under Chap. VII. The SC met and on 31 October demanded the abolition of apartheid and bantustans and an end to violence. On 4 November the SC made the previous voluntary arms embargo mandatory, and decided states should refrain from cooperation with South Africa in nuclear-weapon development. In December the SC established a watchdog committee on arms, and the GA adopted an International Declaration against Apartheid in Sport.

The SC met in January 1978 on prohibiting loans to South Africa, but no action was taken. On 13 June 1980 it again considered the situation in South Africa, condemned massive repression and the killing of peaceful demonstrators, and called on South Africa to grant self-determination and to release prisoners including Mandela. In November 1981 the GA regretted the links of the IMF and World Bank with South Africa.

When South Africa sought to institute a new constitution for three separate parliamentary chambers, without the blacks, the GA declared (15 Nov. 1983) the results of the referendum for whites only was invalid. This was followed in August 1984 by the vote of the coloureds and Indians on the constitution, which both the SC and GA rejected as null and void and aggravating the situation. The SC adopted (23 Oct. 1984) a resolution reiterating its condemnation of apartheid and demanding an end to it and 'massacres'. In December it reaffirmed its seven year old mandatory arms embargo and called on states not to import arms from South Africa.

The SC (12 March 1985) unanimously condemned the arbitrary arrests of United Democratic Front members, called for the unconditional release of political prisoners and detainees, (including Mandela), and also condemned the killings of those protesting against forceable removals. In the name of the SC its Pres. expressed (22 March) its grave concern at the deteriorating situation and violence against defenceless opponents of apartheid. He urged South Africa to end repression and eliminate apartheid.

Following the declaration of a state of emergency (20 July), the SC adopted a French resolution on 26 July (with the UK and US abstaining), which demanded the lifting of the state of emergency, and the unconditional release of prisoners and detainees. It urged suspension of all new investments and of guaranteed export loans, and the prohibition of the sale of Krugerrands, computer equipment for the army and police, and new contracts in the nuclear field.

Reactions at the UN to Pres. Botha's speech of 15 August were critical. The S-G stated it in no way allayed his concerns, and he called for dialogue with representatives of the majority. On 21 August the SC, through its Pres. held that without action to eradicate apartheid and establish a democratic society any Pretoria pronouncements only reaffirmed its attachment to apartheid and 'continuing intransigence'.

A panel organised by the UN Commission on Transnational Corps. had hearings in September 1985 on the activities of transnationals in South Africa and Namibia, respecting apartheid. Its report on 11 October called on transnationals to end new investments and loans, desegregate facilities and observe minimum standards for employees, with a deadline of 1 Jan. 1987 for ending apartheid.

Date	*Case*	*Nature*	*UN bodies involved*
1975–	Belize, UK, Guatemala (ex-colonial)	Independence of Belize and Guatemalan claim	GA (Special Committee on Decolonisation)

UN support for independence and territorial integrity probably discouraged Guatemala from implementing its alleged claim to Belize.

The UK was anxious to grant independence but feared Guatemala would seek to take it over. The GA repeatedly called on all states to recognise the right of Belize to independence and territorial integrity and urged the administering power, UK, in consultation with Belize, to negotiate with Guatemala. Guatemala claimed the GA had no right to intervene, by imposing a political solution on a legal dispute, since it argued Belize was not a decolonisation matter but illegal occupation of territory.

Negotiations took place but to no avail. On 11 Nov. 1980 the GA declared Belize should become independent before the end of its following session in 1981. On 11 March 1981 the UK and Guatemala reached an outline agreement, but failed to achieve a treaty in July. Belize became independent on 21 Sept. 1981 and was admitted to the UN, with only Guatemala voting against, four days later. Some 1800 British soldiers were posted to Belize because of the unresolved Guatemalan claim. After independence talks continued occasionally together with Belize, and Guatemala considerably modified its claim, concentrating on unimpeded access to the Caribbean.

Date	Case	Nature	UN bodies involved
1973–	Comoros, Mayotte, France (ex-colonial)	Independence of Comoro Archipelago and position of Mayotte	SC, GA (Special Committee on Decolonisation), S-G

UN effort to establish the independence of Comoros and to assure its political unity with the island of Mayotte.

In December 1973 and 1974 the GA called for the right to independence and political unity of the four islands of the Comoro Archipelago, then under France. In a referendum of 22 Dec. 1974 three islands voted for independence, which they achieved on 6 July 1975. Comoros became a member of the UN on 12 Nov. 1975.

Mayotte did not accede to independence. On 6 Feb. 1976 France vetoed a draft SC resolution stating that a planned referendum in Mayotte would be interference in the internal affairs of Comoros, and called on France not to hold it. The referendums of 8 February and 11 April 1976 favoured remaining part of France. The GA on 21 Oct. 1976 declared them null and void. It called on France to withdraw from Mayotte and condemned the French presence there as a violation of national unity of Comoros. It invited France to negotiate with Comoros. On 24 Dec. 1976 the French parliament proclaimed Mayotte an integral part of its Republic.

From then on the GA repeatedly asserted the sovereignty of Comoros over Mayotte, called on France to work out a just solution for the political unity of Mayotte with Comoros, mandated the S-G to assist the parties in conjunction with the OAU, and urged negotiations between France and Comoros. Talks were held on several occasions, and some improvement was made in the relationship between the islands, but no integration.

A GA resolution of 11 Dec. 1984 noted the S-G's report, reaffirmed the sovereignty of Comoros over Mayotte, and urged France to open negotiations for the return of the island, honouring its commitment of 15 June 1973 for the independence of the Comoros as a whole. It asked the S-G to report on the problem to the 1985 GA.

Date	Case	Nature	UN bodies involved
1975–	Cyprus, Turkey, Greece	Reunification of Cyprus	SC (UNFICYP), GA, S-G (Special Representatives), UNHCR (Co-ordinator of UN Humanitarian Assistance for Cyprus), HR Commission

Effort by UN to promote the reunification of Cyprus through intercommunal and 'proximity talks'. The UN force in Cyprus effectively held the ring so a solution could be sought peacefully; but the parties were thus shielded from the possible consequences of their failure to agree.

From 1974 the GA adopted basically the same resolution at some half a dozen sessions with a few additions. This affirmed the independence, territorial integrity and non-alignment of Cyprus without interference, demanded the withdrawal of all foreign troops, and called for return of refugees and for negotiations under the S-G between the two communities. Every six months the S-G reported on progress towards a settlement when recommending to the SC the extension of the UNFICYP mandate, which was always granted despite the accumulating deficit. The S-G himself, or through his successive Special Representatives in Cyprus, repeatedly suggested methods for agreement and points on which their views coincided. The efforts were set back by several unilateral actions.

On 13 Feb. 1975 the Turkish Cypriot leader, Rauf Denktash, declared a 'federated Turkish state' of the northern area. The SC regretted the move on 12 March and called for efforts to resume negotiations and on the parties to refrain from actions that would prejudice the sovereignty or territorial integrity of the island or the negotiations. The S-G arranged talks between the two communities 28 April – 3 May, 5–9 June, 31 July – 2 August and 8–10 September. In January 1976 the S-G discussed resumption of talks so a fifth round was held 17–21 Feb. 1976. From 5–31 March 1976 Perez de Cuellar (then the Special Representative to Cyprus) held seven meetings with representatives of the communities on a number of problems. Restriction of the movement of UNIFCYP in the northern area and the problem of persons missing since 1974 were of concern.

On 12 Feb. 1977 Archbishop Makarios (who died on 3 Aug. 1977) and Rauf Denktash met under S-G auspices for the first time in 13 years. They agreed guidelines for inter-communal talks providing for an independent, non-aligned federal and bi-communal republic. Talks were held 31 March – 7 April and 20 May, but not continued after 3 June. In August Cyprus complained to the SC of developments in Famagusta (fearing 'colonisation'). On 15 Sept. 1977 the SC called on the parties to refrain from action adversely affecting negotiations, as did the GA in its annual resolution. On 16 Dec. 1977 the GA also asked the S-G to assist in establishing a body to investigate missing persons with the participation of the International Committee of the Red Cross.

In January 1978 the S-G visited Cyprus, Greece and Turkey to try to resume the talks. In April he received territorial and constitutional proposals from the Turkish Cypriots and passed them on, but the Pres. of Cyprus S Kyprianou and his cabinet found them unacceptable as a basis for talks. At the 10th GA Special Session on Disarmament in June, Kyprianou proposed the demilitarisation of Cyprus and a mixed police force. In July Denktash offered an interim administration of Varosha (the Greek Cypriot suburb of Famagusta) to be free of occupation and under UN control. On 27 Nov. 1978 the SC called on the parties to implement past resolutions within an unspecified time frame, and to resume negotiations, in response to the usual GA resolution which included a recommendation that the SC take appropriate measures for the implementation of UN resolutions, and also called for respect for human rights.

On 18–19 May Pres. Kyprianou and Rauf Denktash agreed on a 10-point procedural plan for talks, based on the guidelines of 12 Feb. 1977. Included was the issue of Varosha. Inter-communal talks were held on 15 June 1979 but recessed on 22 June. The GA annual resolution of 20 Nov. 1979 supported the 10-point agreement and welcomed the proposal for demilitarisation. Efforts continued to restart inter-communal talks. In June 1980 the UN presented a statement on common ground, but this was unacceptable.

Talks were resumed on 9 Aug. 1980 and continued quite regularly within the framework of the 10-point plan, particularly on constitutional and territorial aspirations and the resettlement of Varosha. On 18 Nov. 1981 the S-G submitted an 'evaluation' of the status of the negotiations and an identification of coinciding views, which the parties agreed to use, with some signs of progress.

In May 1983 the GA met on Cyprus, an item of the 37th session postponed over the Christmas recess. Its resolution was basically much like previous ones, however, it reflected frustration at the delay and the urgent need for an early settlement. Denktash then discontinued the inter-communal talks. The S-G sounded out the parties on whether they would accept indicators on territorial delimitation. Kyprianou was reluctant, and Denktash wanted a summit meeting with him. The S-G was trying to arrange one when Denktash declared UDI on 15 Nov. 1983. This was deplored by the SC on 18 November and declared invalid.

In January 1984 the Pres. of Cyprus gave the S-G a 'framework' for settlement of the problem. On 16 March the S-G presented Denktash with a five-point scenario with little response. On 17 April 1984 there was an exchange of so-called ambassadorial credentials between Turkey and Northern Cyprus. On 11 May the SC declared its concern at this further secession act, and called for the transfer of Varosha to UN administration and for further efforts towards a settlement.

In May 1984 the Committee on Missing Persons, which the GA had been calling for since 16 Dec. 1977, started investigating persons missing since 1974, having solved its procedural difficulties. It was composed of a humanitarian person from each community and an official of the International Committee of the Red Cross, agreed by the communities and appointed by the S-G, not an official UN body. A working group of the Commission on Human Rights was also concerned with missing persons in Cyprus.

The S-G met with the parties 6–7 Aug. 1984 and 'proximity talks' were held at intervals in September, October, November, and December. He also provided for a summit 17–20 Jan. 1985 between Pres. Kyprianou and Denktash, with a draft agreement or documentation. Denktash was prepared to accept it, Kyprianou considered it a basis for negotiation. On 25 January, Denktash announced parliamentary elections for the Turkish Cypriot area to be held on 23 June. These followed a vote on a constitution (5 May 1985) and for him to be President (9 June), and delayed further progress on agreement apart from the S-G's draft modified proposals of April, which were acceptable to the Greek Cypriots but not to Denktash or Turkey. In an oral report of 20 September to the SC the S-G considered the two sides had never been closer. Through its Pres. the SC then called on all parties for a special effort to agree soon.

Date	*Case*	*Nature*	*UN bodies involved*
1975–	East Timor, Indonesia, Portugal (colonial)	Decolonisation, civil war, Indonesian takeover	SC (Special Representative), GA (Special Committee on Decolonisation), S-G, UNICEF, UNHCR, HR Commission

UN attempt to assure East Timor exercised its right to self-determination. Portugal acknowledged the right of self-determination for its territories in 1974. Its plans for a transitional government were interrupted by civil war in August 1975 between FRETILIN and two smaller parties. The S-G called for an end to hostilities on 26

Aug. 1975. FRETILIN declared independence on 28 November, the other parties were for integration with Indonesia.

On 7 Dec. 1975 Portugal informed the SC that Indonesia had attacked. The GA deplored this intervention on 12 December and called for withdrawal. On the 17th the pro-Indonesian parties established a provisional government. On 22 December the SC called for Indonesia to withdraw, for Portugal to cooperate with the UN in enabling East Timor to exercise its right of self-determination, and asked the S-G to send a Special Representative to assess the situation.

The Special Representative reported on the need for consultations in view of the differences on how East Timor should determine its future. On 22 April 1976 the SC called on Indonesia to withdraw and for the Special Representative to pursue his consultations. It again supported East Timor's right to self-determination, which Indonesia insisted the people had already exercised. The GA rejected this claim on 1 Dec. 1976 and called on Indonesia to withdraw.

On 28 Nov. 1977 the GA asked the S-G, in consultation with the Special Committee on Decolonisation, to send a representative to assess the situation and prepare for the visit of the Special Committee mission. On 13 Dec. 1978 the GA again asked for the dispatch of a Special Committee visiting mission, and recommended that the SC should implement its resolutions on East Timor. Indonesia considered the matter an interference in its internal affairs. A GA resolution of 21 Nov. 1979 declared East Timor should determine its future under UN auspices and called for humanitarian relief by UNICEF and UNHCR.

Portugal proposed consultations between all parties concerned to break the impasse. The GA welcomed this initiative on 11 Nov. 1980 and urged cooperation with it as a step towards self-determination. The GA repeated its usual resolution on 24 Nov. 1981 and called on UN agencies (UNICEF, UNHCR and WFP) to provide assistance. On 23 Nov. 1982 it requested the S-G to initiate consultations for a comprehensive settlement by a vote of 50 to 46 with 50 abstentions. In 1983 it deferred consideration. Reporting to the GA in July 1984 the S-G reviewed his efforts since 1982 to promote a comprehensive settlement and improve the humanitarian situation in East Timor, through contacts with Portugal and Indonesia. The GA deferred consideration in 1984 and 1985.

Date	*Case*	*Nature*	*UN bodies involved*
1965–	Falklands (Malvinas), UK, Argentina	Claim to the Falklands (Malvinas)	SC, GA (Special Committee on Decolonisation), S-G

UN attempt to induce Argentina and the UK to negotiate a settlement of their claims to the islands, subsequently to end hostilities and to reach a diplomatic solution of their dispute.

The Falklands were listed in 1946 as one of the non-self-governing territories. Argentina periodically claimed them as an integral part of its territory. The Falklands were considered by the Special Committee on Decolonisation and the GA from 1964; in 1965 the GA invited the two parties to negotiate for a peaceful settlement. Discussions began July 1966 and continued at intervals. GA consensus noted progress in talks and urged them to continue. Measures on communications were reported to the S-G in notes of 1969, 1971, with agreement for Argentina to provide an air link and the UK a sea link.

The GA resolution December 1973 declared the need to accelerate negotiations to solve the sovereignty conflict peacefully and to end the colonial situation – a basic attitude of the GA in following years. Talks continued periodically until February 1982 and included sovereignty, with the UK holding a transfer could only be with the agreement of the islanders.

In March 1982 scrap iron merchants raised the Argentinian flag on South Georgia, followed by Argentinian naval movements. The SC met on 1 April in response to a UK complaint and its Pres. urged the parties to refrain from the use or threat of force and to seek a diplomatic solution. On 2 April Argentina took the Falklands. The SC, on 3 April, adopted resolution 502 for an end to hostilities, withdrawal of Argentinian forces and a diplomatic solution.

During the next month the S-G repeatedly called for the implementation of resolution 502. He did not interfere with the efforts of the US Secretary of State to find a solution, but had contingency proposals prepared for UN assistance. On 19 April he outlined them to the representatives of Argentina, UK and US, including possible UN observers and a temporary UN administration. On 2 May he gave the two parties an aide-memoire suggesting a series of steps. On 5–6 May these were accepted by both as a basis for a framework. The S-G had some 30 separate meetings with both to assist an agreement and thought it was near. He received drafts of interim agreements from both 17–19 May, which did not reflect the progress he thought had been made.

The S-G phoned Pres. Galtieri and PM Thatcher on 19 May making certain suggestions. He informed the SC of his efforts on 21 May (the day a bridgehead was established at Port San Carlos). By SC resolution 505 of 26 May the S-G was asked to renew his good offices to achieve a cessation of hostilities and to negotiate terms which could include dispatch of UN observers. He reported on 2 June that the positions of the two sides did not allow for an acceptable ceasefire. The draft SC resolution of 4 June provided for a ceasefire and the implementation of resolution 502 and resolution 505, but was vetoed by the UK and also the US, although the US informed the SC afterwards that it would have abstained had it been possible to change its vote. On 14 June the Argentinians surrendered.

On 4 Nov. 1982 the GA asked Argentina and the UK to resume negotiations to find a peaceful solution of their sovereignty dispute and requested the S-G to undertake his good offices. The preamble said colonial situations were 'incompatible with the UN's ideal of universal peace' and that the 'interest' of the islanders should be taken into account. The UK insisted on their right to self-determination. The GA adopted much the same resolution on 16 Nov. 1983, when the S-G reported to the GA that he had held exchanges with both parties, but their agreement was necessary for negotiations to begin. He was informed by both of the respective positions they took at their abortive Berne meeting in July 1984. On 1 Nov. 1984 the GA adopted a resolution similar to the ones in 1982 and 1983, and on 9 Aug. 1985 the Special Committee on Decolonisation urged the two countries to resume negotiations and regretted that the UK would not consider sovereignty within comprehensive negotiations.

Date	*Case*	*Nature*	*UN bodies involved*
1964–	Gibraltar, UK, Spain	Future of Gibraltar, Spanish claim on grounds of territorial integrity	GA (Special Committee on Decolonisation)

Part of UN efforts to implement the Declaration on the Granting of Independence to

Colonial Countries and Peoples 1960, and to induce Spain and UK to settle their differences over Gibraltar.

Gibraltar was ceded by Spain to Britain in the Treaty of Utrecht 1713. Spain claimed it was ceded as a military base and then turned into a British colony which contravened the above declaration and violated Spain's territorial integrity. Gibraltar was listed in 1946 as one of the non-self-governing territories.

The GA, in 1965, endorsing proposals of the Special Committee on Decolonisation in 1964, called on the parties to negotiate in line with the declaration and the interests of the people. The UK and Spain told the S-G, March 1966, they would hold talks. These lasted May–October 1966 and included suggestions to refer the matter to the ICJ (not taken up by Spain). The GA then asked the parties to continue negotiations. In the September 1967 Gibraltar referendum a large majority was for continued association with UK. GA declared the referendum contravened its resolutions for negotiated settlement and called for resumption of talks. Meetings were held in March 1968; later in 1968 the GA asked UK for more talks to end the colonial situation by 1 Oct. 1969. UK introduced a new constitution May 1969.

Spain closed all land access to Gibraltar in 1969. The GA postponed consideration of Gibraltar for several years. On 14 Dec. 1973 it adopted a consensus which reiterated hopes that negotiations between Spain and the UK would soon be resumed 'with a view to the final solution of this problem' of sovereignty. Thereafter annual GA resolutions were along the same lines, while noting certain meetings and exchanges between the parties they continually urged actual negotiations on all differences.

On 10 April 1980 the Spanish Foreign Minister and UK Foreign Secretary agreed in Lisbon to open the frontier, together with a statement of each party's position on the status of Gibraltar. The GA consensus of 1980 noted this declaration to begin negotiations. In January 1982 Spain and the UK agreed to begin them on 20 April, but with the invasion of the Falklands by Argentina they were postponed until 25 June and then indefinitely.

A new Spanish government opened the border to pedestrians on 15 Dec. 1982. Stalemate continued. On 27 Nov. 1984, after a meeting in Brussels, a joint communiqué was issued to apply the Lisbon Declaration by 15 Feb. 1985 for free movement of people, vehicles and goods and a negotiating process to overcome all differences. The GA noted this, in a decision of 5 Dec. 1984, and urged the governments to initiate negotiations for a lasting solution within the spirit of the Charter. The border was opened at midnight on 4 Feb. 1985 and the Spanish Foreign Minister and UK Foreign Secretary agreed on 5 February to hold regular annual meetings to discuss 'matters of mutual interest' (presumably including sovereignty). They agreed to set up working groups to consider practical problems of aviation, tourism etc. The UK Prime Minister said in Parliament the Government would not hand over the sovereignty of Gibraltar against the people's wishes.

Date	*Case*	*Nature*	*UN bodies involved*
1982–	Guyana, Venezuela	Venezuelan territorial claims	S-G

S-G effort to advise on a method of settling the dispute over territory in Guyana claimed by Venezuela.

Venezuela claimed some two-thirds of Guyana, but the two governments agreed to a 12-year moratorium on claims in 1970. This expired in June 1982 and Venezuela would not renew it. Accordingly the parties were obligated, under the Geneva Agreement of 1966 between the UK and Venezuela and adhered to by Guyana when it became independent, to seek a negotiating procedure for a peaceful settlement. As they did not achieve this, they asked the S-G to advise them. He stated on 30 Aug. 1983 that to discharge 'his responsibility under the terms of Art. IV (2) of the Agreement signed at Geneva on 17 February 1966' he was sending an Under-Secretary-General to assemble the necessary information to make the choice of the procedure for a settlement. Diego Cordovez visited Guyana and Venezuela 21–26 Aug. 1983 to collect the necessary information.

Date	*Case*	*Nature*	*UN bodies involved*
1972–	India, Pakistan	Kashmir and border problems	SC (UNMOGIP)

UN role in the Kashmir dispute dormant, although the UN Military Observer Group in India and Pakistan (UNMOGIP) of 40–45 military observers continued operating. UNMOGIP's activities have been restricted on the Indian side since 1971.

Under the Simla Agreement of July 1972 India and Pakistan agreed to find a solution to the Kashmir problem through bilateral negotiations. In December 1972 they agreed on a 'line of control', similar to the ceasefire line of 1949 with a few deviations. But a section of this has been in dispute. Pakistan mentioned the Kashmir problem in several sessions of the GA and referred to past UN resolutions, while India insisted that the Simla Agreement decided the issue should be settled bilaterally, not internationally. In 1984 and 1985 Indian and Pakistani patrols clashed in the disputed Siachen glacier area.

Date	*Case*	*Nature*	*UN bodies involved*
1980–	Iran, Iraq	Hostilities	SC, GA, S-G (Special Representative, team to assess civilian damage, mission to investigate use of chemical weapons, two inspection teams stationed in capitals to investigate attacks on civilian areas, mission to investigate prisoner of war camps), HR Commission

Repeated efforts by the UN to end the hostilities and to humanise them. Iraq was more receptive then Iran, which considered the SC biased as it had not condemned the aggression by Iraq. But Iran showed confidence in S-G.

Amid growing animosity between the two countries, Iraq denounced the Algiers Agreement of 6 March 1975 on 17 Sept. 1980. Its forces crossed the frontier in strength on 22 September and the S-G immediately appealed to the parties to stop fighting, suggesting the SC should meet. On 28 Sept. 1980 the Council unanimously called on the parties to end hostilities and settle the dispute peacefully. Iraq prepared to do so if Iran would, Iran would not while Iraq violated its territory. On 10 October the S-G appealed to both to allow peaceful shipping to leave the Shatt al-Arab area under UN flag. Iran agreed but Iraq insisted on its own flag (claiming sovereignty over the river).

The SC held five meetings from 15–29 Oct. 1980. Its Pres. stated the members' concern and support for S-G good offices. The S-G sent Olof Palme as his Special Representative to both countries in November. He reported an agreement, in principle (not fulfilled), to free passage for over 60 commercial ships in the river. Palme repeated his visits in January, February and June 1981.

In January 1982 the S-G reached an agreement with both parties to enable families to visit prisoners of war, and on his fifth trip, at the end of February 1982, Olof Palme reported the arrangements for the visit of over 30 000 were proceeding.

The SC met on 12 July 1982 and unanimously called for a ceasefire and withdrawal to internationally recognised boundaries with UN observers. Iraq claimed to have withdrawn from Iran, but Iran disputed this and dissociated itself from action by the SC. The Council renewed these calls on 4 October and on the 22nd the GA called for a ceasefire, a withdrawal, and asked the S-G to continue his efforts.

The S-G continued frequent contacts with both parties looking for an opportune time to act. Palme agreed to continue his efforts when he became PM of Sweden. On 21 Feb. 1983 the Pres. of the SC, in its name, called for a ceasefire together with withdrawal to international recognised boundaries and asked the S-G to continue his efforts.

At Iran's request, and with Iraq's agreement, the S-G sent a team (May 1983) to assess damage to civilian areas in both countries, which the team reported was heavy, especially in Iran. On 31 Oct. 1983 the SC called for an end to attacks on civilian targets, affirmed the right of free navigation in the Gulf, and asked the S-G to consult with the parties on verification of an end to hostilities with possible use of UN observers. Iraq agreed but Iran dissociated itself from the resolution.

In December the S-G proposed that, in line with the October resolution, he would send a mission to explore 'the most effective means of conducting the consultations' (not accepted by Iran). He informed both countries in February 1984 that he felt it his duty to send a mission, because of the attacks on civilian targets. Iran wanted the mission to up-date the previous report, but Iraq wanted comprehensive discussions, so it did not get off the ground.

Iran was pressing the S-G to look into the use of chemical weapons. He sent experts who reported unanimously on 21 March that mustard gas had been used against Iran. On 30 March a SC declaration strongly condemned the use of chemical weapons without naming Iraq, which denied it had used them. The SC urged both to observe their obligations under international conventions.

On 1 June 1984 the SC condemned attacks on ships in the Gulf not party to hostilities. In accordance with which the S-G later reported to the SC that there had been 42 incidents involving merchant shipping in the Gulf from 1 June – 31 Dec. 1984. Then the S-G appealed again to both countries to stop attacks on civilian targets. They agreed as of 12 June, and two UN inspection teams were stationed in Baghdad and Teheran by early July, chiefly drawn from UNTSO, agreed to by the SC. On 29 June the S-G appealed to both countries that as they had agreed to stop attacks on civilian areas, to also undertake not to use chemical weapons. Iran replied it was committed not to use them. UN inspection teams investigated attacks on civilian targets during January 1985 in both countries.

Reported deaths of six Iraqi prisoners of war at the Iranian Gorghan camp prompted the S-G to offer to send a humanitarian mission to investigate camps in both countries. This was agreed and then cancelled because Iran held the mission should first visit Iraq. The mission was sent in January 1985 when Iraq had agreed. It reported to the SC (22 Feb. 1985) that the situation was a cause for serious concern, specifically the use of force in Iraq and of 'ideological and religious pressures' in Iran, and made specific recommendations.

On 5–6 March 1985 the SC Pres. and S-G expressed alarm at reports of attacks on civilian areas and appealed to both countries to respect their commitments of June 1984. On 15 March the SC Pres. again expressed the SC's concern and the need for a moratorium on attacks against civilians. Iraq held the UN and SC should tackle the problem of a comprehensive settlement. Iran appealed to the S-G for a team to inspect the use of chemical weapons.

On a visit to the Gulf states the S-G paid unscheduled side-trips to Teheran (7 April) and Baghdad (8 April). He reported to the SC that both governments reaffirmed their desire for peace and confidence in him and his efforts. He proposed that the SC invite them to take part in an examination of all aspects of their dispute and hopefully 'to explore every avenue that might end the conflict'. The SC, through its Pres. on 25 April, stated it was ready to issue such an invitation when appropriate; it also condemned all violations of international humanitarian law, having seen a report of a specialist who had examined Iranian patients – victims of chemical weapons. On 28 May the S-G regretted the resumption of attacks on civilian targets. On 17 June he welcomed Iraq's decision to stop attacking Iranian cities until the end of June, but he was dismayed (2 July) at Iraq's announcement to resume targeting civilian areas; he again offered to assist towards reaching a settlement in any way both sides considered appropriate.

Date	*Case*	*Nature*	*UN bodies involved*
1979–	Kampuchea, Vietnam, ASEAN countries	Vietnam attacked 'Democratic Kampuchea' (Khmer Rouge) and helped create the 'People's Republic of Kampuchea'	SC, GA (International Conference and ad hoc committee), S-G (Special Representative, Special Representative for Coordination of Kampuchean Humanitarian Assistance Programmes), UNICEF, UNHCR WFP, Programme of Humanitarian Assistance to Kampuchean People, UN Border Relief Operation, HR Commission

UN effort to rid Kampuchea of foreign intervention, and to alleviate suffering.

In the hostilities between Vietnam and Democratic Kampuchea (Pol Pot's regime) the capital was taken on 7 Jan. 1979. A SC draft resolution of 15 Jan. 1979 calling for a ceasefire, withdrawal of troops and non-interference, was vetoed by the USSR. Two conflicting SC draft resolutions on South East Asia in February could not be reconciled, so neither was put to a vote. They separately condemned Vietnam for aggression in Kampuchea and China for aggression against Vietnam. In March a combined SC draft resolution, for all parties in South East Asian conflicts to end hostilities and withdraw was vetoed by the USSR.

On 14 Nov. 1979 the GA called for the withdrawal of foreign forces from Kampuchea and non-interference in their democratic choice of government. Also it asked the S-G to explore the holding of an international conference and appealed for humanitarian help. An effort to block the credentials of the Democratic Kampuchean representative to the GA had failed in 1979 and subsequently, on the ground that the People's Republic of Kampuchea was imposed by foreign forces.

On 22 Oct. 1980 the GA called for an international conference to find a comprehensive solution to the Kampuchean problem, and for UN observers on the Thailand border to establish safe areas. The conference was held 13–17 July 1981 with 93 UN member states attending, but the USSR and Vietnam declined. It adopted a declaration for a comprehensive settlement and also a resolution for negotiations on a ceasefire, the withdrawal of troops and free elections both under UN supervision. It established an ad hoc committee to advise the S-G and requested the GA to ask him for a preliminary study of a possible UN role. The conference considered it essential that states should respect Kampuchea's future non-alignment and not interfere with it.

The GA reaffirmed its previous resolutions on Kampuchea 21 Oct. 1981, adopted the Declaration of the International Conference and accordingly asked the S-G to study a future Kampuchean role for the UN. It appealed for continued assistance for the Kampucheans, and foresaw a programme of reconstruction. The GA resolutions of 28 Oct. 1982, 27 Oct. 1983 and 30 Oct. 1984 reiterated its past policies and asked the S-G to continue his good offices, which he had been doing together with his Special Representative, Rafeeuddin Ahmed.

The S-G and officers of the Kampuchean Conference and its ad hoc committee expressed concern at the attacks on the Thai-Kampuchean border early in the spring of 1984. The ad hoc committee repeated its concern 17 Jan. 1985, calling for conditions for a constructive dialogue to achieve a settlement. The S-G visited Thailand, Laos and Vietnam in January 1985 seeking a common ground. Again the ad hoc committee deplored the military border actions. In a letter to the S-G of 19 February Thailand alleged chemical agents had been used by Vietnamese forces, which Vietnam denied. On 13 March 1985 the S-G expressed his special concern at the reports of incidents between Thai and Vietnamese troops. A mission of the ad hoc committee consulted with the ASEAN foreign ministers 6–8 July at Kuala Lumpur.

According to the S-G's report of October 1985 his discussions and those of his Special Representative led him to believe there was a reasonable coming-together on elements of a settlement, which could only be achieved through dialogue.

The HR Commission considered the problem of Kampuchea repeatedly and held that the primary violation of human rights was the deprivation of the right of self-determination due to foreign occupation. In 1985 it condemned persistent HR violations, attacks on civilians and demographic changes, and reaffirmed Kampuchea's right to self-determination, non-interference and non-alignment with foreign troops withdrawn.

The UN's humanitarian efforts were in three fields, providing for the people in Kampuchea, those on the Thai border and refugees in camps within Thailand. They involved a number of its agencies as well as the Programme of Humanitarian Assistance to the Kampuchean people and the UN Border Relief Operation. UNICEF started as the lead agency in association with the World Food Programme (WFP) and the International Committee of the Red Cross. The demands necessitated a special relief organisation headed by Sir Robert Jackson until March 1984, when he was succeeded by Tatsuro Kunugi. Donor-pledging conferences were held repeatedly; requirements were varied and changed with the harvests and the ebb and flow of fighting on the Thai border.

Date	*Case*	*Nature*	*UN bodies involved*
1966–	North Korea, South Korea, US	Armistice continuation and problem of reunification	GA (UNCURK, UN Command), S-G

The UN's aim was to bring about peacefully a unified, independent, democratic Korea, and for this purpose to have free elections. The GA noted that any UN forces remaining would be withdrawn at the request of the Republic of Korea (South Korea), or if conditions for a settlement were achieved. Efforts at reunification talks were left to the parties involved; a complicating factor was the role of the US which had troops in South Korea under a separate agreement with Seoul.

From 1966 a number of states proposed dissolution of the UN Commission for the Unification and Rehabilitation of Korea (UNCURK) as actually blocking unification. Direct negotiations in 1971 on divided families, between Red Cross societies of North and South Korea, encouraged hope for other negotiations, but they floundered in 1973.

On 4 July 1972 the two Koreas issued a joint communiqué for three principles of reunification, that it should be done independently, without outside interference, peacefully, and should promote national unity. They established a South-North Coordinating Committee and 'hot line'. Because of these moves UNCURK suggested its own dissolution. A GA consensus statement of 28 Nov. 1973 ended UNCURK and expressed the hope the parties would continue the dialogue to hasten independent, peaceful reunification.

On 17 Dec. 1974 the GA urged the two Koreas to continue their dialogue to expedite reunification and the SC to consider, in due course, dissolving the UN Command and making appropriate arrangements to keep the Armistice Agreement pending reconciliation. But on 18 Nov. 1975 the GA adopted two incompatible resolutions on Korea: one urged the parties concerned to hold talks so that the UN Command could be dissolved and arrangements be made for maintaining the Armistice, the second for the 'real parties' (presumably excluding South Korea which was not a signatory to the Armistice) to replace the Armistice with a peace agreement in the context of dissolving the UN Command and withdrawal of foreign troops under the UN flag.

The killing of two US officers of the UN Command on 18 Aug. 1976 by North Koreans, when pruning a poplar at Panmunjon, led to an agreement of 6 Sept. 1976 between North Korea and the UN, establishing a joint security area divided in two equal parts to ensure separation.

South Korea was anxious to join the UN, but North Korea feared that if both had membership their division would be perpetuated; they have observer status. There were various efforts of North and South Korea to meet on reunification which did not succeed. A series of talks was held unsuccessfully from February to September 1980. Other attempts at dialogue on reunification, economic cooperation and humanitarian issues were spoilt by confidence-destroying incidents, but were continued.

Date	*Case*	*Nature*	*UN bodies involved*
1978–	Lebanon, Israel, Syria, PLO	Israeli intervention in Lebanon and sectarian strife	SC (UNIFIL, UNTSO, OGB, ILMAC), GA (UNRWA, UNICEF, UNHCR, committees for assistance to Lebanon), S-G

The UN's efforts to restore Lebanon's authority over its territory were jeopardised by Israel's intervention and the sectarian discord in Lebanon.

UNIFIL was prevented from occupying to the Lebanese border by the Israelis handing over a strip to an irregular Christian client group ('de facto' forces under Major Haddad), which also prevented Lebanese regular soldiers from establishing their authority. UNIFIL was obligated 'not to use force except in self defence'. Its mandate was extended from September 1978 to 19 Jan. 1979.

On 6 Oct. 1978 the SC called for a ceasefire to facilitate national reconciliation. The next day Prince Sadruddin Aga Khan went to Beirut and then to Damascus on a good offices mission for the S-G to help establish a ceasefire, which took effect spasmodically. In a consensus statement on 8 Dec. 1978 the SC demanded removal of obstacles to the deployment of UNIFIL and called on Israel particularly 'to desist' from interfering with UNIFIL's operations. The GA also adopted a resolution in December for coordinating and providing assistance and advice to Lebanon in reconstruction.

The SC extended UNIFIL's mandate from 19 Jan. 1979 to 19 June 1979, deploring Israel's lack of cooperation and inviting Lebanon, in consultation with the S-G, to formulate a programme for the restoration of its authority. Brian Urquhart went to Lebanon for these consultations and reported some progress in the deployment of civilian personnel and the Lebanese army despite opposition from the 'de facto' forces which shelled UNIFIL headquarters in April. On 14 June the SC extended UNIFIL's mandate until 19 Dec. 1979 and again called on Israel to cease incursions into Lebanon and its assistance 'to irresponsible armed groups'. It asked for the reactivation of the Mixed Armistice Commission (ILMAC).

The duel between Major Haddad's 'de facto' forces and 'armed elements' (allegedly Palestinians with left-wing Lebanese) continued often above and across UNIFIL's area, with periodic ceasefires. The SC Pres. called for a permanent ceasefire on 30 Aug. 1979. The SC extended UNIFIL's mandate from 19 Dec. 1979 to 19 June 1980.

Incidents escalated in January and February 1980 with UNIFIL disarming infiltrators from the North and subjected to 'de facto' force attacks from the South. On the night of 6–7 April Palestinian elements attacked Misgav Am in Israel causing some 18 casualties. A UN spokesman noted that if they had gone through UNIFIL's area, they must have crossed Haddad's enclave. Next day Israeli and 'de facto' forces drove tanks and armoured carriers into the UNIFIL zone and attacked its headquarters on 12 April, damaging its hospital, four helicopters and destroying 15 buildings etc. They withdrew, but on 18 April 'de facto' forces murdered two Irish UNIFIL soldiers, which was immediately condemned by the SC. A SC resolution of 24 April condemned the violation of Lebanon and acts against UNIFIL and UNTSO, again it called for UNIFIL's control to the frontier and asked the S-G to revive the Mixed Armistice Commission, which he was vainly trying to reactivate. On 17 June the SC renewed UNIFIL's mandate until 19 Dec. 1980 and then again until 19 June 1981.

The situation escalated in August and December 1980 with 'de facto' attacks on villages in UNIFIL areas and obstruction of UNTSO observation, while 'armed elements' tried to infiltrate the area, despite PLO's commitment to cooperate with UNIFIL. A few reports of the encroachments reached the SC. On 20 March 1981 the Pres. strongly condemned the 'de facto' forces for killing two UNIFIL soldiers and wounding 20, as well as two members of the Lebanese army. He called for an end to acts threatening security and to the assistance provided to forces interfering with UNIFIL, and for the release of Lebanese soldiers and others kidnapped. In June the SC Pres. condemned 'armed elements' (PLO), infiltrating from the North, for killing two UNIFIL soldiers.

Renewed violence occurred in early 1981 between the Arab deterrent forces (Syrian) and right wing Lebanese Phalangists (backed by Israel) in the Zahle area. The S-G deplored the loss of life and continually pressed for a ceasefire. UNIFIL's mandate was renewed 19 June to December 1981 with the SC supporting deployment of Lebanese army contingents (then numbering 1350) in UNIFIL's area. Lebanon brought to the SC Israel's bombing of civilians in Beirut and the situation in Southern Lebanon, and Israel complained of indiscriminate shelling of Israeli towns from beyond and over UNIFIL's area. On 21 July 1981 the SC's Pres. called for an end to all armed attacks. The S-G instructed UNIFIL and UNTSO to arrange a ceasefire, which the PLO agreed to, while the US contacted the Israelis. A temporary ceasefire was established 24 July which lasted, with a couple of brief interruptions, until Israel invaded in June 1982. UNIFIL's mandate was renewed twice with a provision for an increase to 7000 men (25 Feb. 1982).

Israel attacked Lebanon on 5 June 1982. UNIFIL had neither the authority nor capacity to counter it. The SC unanimously called for a ceasefire by 6 June and then for a withdrawal, but the US vetoed another resolution condemning Israel for not complying with the SC's two previous ones. The SC extended UNIFIL's mandate from 19 June to 19 Aug. 1982 and authorised it to undertake humanitarian and administrative tasks. On 19 June the SC called for all conflicting parties to alleviate civilian sufferings and facilitate the distribution of aid, while appealing to member states for such aid.

On 26 June the US vetoed a draft resolution for an immediate ceasefire and Israeli withdrawal to 10 km. from Beirut as a preliminary to complete withdrawal, and the simultaneous evacuation of Palestinian forces from Beirut, with possible provision of UN observers and consideration of a UN force to support Lebanese interposition forces. The same day the GA seventh emergency special session on the Question of Palestine resumed and supported SC's demands for an Israeli withdrawal and the cessation of military activities in Lebanon.

In June 1982 the S-G appointed a coordinator of emergency relief from UN agencies, and in July had an inter-agency mission survey the needs and make recommendations. On 4 July the SC called for provisions of water, electricity, food and medicines for civilians.

Responding to the seige of West Beirut on 29 July 1982 the SC demanded Israel lift its blockade and permit distribution of supplies and international aid, the US did not participate in the vote. On 1 August the SC called for an immediate ceasefire and authorised UN observers to monitor it, but their deployment was hampered by the Israelis, although the Observer Group Beirut (OGB) assigned to the ILMAC was established in Beirut. The SC on 4 August called for an Israeli pull-back to their positions on 1 August and noted that the PLO had decided to move its forces from Beirut.

A draft resolution of 6 August condemned the continuing Israeli bombardment and called for an end to military aid to Israeli forces until they withdrew from Lebanon, but was vetoed by the US. A resolution of 12 August was unanimously adopted which called for a ceasefire, the lifting of restrictions against West Beirut and for aid and UN observers. The SC extended UNIFIL's mandate for two months until 19 Oct. 1982. The GA seventh special session on Palestine reconvened 16–19 August. It condemned Israel for non-compliance with UN resolutions and requested measures to safeguard civilians, assess losses in Lebanon and to investigate Israel's application of the 1949 Geneva Convention.

PLO forces left West Beirut by 1 Sept. 1982, supervised by a temporary multinational force (not UN) from France, Italy and the US. Israeli troops moved in on 15 September. The SC condemned this intrusion on 17 September and demanded a return to their previous positions. The Phalangist massacre of Palestinians in Shatila and Sabra camps was reported on the 18th, and at dawn next day the SC unanimously condemned them, authorised an increase of UN observers from 10 to 50, and requested the S-G to consult with Lebanon on additional help such as the possible deployment of UN forces. The GA's seventh special session resumed on 24 September, condemned the massacres, urged the SC to investigate them and supported SC past resolutions for Israeli withdrawal to recognised boundaries. The multinational force was reconstituted, including also a British detachment, and remained until February 1984.

After a statement by Pres. Gemayel, the SC extended UNIFIL for three months until 19 Jan. 1983, asking the S-G to consult on means to fulfil its original purpose of helping to restore Lebanon's authority over its territory, and authorised UNIFIL to help protect the inhabitants. On 16 Dec. 1982 the GA condemned the massacres of Palestinians and supported Lebanon's efforts to extend its authority to its frontiers. At Lebanon's request UNIFIL's mandate was renewed from 19 January to July 1983, then to 19 Oct. 1983 and 19 April 1984. Its operations were not extended to all Lebanon as Beirut then wanted. UNIFIL was called on to prevent local armed groups from operating in its area, although Israel continued to recruit them from villages there.

In November 1983 PLO factional strife swelled in Northern Lebanon. On 23 November the SC called for a ceasefire and settlement. With the support of the SC the S-G authorised use of the UN flag on Greek ships evacuating PLO fighters from Tripoli on 20 Dec. 1983.

In February 1984 France urged that a UN force be positioned in Beirut when all multinational forces had withdrawn, and that the OGB monitor a ceasefire. On 29 February the USSR vetoed this SC resolution in the absence of withdrawal of foreign warships and guarantees of non-interference by multinational forces. The S-G again pressed for an extended role for UNIFIL, for instance in the Sidon area, and in assisting Lebanon's restoration of authority as Israel withdrew. The SC renewed UNIFIL's mandate until 19 Oct. 1984 but did not extend its functioning.

The S-G visited Lebanon 9–10 June during his tour of five nations in the Middle East and discussed an extended role for UNIFIL in the South, which he again considered with the Lebanese PM on 2 October, prior to the SC's renewal of UNIFIL's mandate from October to 19 April 1985.

In September the SC considered a resolution calling on Israel to lift its restrictions on movement between the area it was occupying and the rest of Lebanon, and to observe the 1949 Geneva Convention in its treatment of civilians. But the US vetoed it on 6 September. The S-G convoked a conference of Israeli and Lebanese military representatives on security arrangements pertaining to Israel's withdrawal, which opened on 8 November at UNIFIL headquarters and continued spasmodically until broken off on 24 Jan. 1985 despite UN efforts to get a compromise.

Attacks and counter-attacks escalated. UNIFIL contingents trying to protect local inhabitants clashed with Israeli forces and their surrogates. A draft SC resolution condemning Israel for violating the principles of international law in its treatment of civilians was vetoed on 12 March 1985 by the US. Ten countries contributing troops to UNIFIL urged the SC to establish conditions in which it could function effectively, but the mandate was renewed to 19 Oct. 1985 without tackling this.

Violence accelerated in the Beirut Palestinian refugee camps. On 24 May the Pres. of the SC, on its behalf, supported the S-G's concern of two days earlier and appealed for restraint. The SC unanimously adopted, on 31 May, a resolution calling for all parties to end violence against civilians, particularly in Palestinian refugee camps, and to help alleviate the suffering therefrom. Lebanon regretfully held that this was interference in its internal affairs.

The Southern Lebanon Army (SLA surrogate of Israel) took 21 Finnish UNIFIL soldiers prisoner, allegedly for helping the Amal militia detain 11 SLA men (7 June). The Finns were released, it was found the SLA personnel had defected of their free will.

On 25 June the S-G stated his concern at the violence in Southern Lebanon, particularly the SLA shelling of Yatar on 20 June which caused casualties and displaced more than 2000 people. He called for a ceasefire so UNIFIL could function effectively, which was echoed by UNIFIL.

The S-G's report to the SC for April to October 1985 stated he and his colleagues had pointed out that the hand-over of the border area by the Israelis to the so-called 'South Lebanon Army' was a breach of SC resolutions and Lebanese sovereignty and 'likely to give rise to a whole new round of violence in the area', which would be a great strain on UNIFIL.

By mid-September UNIFIL had lost 111 soldiers in the line of duty. The Netherlands gave notice of withdrawal of its contingent from 19 October, because UNIFIL's mandate could not be fulfilled. The S-G recommended the mandate be extended 'as an extremely important factor in whatever peace and normality exists in Southern Lebanon'. The SC extended it on 17 October until 19 April 1986.

The UN and many of its agencies were involved in assistance to Lebanon as part of its peace efforts. The relief and reconstruction needs were too varied and changing to enumerate. Of over 19 000 killed in 1982 alone 84 per cent were civilians, some half a million were reported displaced in March 1984, and there were 255 685 Palestinian refugees in Lebanon in June 1984. The demands over-taxed the funds and capacity, particularly of UNRWA.

Date	*Case*	*Nature*	*UN bodies involved*
1979–	France, Madagascar (ex-colonial)	Claim to Malagasy Islands	GA, S-G

A UN effort to assure the territorial integrity of an ex-colony on independence. On 12 Dec. 1979 the GA reaffirmed that colonial territorial integrity must be respected at independence. It invited France to negotiate with Madagascar for the reintegration of the Malagasy Islands (Glorieuses, Juan de Nova, Europa and Bassas da India) separated from Madagascar when it became independent in 1960. France claimed the islands and regarded the resolution as interference.

On 11 Dec. 1980 the GA noted the S-G's report and the OAU's resolution on the question, and reiterated its previous year's resolution. France held that the GA was not competent to act because of Art. 2 (7). The GA deferred action in the following three years, and also in 1984 because meetings were taking place between the parties. In 1985 the GA decided the matter should go on its next provisional agenda.

Date	*Case*	*Nature*	*UN bodies involved*
1947–	Micronesia, US	Future of Strategic Trust Territory administered by US	SC (TC authorised by the GA, but responsible to the SC), GA (Special Committee on Decolonisation), S-G

UN effort to foster the development and independence of the Trust Territory of the Pacific Islands. The area comprises 2141 islands sprinkled over three million square miles – only 95 of which are inhabited by 136 500 people; they include the Marshalls, the Carolines and the Marianas (excluding Guam). Because it is a Strategic Trust Territory the TC functions under the authority of the SC rather than the GA.

On 26 Feb. 1947 the US submitted a draft Trusteeship Agreement to the SC for the islands, formerly under mandate from the League of Nations to Japan. SC adopted the Agreement with amendments on 2 April 1947. On 7 March 1949 the SC defined how it would make use of the TC in fulfilling its functions under the Trusteeship system. The TC has made regular visits to the territory, and the US has submitted annual reports to the TC which reports to the SC. The Special Committee on Decolonisation has considered the territory frequently and wanted to send its own mission, but the US provides for visits of the TC and not the Special Committee on Decolonisation.

The SC has continually urged Micronesian participation in the executive, an extension of powers of legislature, long-term economic planning and improvements in communications and education. It wanted the territory to adopt political unity, but recognised the right of groups of islands to make their own choice, and that the decision of 'free association with the US' was not incompatible with the Trusteeship Agreement if confirmed by free choice. But the Agreement continues to apply to all areas until formally ended.

The Northern Mariana Islands had a plebiscite observed by the UN on 17 June 1975, and approved a Covenant for a Commonwealth in Political Union with the US when the Trusteeship Agreement ends.

When the Federated States of Micronesia voted on their constitution for a republic in free association with the US, on 13 July 1978, the entities Kosrae, Ponape, Truk and Yap approved, but the Marshalls and Palau wanted separate agreements. The US signed Compacts of Free Association with the governments of the Federated States of Micronesia, the Marshall Islands and Palau (Belau) giving authority over defence and security to the US, and leaving internal and foreign affairs to the Islands. These agreements had to be submitted to plebiscites by the three governments. The draft Compact was approved under UN observation by the Marshall Islands and the Federated States of Micronesia (1983), and transmitted to the US Congress for approval (30 March 1984).

Palau endorsed the revised proposals on 10 Feb. 1983 but did not give the 75 per cent required to amend its nuclear-weapon-free constitution, which was not compatible with the Compact. Another referendum was held in Palau on 4 Sept. 1984 observed by a UN mission, but again the required 75 per cent was not reached. A visiting mission of the TC toured Micronesia 15 July – 3 Aug. 1985. On 16 September the US asked the S-G for a special session of the TC on the future of Micronesia and question of self-determination.

While the TC approved the reports of the missions, the USSR voted against them. The TC expressed the hope that the different islands would establish some form of unity, which they agreed to in Molokai (October 1977).

Date	*Case*	*Nature*	*UN bodies involved*
1974–	Israel, US, Arab countries, Palestinians	Middle East dispute	SC (UNEF, UNDOF, SC Commission [1979]), GA (Special Committee to Investigate Israeli Practices Affecting the Human Rights of the Population of the Occupied Territories [1968], Committee on Exercise of the Inalienable Rights of the Palestinian People [1975], seventh Emergency Special Session on the Question of Palestine People [1980], International Conference on Palestine [1983]), S-G, UNRWA, HR Commission

The UN effort to proceed to a comprehensive settlement of the Middle East problem was thwarted, as were bilateral efforts. UN policy followed resolution 242 of 1967 including return of occupied territory, and the right of states to secure boundaries. In addition it advocated self-determination for the Palestinians and the convening of a Middle East peace conference with the PLO represented.

At the GA session in 1974 the inalienable rights of the Palestinians were reaffirmed, including independence (22 Nov. 1974), and the PLO was given observer status. Yasser Arafat had already addressed the GA on 13 November.

On 24 July 1975 when renewing the UNEF mandate the SC urged Egypt and Israel to implement the resolution 338 (1973) for negotiations towards their disengagement and a settlement. Egypt and Israel signed an agreement for the separation of their forces in the Sinai on 4 Sept. 1975 witnessed by the Chief Coordinator of UN Peacekeeping Missions in the Middle East. A protocol was completed by 22 September, under which the UN buffer zone and its tasks were extended, and the US together with Egypt and Israel set up an early warning system in the UNEF zone at the Giddi and Mitla Passes. The UNEF mandate was renewed for a year until 24 Oct. 1976 and periodically until ended on 24 July 1979 after the Camp David Agreement.

On 10 Nov. 1975 the GA asked the SC to enable the Palestinians to exercise their national rights, and established a Committee for the Exercise of the Inalienable Rights of the Palestinian People (Palestinian Rights) to prepare a programme for the implementation of those rights, but Israel would not participate. On 5 December the GA asked the SC to take measures for a Middle East settlement and requested all states to desist from military or economic aid to Israel.

As arranged the SC met on 12 Jan. 1976 with the PLO present, but Israel would not participate. After lengthy debate a resolution was vetoed by the US on 26 January to enable the Palestinians to exercise their right to self-determination and to an independent state, for the return of all Arab territories occupied since June 1967, and for arrangements to guarantee to all states in the area peaceful existence within secure boundaries.

The SC met in March with both the PLO and Israel present. The US vetoed a draft resolution approved by all other members calling on Israel to refrain from measures against Arabs and their property in occupied territories and the establishment of settlements or any change in the legal status of Jerusalem, and to respect the inviolability of holy places. The SC again took up this problem in May and on the 26th its Pres. made a statement on behalf of the majority of the SC (not the US) that the fourth Geneva Convention of 1949 applied to the territory occupied since 1967. He called on Israel to comply strictly with it, and deplored any demographic changes particularly Jewish settlements as an obstacle to peace.

The Palestinian Rights Committee report went to the SC in June. It proposed a two-phase return of Palestinians – those displaced in 1967 and those in 1948–67, withdrawal from areas occupied in 1967 by 1 June 1977 and possible temporary UN administration until transferred to the PLO.

On 29 June 1976 the US vetoed a SC draft resolution affirming the right of the Palestinians to self-determination and independence, and taking note of the report of the Palestinian Rights Committee. A consensus statement of the SC on 11 November 'strongly deplored' measures changing the demography of the occupied territories, specifically new Jewish settlements, and reaffirmed the applicability of the 1949 Geneva Convention. It held invalid any legislative or administrative measures to change the legal status of Jerusalem, asking Israel to rescind them.

The GA, on 24 November, endorsed the recommendations of the Palestinian Rights Committee and authorised it to promote them. On 9 December it adopted two resolutions for convening a Middle East peace conference, one proposing it should be held under UN auspices co-chaired by the US and USSR not later than March 1977.

The S-G toured the Middle East in February 1977 and reported to the SC that reconvening the Geneva Peace Conference hinged on the participation of the Palestinians or PLO, which Arab countries favoured and Israel opposed. The SC met on the report at the end of March and adjourned without a resolution on 29 March 1977. In July the new Begin government legalised three settlements and authorised others. The S-G and the SC Pres. considered this a threat to peace and referred to the SC's consensus of 11 Nov. 1976. A joint US-USSR declaration of 1 October called for reconvening the Geneva Conference, as did the GA on 25 Nov. 1977.

On 28 October the GA again called on Israel to comply with the 1949 Geneva Convention and halt efforts to change the status of occupied territory, followed by a resolution of 2 December which endorsed recommendations for an Israeli withdrawal and a plan for the return of Palestinians.

On 19–20 November Pres. Sadat of Egypt had visited Jerusalem, which was followed by much bilateral diplomacy, Israel's advance into Lebanon (March 1978), and Camp David (September 1978). The S-G and GA continued to advocate a Geneva type conference. On 7 Dec. 1978 a GA resolution called for a peace conference under UN auspices, chaired by the US-USSR with the PLO present. Prompted by the Palestinian Rights Committee it asked the SC to act on its previous recommendations, and on 14 December it proposed the Council adopt a mandatory embargo on all arms to Israel.

In 1979 the consequences of the Camp David accords influenced the Middle East situation. The UN was chiefly concerned with trying to halt the Israeli practices in the occupied Arab territories (including Jerusalem) which contravened the 1949 Convention, and also with favouring a peace conference under UN auspices with PLO participation.

After eight meetings the SC, on 22 March, declared Israeli settlement practices invalid and an obstruction to peace, and it established a SC three-member commission to report on the situation. Israel refused to cooperate, so the commission visited adjoining states and reported to the SC, which on 20 July called for an end to settlements.

The UNEF mandate ended on 24 July 1979 as the USSR, which disapproved of Camp David accords, intended to veto UNEF's proposed supervision of the Israeli withdrawal from Sinai. The SC considered the recommendations of the Palestinian Rights Committee at numerous meetings but did not act on a resolution.

The GA adopted a number of resolutions on the Middle East in November and December 1979. On 29 November it rejected the Camp David accords as invalid over the rights of the Palestinians, and condemned partial agreements and separate treaties. On 6 December the GA called for a settlement under UN auspices through a peace conference with PLO participation. It again urged the SC to consider the recommendations of the Palestinian Rights Committee, and deplored Israel's violation of the 1949 Geneva Convention.

The UN continued its efforts to halt Israeli encroachments in Arab occupied territories. Of the SC's 77 meetings in 1980, 38 were related to the Middle East. On 1 March the Council described Jewish settlements as a violation of the 1949 Geneva Convention and accepted the recommendations of the commission it established in 1979. On 30 April the US vetoed a SC draft resolution that Israel should withdraw from the territories occupied in 1967 (including Jerusalem), that the Palestinians had a right to an independent state and that there should be security guaranteed for all states in the area.

In anticipation of Israeli measures to incorporate Jerusalem the SC, on 30 June, declared any change in its status null and void. The GA seventh emergency special session met on 22 July and was reconvened subsequently. It adopted a resolution on 29 July that peace could not be established without Israeli withdrawal which should start before 15 November, that the Palestinians had a right to self-determination and an independent state, and that the PLO should participate in deliberations within the UN. It requested the SC to consider measures under Chap. VII if Israel did not comply. The following day Israel declared Jerusalem its indivisible capital. On 20 August the SC affirmed this violated international law and obstructed peace. It called on UN members with missions in Jerusalem to withdraw them elsewhere, which they did.

On 15–16 December the GA adopted a number of resolutions covering the same ground as previous ones for Israeli withdrawal, a guarantee of the political independence of the states in the area, Palestinian right of self-determination, the PLO right to participate in deliberations, and against partial agreements, and Israel's claim to Jerusalem as its capital. It asked the SC to consider measures under Chap. VII and authorised its Palestinian Rights Committee to promote implementation of its recommendations.

Much the same substance was adopted by the GA in its resolutions of December 1981. It also decided to convene an International Conference on the Question of Palestine no later than 1984. On 16 December the GA demanded Israel cease its 'canal' project linking the Dead Sea and Mediterranean and asked the S-G to prepare a study of its effect on Jordan and occupied territory.

The SC unanimously declared on 17 Dec. 1981 that Israel's decision of the 14th to impose its jurisdiction on the Syrian Golan Heights was null and void and that acquisition of territory by force was inadmissible. It called on Israel to rescind the decision, otherwise the Council would meet no later than 5 Jan. 1982 to consider appropriate measures. The GA also on 17 December condemned Israel's annexation policies on the Golan Heights and declared them null and void. The SC continued to renew the mandate of its UNDOF on the Golan Heights every six months. On 21 May 1985 it was extended until 30 Nov. 1985.

Tension grew in 1982. SC attempts to halt Israeli measures in occupied territories were vetoed by the US. The GA seventh emergency special session was reconvened four times, two on the Middle East, two on Israel's actions in the Lebanon.

On 20 Jan. 1982 the US vetoed a SC draft resolution that Israel's action on the occupied Syrian Golan Heights was an act of aggression and states should consider applying measures under Chap. VII to nullify the annexation and refrain from all aid to Israel. On 28 January the SC voted for reconvening the GA seventh emergency special session which met the next day and on 5 Feb. 1982 declared Israel's action on the Golan Heights aggression, illegal and a continuing threat to international peace. It called on states to stop all forms of dealings with Israel and to sever relations. It deplored the veto that prevented SC action under Chap. VII.

On 2 April 1982 the US vetoed a SC draft resolution which would have called on Israel to rescind its disbanding of the elected municipal council of El-Bireh and its removal of the mayors of Nablus and Ramallah. It would have called on Israel to cease measures contrary to the 1949 Geneva Convention. The GA seventh emergency special session reconvened 20–28 April, condemned disbandment of El-

Bireh municipal council and dismissal of the two mayors, violation of holy places (11 April incident of shootings at Al-Haram Al-Shareef), repressive measures and failure to comply with its obligations under the 1949 Geneva Convention. It asked the S-G to initiate contacts towards a comprehensive peace.

The third (16–19 August) and fourth (in September) GA seventh emergency special sessions were chiefly concerned with Lebanon.

As Israel announced new settlements in the occupied Arab territories the SC met on 12 Nov. 1982 and decided to continue consideration later, as it did in 1983. In December 1982 the GA adopted a five-part resolution on Palestine and a six-part resolution on the Middle East, which reaffirmed much of its previous policy. It reiterated UN responsibility for a solution, the inadmissibility of acquisition by force, and the need for an Israeli withdrawal. It asked the SC to recognise and implement the Palestinian right to self-determination and an independent state, endorsed the recommendations of its Palestinian Rights Committee and held SC action on it long overdue. It recommended a transitional period under UN auspices when Palestinians would exercise their right to self-determination and a comprehensive peace under UN auspices in which the PLO would participate.

The GA also demanded Israel rescind its actions in the Syrian Golan Heights, calling on all parties to respect the 1907 Hague and 1949 Geneva Conventions. It deplored the veto in the SC, which blocked appropriate measures under Chap. VII. It called on states to suspend all assistance to Israel and sever relations, and deplored the transfer of some diplomatic missions to Jerusalem. It condemned Israel's continued occupation of Arab territories and held peace could not be achieved without Palestinian exercise of their rights and PLO participation, rejecting all arrangements that violated those rights, and stated that US-Israel strategic cooperation encouraged Israeli expansionist policies.

The GA again considered the 'canal' project from the Dead Sea to the Mediterranean which UN experts had visited in May 1982. The GA held it would be a violation of the rules of international law relating to the rights and duties on belligerent occupation of land.

The S-G described 1983 as a 'year of frustration' in his report to the GA on the Middle East. Efforts continued to get the SC to implement the recommendations of the GA Palestinian Rights Committee, but failed. The SC continued its considerations of 12 Nov. 1982 during 1983: 11, 14, 16 February, 20 May, 28–29 July, and 1–2 August. The US vetoed a SC draft resolution on 2 April, although it did not approve of Israel's settlement policy and considered the Hague regulations of 1907 and 1949 Geneva Convention applicable. The draft held Israeli settlement policies illegal and a 'major obstacle to all efforts and initiatives towards a comprehensive, just and lasting peace'; called on Israel to dismantle them, not to change the legal or demographic status of the Arab occupied territories; and condemned recent attacks on civilians particularly the wounding of students on 26 July 1983. It called on states not to provide any assistance connected with settlements and for the SC to examine implementation measures in the case of non-compliance.

From 29 August to 7 September the UN International Conference on the Question of Palestine was held in Geneva with 137 states and the PLO represented, but the US and Israel would not participate. It adopted a declaration as a guideline to its Programme of Action. The declaration held a UN role essential. The guidelines declared the Palestinian right to self-determination, an independent state, right of return and PLO participation, while all states in the area had the right to secure boundaries. It stressed the need for withdrawal, and rejected measures contrary to international law (especially settlements) and changes to the character of Jerusalem particularly the 'basic law' proclaiming it the capital. To effect these guidelines a Middle East peace conference under the UN and including the US, USSR and PLO was deemed essential with the SC responsible for implementing any peace accords.

The Programme of Action outlined specific measures to fulfil the Declaration, amongst them: states to refrain from all forms of aid to Israel encouraging its aggression or occupation; to undertake efforts for the protection of holy places; to enable Palestinians to control their resources, particularly water; and to see that detained Palestinians were given prisoner of war status. It asked the SC to suppress growing acts of aggression and to facilitate a Middle East peace conference, to guarantee Palestinians' safety pending withdrawal and provide a short transitional period under the UN for self-determination and elections (if necessary for a peacekeeping force), and to consider appropriate measures to ensure compliance with past resolutions.

The GA approved 10 resolutions on Palestine and the Middle East on 13 and 19 Dec. 1983 much along past policy lines. It endorsed the 1983 Geneva Declaration on Palestine and welcomed the call for a Middle East peace conference asking the S-G, in consultation with the SC, to prepare for a conference. It declared illegal all practices aimed at annexation, rejected acts violating Palestinian rights, called on states to refrain from any assistance to Israel and to sever relations, deplored any transfer of missions to Jerusalem and considered the strategic cooperation of US and Israel (30 Nov. 1981) would encourage Israeli aggression.

Once again the GA pointed out that SC consideration of the recommendations of its Palestinian Rights Committee (established 1975) was long overdue. The recommendations in that committee's report of 1983 included: Part I a Middle East solution must take into account the legitimate aspirations of the Palestinians with PLO participation and conferences under UN auspices; Part II 'the right of return'; and Part III 'the right to self-determination, national independence and sovereignty'. It also recommended that the SC establish a time-table for withdrawal and provision for temporary peacekeeping forces to facilitate withdrawal and takeover.

A separate GA resolution demanded that Israel not construct a 'canal' between the Dead Sea and Mediterranean. The S-G issued a second report after a visit of UN experts in the summer of 1983.

On 26 Jan. 1984 the SC Pres. stated its concern at Israeli extension of emergency regulations in occupied territories (2 Jan. 1982) stressing the applicability of the 1949 Geneva Convention. On a visit to the Middle East 5–13 June 1984 the S-G helped arrange for the exchange of Israeli and Syrian prisoners of war. Having met the five permanent members of the SC and Yasser Arafat, he reported on the replies he had from 19 governments (15 of the SC) and the PLO on the proposed peace conference. Most were for a conference, but Israel and the US were against and would not participate. In the S-G's report to the GA he said that a 'framework for negotiation' and 'umbrella' for contact was needed, and a peace conference did not have to be in 'permanent session', but that there were not then the conditions for the success of such a conference.

Again in December 1984 the GA adopted resolutions on the Middle East and question of Palestine, and one on the Dead Sea canal, all on much the same lines as the previous year's.

A draft SC resolution, deploring Israel's repressive measures against Palestinians in occupied territories since 4 Aug. 1985, was vetoed by the US on 13 Sept. After the killing of three Israelis on a yacht in Cyprus, which the S-G condemned, the Israelis bombed a suburb of Tunis (1 October) where PLO headquarters were located, killing over 60 people. The SC adopted a resolution on 4 October, with the US abstaining, which condemned 'the act of armed aggression', demanded Israel refrain from such acts and requested that states help to dissuade it from them. The resolution held Tunisia had the right to reparations.

On 9 October, through its Pres., the SC welcomed the release of the cruise ship Achille Lauro, deplored the death of a passenger and condemned 'criminal hijacking'. During the next two days the SC considered the Middle East and question of Palestine and resumed the debate later.

In a speech to the GA on 21 October Prime Minister Peres called for talks with Jordan on ending the state of war, with the support of an international forum (but restricted participation), in which the UN could have a role.

Date	*Case*	*Nature*	*UN bodies involved*
1979–	Namibia, SWAPO, South Africa, Angola	Effort to achieve independence for Namibia	SC (Contact Group), GA (UN Council for Namibia, UN Commissioner for Namibia), S-G (Special Representative, Commander-designate of UNTAG), Special Committee on Decolonisation, ECOSOC and HR Commission

The SC plan (resolution 435 of 1978) for the independence of Namibia was well advanced with high hopes for a speedy settlement, which were eroded by repeated manoeuvrings of South Africa and attacks into Angola. The S-G's Special Representative Martti Ahtisaari visited South Africa, Namibia and the frontline states in January 1979. The S-G hoped for a ceasefire by 15 March, but South Africa questioned his interpretation of the SC plan on SWAPO bases.

South African forces attacked SWAPO bases in Angola, for which it was condemned by the SC on 28 March 1979. The Pretoria government then transformed the constituent assembly in Windhoek into a legislative one (21 May). The GA immediately reconvened its 33rd session and on 31 May recommended the SC take enforcement measures under Chap. VII. It reaffirmed SWAPO as the sole authentic representative of Namibians and Namibia's right to independence including Walvis Bay.

On 2 November the SC again condemned South Africa for aggression in Angola and called on it to withdraw. The S-G called for a conference 12–16 November with the Contact Group, frontline states, SWAPO and South Africa to consider proposals for a demilitarised zone (DMZ) on the Namibian-Angolan border. South Africa agreed conditionally subject to satisfaction on six questions. On 12 December the GA asked the SC to impose mandatory comprehensive sanctions against South Africa, called on states to sever all economic relations with it that concerned Namibia, and condemned foreign corporation exploitation of Namibian resources.

On the S-G's recommendation the GA appointed Martti Ahtisaari as UN Commissioner for Namibia in 1980.

Border problems featured in 1980. The S-G appointed Lt. Gen. Prem Chand Commander-designate of UNTAG. In February and March he with senior UN political experts visited Angola, Zambia, Botswana and South Africa particularly on the DMZ. On 31 March the S-G reported to the SC that at these discussions South Africa had reaffirmed its acceptance of the resolution 435 (1978). In answer to this on 12 May South Africa informed the S-G of issues needing clarification relative to the DMZ, and brought up the question whether the S-G and Secretariat would refrain from recognising SWAPO as the sole authentic representative of Namibians. In a letter of 20 June the S-G assured South Africa impartiality would be followed in the implemention of the SC resolution 435 (1978). South African incursions from Namibia continued; in April the SC condemned it for an attack against Zambia and in June for an attack in Angola.

In October a high-level UN team went to Pretoria to discuss a time-frame for the implementation of the SC plan. The S-G called for a pre-implementation conference in January 1981, so the GA postponed its Namibian debate.

In 1981 South Africa pursued the issue of UN partiality, although the S-G's report S/12827 of 1978 required UNTAG to act with complete impartiality and this had been approved by the SC in its resolution 435. The conference 7–14 Jan. 1981 was attended by the Contact Group, frontline states, Nigeria, OAU, South Africa, its Administrator-General for Namibia, and SWAPO, but failed to get an agreement on dates for a ceasefire or for starting the implementation of the plan. SWAPO was prepared for both, but the Administrator-General of South-West Africa/Namibia declared it would be premature to set a date for implementation as the UN had failed to prove its impartiality.

The GA resumed its 35th session on 2 March and on the 6th condemned South Africa for its illegal occupation of Namibia, called for material and military assistance for SWAPO, which it reaffirmed as the sole authentic representative of the Namibians, and called on the SC for comprehensive, mandatory sanctions. The SC held 11 meetings and on 30 April France, the UK and US vetoed such sanctions.

In August 1981 South Africa again attacked Angola, and the US vetoed a SC draft resolution condemning it and calling for withdrawal. The GA then met for its eighth emergency special session 3–14 September. It called on the SC for mandatory comprehensive sanctions to speed implementation of its plan and for states to isolate South Africa economically, militarily and culturally. The resolution repeated many previous provisions, as did the GA again on 10 December when it urged the SC to act decisively against the dilatory manoeuvres of South Africa.

In 1982 the South African demand (espoused by the US) for the withdrawal of Cuban troops from Angola and the matter of procedure for elections of a Namibian constituent assembly (proportional representation or constituency system), featured in blocking Namibian independence. Increasingly the US took over negotiations concerning Namibia. No UN body would countenance the linkage of Cuban troop withdrawal with the SC plan. Angola and Cuba agreed on 4 Feb. 1982 that the forces would go when acts of aggression ended. Meanwhile South Africa repeatedly invaded Angola, and it reasserted its rule over Walvis Bay.

From 1 April 1982 Brajesh Chandra Mishra became UN Commissioner for Namibia on the proposal of the S-G, approved by the GA. He was reappointed by the GA from 1 Jan. 1983. On 20 Jan. 1982 the GA adopted a five-part resolution on Namibia, which again repeated previous provisions and insisted Walvis Bay was an integral part of Namibia. It demanded withdrawal of transnationals that exploit Namibian resources and deplored IMF collaboration with South Africa, called for the isolation of South Africa and rejected linkage with Cuban troop withdrawal.

Minimal progress was made in 1983. The S-G visited the frontline states, Kenya and Uganda in February. An international conference on Namibia of over 130 countries was held in Paris 25–29 April, which rejected linkage, called on all the Contact Group to dissociate themselves from it as France had done, expressed dismay that the SC had failed to consider mandatory comprehensive sanctions and called on states to prohibit their corporations from dealing with Namibian uranium. It followed GA resolutions in declaring Namibia's right to independence, SWAPO's authenticity in representing Namibians, the illegality of South African's annexation of Walvis Bay, and held that foreign corporations illegally exploiting Namibian resources should be liable for reparations.

On 31 May the SC unanimously condemned South Africa for its illegal occupation of Namibia and asked the S-G to seek implementation of its plan. Accordingly the S-G visited Angola, Namibia and South Africa 22–26 August. He reported that outstanding issues had been resolved except for South Africa's demand for linkage. The SC met 20–28 October when it rejected linkage insisting its plan could not be held hostage to issues alien to it, and called on South Africa to communicate its choice of electoral system for a constituent assembly.

The GA adopted its usual set of resolutions on Namibia 1 Dec. 1983, endorsing the SC plan and urging it to exert pressure on South Africa. France withdrew from the Contact Group as powerless to fulfil its mandate.

South Africa launched a major strike far into Angola in December, but in a letter to the S-G of 15 December proposed disengagement of its forces starting on 31 Jan. 1984 for 30 days provided others reciprocated and did not take advantage of the situation. The SC met 16–20 December and demanded South Africa cease violating Angolan sovereignty and considered Angola entitled to redress. On 29 December the S-G reported that despite his repeated requests South Africa had not declared its choice of electoral system and was still insisting on linkage.

An active start to 1984 petered out. The Contact Group practically ceased to function, while the US continued shuttle diplomacy. The SC met 4–6 January when it demanded South Africa stop all bombing, withdraw unconditionally, and condemned its continuing occupation of Angola. South Africa rejected this, although its Defence Minister said they had reached their goal and started to withdraw, but Angola reported no change. In February Angola and South Africa agreed to phased withdrawal supervised by a joint military commission, but protracted over more than one year. South Africa sought a ceasefire agreement with SWAPO outside the UN plan but to no avail.

In a letter to the S-G of 17 Nov. 1984 Angola proposed a phased withdrawal of 20 000 Cuban troops over three years from the entry of UN troops into Namibia, and conditional on South Africa implementing the UN plan. South Africa replied to the S-G calling for withdrawal of Cuban troops within 12 weeks of the start of implementation of the UN plan.

On 12 Dec. 1984 the GA adopted a comprehensive resolution of 69 do's and don'ts. Like others this was passed without a negative vote but with numerous abstentions. As previously it established Namibia's right to independence; it reaffirmed SWAPO as the authentic representative of Namibians and supported its armed struggle and the SC plan. It called for mandatory sanctions by the SC under Chap. VII, denounced the US liaison office in Windhoek, and condemned South

Africa's imposition of military conscription and its promotion of an internal settlement through a so-called multi-party conference.

The multi-party conference duly produced a 'puppet regime'. The S-G expressed dismay at the prospect in April 1985. The SC Pres. declared on 3 May it would be null and void, and on 19 June the SC condemned the installation on 17 June of the interim government in Windhoek. It 'strongly' warned that if South Africa did not cooperate on effecting the SC plan, the Council would consider appropriate measures to compel compliance. It urged UN states to take voluntary measures which could include stopping new investments, and ending krugerrand sales etc.

On 20 June the SC acted on the South African commando unit which was intercepted close to the oil complex near Cabinda (North Angola) presumably bent on sabotage. It unanimously condemned this aggression against Angola, the violation of its sovereignty, and declared Angola was entitled to appropriate redress.

The S-G reported to the SC on 6 September that there had been 'no progress' in his discussions with South Africa on implementation of the UN plan. The UN Council for Namibia held a conference 11–13 September for intensification of international action for the independence of Namibia.

In a resolution of 20 Sept. 1985 the SC condemned South Africa 'for its premeditated, persistent and sustained armed invasions' of Angola and decided to send a mission to ascertain the damage caused. On 7 October the Council condemned South Africa for its aggression in, and occupation of, Angolan territory and for use of Namibia as a springboard. The US abstained on the sixth paragraph urging states to extend assistance to Angola needed for strengthening its defence.

Date	*Case*	*Nature*	*UN bodies involved*
1982–	Nicaragua, US, Contadora Group, Central American states	Destabilisation in Central America	SC, GA, S-G, ICJ

UN effort to prevent destabilisation in Central America, particularly Nicaragua, and to promote a peaceful solution of the controversy through support of the Contadora group proposals for a settlement.

Nicaragua brought the danger of US military intervention in Central America to the SC in March 1982. The US alleged Nicaragua was fostering civil war in El Salvador with arms shipments. After eight meetings a draft resolution was vetoed by the US on 2 April 1982, which would have called on states to refrain from 'overt or covert' use of force in Central America and the Caribbean, and for dialogue and support for a peaceful settlement.

Four states met 8–9 Jan. 1983 forming the Contadora Group (Colombia, Mexico, Panama and Venezuela) to seek a peaceful settlement. They met 12 times as a group in the next 12 months including five times with the foreign ministers of Costa Rica, El Salvador, Guatemala, Honduras and Nicaragua.

In 1983 and 1984 Nicaragua was a member of the SC. It brought complaints of acts of aggression to the SC in March, May and September 1983. After eight meetings in March 1983 the Pres. of the SC said the 'present stage' of the consideration was concluded. On 19 May the SC unanimously adopted a resolution urging the Contadora Group 'to spare no effort to find a solution' and for states to cooperate with it. It reaffirmed the right of all countries to live in peace and security and asked the S-G to keep the SC informed. At the 13 September meeting Nicaragua reported flagrant attacks on 8 and 9 September; the matter remained on the SC agenda.

Contadora Group efforts were spurred by their Presidents' meeting at Cancún on 17 July, which adopted the Cancún Declaration, a general programme for Central America. The Contadora Group met 7–9 September with the foreign ministers of the five Central American states. This formulated the Document of Objectives (21 basic points for peace) which included: promoting detente, respect for human rights, democratic system and international security; stopping the arms race and trade; excluding military bases, advisers and destabilisation; and undertaking economic and social development.

A GA consensus of 11 Nov. 1983 condemned attacks from outside on Nicaragua's strategic installations, the loss of life in El Salavador and Honduras and destruction of public works. It supported the Contadora Group, welcomed the Cancún Declaration and the Document of Objectives.

In January 1984 the Contadora met with the five ministers of Central American states to fulfil the commitments of the Document of Objectives and set up three working groups to deal with (1) security – monitoring and guidelines restricting military activities, (2) political reconciliation and elections, (3) economic and social problems, trade and investment and assistance to refugees etc.

On 3 Feb. 1984 the SC met on Nicaragua's complaint of incursions by air and water, then again on 30 March, and 2–4 April. On 4 April the US vetoed a resolution that would have called for an end to attacks on Nicaraguan sovereignty, particularly the mining of ports, and on all states to refrain from acts that hinder the Contadora peace objectives. It also would have reaffirmed the right of free navigation in international waters. Anticipating that Nicaragua was to take the matter to the ICJ the US declared, on 6 April, that its acceptance of the Court's compulsory jurisdiction would not apply for two years to Central American cases. On 9 April Nicaragua started proceedings with the Court. On 10 May the Court ruled that the US should cease restricting access to Nicaragua's ports, particularly by mining, and rejected the US request for dismissal of the case on jurisdictional grounds. The US questioned the Court's jurisdiction but announced it would act in accordance with the Court's ruling.

At the GA on 2 October Daniel Ortega announced Nicaragua had decided to sign the Contadora Act for Peace and Cooperation in Central America immediately. It appeared El Salvador and Honduras were likewise inclined, but on 8 October Pres. Napoleon Duarte at the GA called for verification measures. On 26 October the GA adopted without a vote a resolution urging the five central American Governments to speed negotiations for an early signing of the Contadora Act on Peace and for all states to respect its commitments and principles.

The SC had met on 7 September to consider an alleged 'fresh escalation of aggression' by a plane from Honduras, then again on 9 November owing to mounting tension over reports of shipments of MiGs to Nicaragua, which proved incorrect. The date of the next meeting was left to consultations.

In May 1985 the SC met on the embargo instigated by the US against Nicaragua. There were a series of votes on 10 May, the US vetoed parts of the resolution for ending the trade embargo and calling on states not to destabilise other states. The parts of the resolution supporting the Contadora peace efforts and calling on Central American states to refrain from military, political or economic measures against each other were adopted. The US abstained on the provision that it and Nicaragua should resume dialogue.

The S-G reported to the GA in October 1985 that the situation in Central America had been 'steadily deteriorating'. He cited the increase in 'bilateral incidents', including tension between Nicaragua and Costa Rica. The report called for support of Contadora's efforts and the political will for a solution.

Date	*Case*	*Nature*	*UN bodies involved*
1963–	Western Sahara (Spanish Sahara), Spain, Morocco, Mauritania, Algeria (colonial)	Self-determination and claims of neighbouring states	SC, GA (Special Committee on Decolonisation), S-G (Special Representative), UNHCR, HR Commission, ICJ

UN efforts to obtain self-determination for the people of Spanish Sahara bordering on Algeria, Mauritania and Morocco. Subsequently it gave full support to the OAU when that organisation took over the problem.

Spanish Sahara was added to the GA list of non-self-governing territories in 1960. The Special Committee on Decolonisation considered it from 1963. In 1965 the GA asked Spain to negotiate an end to colonial domination. Spain accepted the principle of self-determination, but did not implement the repeated GA resolutions, from 1967 onwards, for consultation with Mauritania and Morocco on the procedures for a referendum under the UN, and for a visiting UN mission to prepare for it. The GA strengthened its resolutions and asked states to refrain from investments there in order to speed self-determination. On 21 Aug. 1974 Spain announced it would hold a referendum in Spanish Sahara in the first half of 1975 under UN auspices. On 13 December the GA reaffirmed the right of Spanish Sahara to self-determination and decided to ask the ICJ for an advisory opinion on the historical claims. It requested Spain to postpone the referendum until the GA decided its policy in the light of the ICJ opinion.

At the invitation of Spain the Special Committee on Decolonisation sent a fact-finding mission in May and June 1975 to Spanish Sahara and the bordering states. On 23 May Spain announced it was ready to end its presence there and would like a conference under UN auspices to harmonise positions and permit peaceful evolution. Spain asked the S-G to send observers. Mauritania approved. Morocco disapproved. The S-G visited the parties concerned 9–13 June. The UN visiting mission reported that the population it encountered wanted independence and should decide its own future.

On 16 Oct. 1975 the ICJ held the territory belonged to no one when Spain colonised it, although there were some legal ties with Morocco and the Mauritanian entity, but not such as to affect the principle of self-determination. The same day King Hassan of Morocco announced a march of unarmed Moroccans into Spanish Sahara to claim it. Spain called a SC meeting, which on 22 October asked the S-G to consult with the concerned parties, which he did from 25–28 October. On 2 November the SC adopted a resolution urging all parties to avoid action that would escalate the tension and asked the S-G to intensify his consultations. On 5 November the SC authorised its Pres. to request the King to end the march; the following day the King replied the Green March had begun. The SC agreed a consensus resolution 6 November calling on Morocco to withdraw and deploring the march. On the 9th the King asked the volunteer marchers to return, and on 14 November Spain,

Mauritania and Morocco concluded the Madrid Declaration to end Spain's presence in Spanish Sahara by 28 Feb. 1976 and transfer its powers to a temporary tripartite administration working in collaboration with the Jemma (representing the Saharan population). Algeria regarded it as against SC resolutions and therefore null and void.

On 10 Dec. 1975 the GA called on Spain to take measures enabling Spanish Sahara to exercise its right to self-determination under UN supervision and on the interim administration to ensure the Saharans exercised that right through free consultations with the assistance of a UN representative appointed by the S-G. On 31 Jan. 1976 the S-G appointed Olof Rydbeck of Sweden as his Special Representative.

Spain completed its withdrawal from Spanish Sahara on 26 Feb. 1976 without the exercise of self-determination. The transfer of authority to Mauritania and Morocco was endorsed by the Jemma, but the active liberation movement, Polisario, held it had not been democratically elected and most of its members had joined them. The Polisario proclaimed a 'Saharan Arab Democratic Republic' (SADR) on 27 February.

By an agreement on 14 April 1976 Mauritania and Morocco partitioned the territory. Fighting continued between the factions. In July 1976 the OAU considered assuming a role in the problem with a decision to hold an extraordinary session on the Western Sahara, but this was postponed for two years. The GA took note of the OAU's decision and deferred its debate until the 1977 Assembly. On 28 Nov. 1977 it reaffirmed the principle of self-determination and asked the OAU to inform the S-G on implementation of its decisions. It hoped a just solution would be achieved in accordance with UN principles at the OAU session. On 23 Dec. 1977 the S-G, exercising his 'good offices', obtained the release of eight Frenchmen abducted by the Polisario in Mauritania the previous May.

The OAU session of 19–22 July 1978 made no real progress itself on Western Sahara, but established an ad hoc committee of 'wise men', which later proposed a settlement plan. On 13 Dec. 1978 the GA adopted two resolutions on its commitment to self-determination and the UN's responsibility to decolonise Western Sahara. It invited the OAU to find a just settlement of the problem and requested it to keep the S-G informed.

On 1 Jan. 1979 Mauritania's head of state announced his country was prepared to pull out of the war, which it did by confusing stages. Morocco asked for an SC meeting, held 20–25 June, regarding its complaint of Algerian aggression on its territory, but at the intercession of the OAU Pres. it requested the Council to suspend action. On 5 Aug. 1979 Mauritania signed a peace settlement with the Polisario, and Morocco then claimed the whole area. On 21 Nov. 1979 the GA welcomed this peace agreement, urged Morocco to follow suite and deplored its continued occupation of the area evacuated by Mauritania. It recommended that the Polisario, which represented the people of Western Sahara, should participate in seeking a solution conforming with UN and OAU decisions.

The OAU Committee met 9–12 Sept. 1980 but Morocco rejected its peace plan for a ceasefire, referendum and use of UN troops, holding the committee was biased. The GA resolution of 11 Nov. 1980, after reaffirming Western Sahara's right to self-determination and the legitimacy of the struggle, called on Morocco to end its occupation and to negotiate with the Polisario, deplored Morocco's occupation of the part previously held by Mauritania, welcomed the efforts of the OAU and its committee, and reaffirmed the UN's determination to cooperate with the OAU to enable Western Sahara to exercise its right to self-determination.

At the OAU meeting of 24–27 June 1981 a major issue was again the recognition of the SADR. King Hassan announced acceptance of 'a procedure of controlled referendum'. The OAU committee recommended an OAU and UN supervised referendum, a ceasefire and a return to barracks. An action committee was set up to implement the recommendations but was stalled by a new Polisario attack.

On 24 Nov. 1981 the GA appealed to Morocco and the Polisario to negotiate and observe a ceasefire and a peace agreement permitting self-determination. It reaffirmed the UN's intent to cooperate with the OAU in the fair and impartial organisation of a referendum. A year later on 23 Nov. 1982 the GA adopted a similar resolution.

In 1983 the OAU meeting of 6–12 June adopted a resolution which referred to King Hassan's acceptance of a referendum, urged the parties to negotiate for holding one under OAU and UN auspices which were requested to provide peacekeeping forces during it. The GA approved the OAU resolution without a vote on 7 Dec. 1983, requesting the S-G to take the necessary steps for participation. At the delayed OAU meeting in Addis Ababa (November 1984) the SADR occupied its seat for the first time, and Morocco walked out. On 5 December the GA again supported the OAU resolution for direct negotiations on a ceasefire and the creation of conditions for a referendum under the OAU and UN.

On 23 Oct. 1985 the Moroccan PM, in a speech to the GA, defended Morocco's claim, announced a unilateral, immediate ceasefire if there was no aggression against territory under its responsibility, offered to have it verified by neutral observers, and said a referendum could be held under UN auspices early in January 1986.

INTERNATIONAL COURT OF JUSTICE CASES

Date and case	*Nature*	*Decisions*
1947–49 UK v. Albania	Mine damage to British warships in Corfu Channel	28 March 1948 ICJ upheld its jurisdiction; 9 April 1949 ICJ found Albania responsible; 15 Dec. 1949 ICJ assessed damages

The Court's judgment and assessment of damages were disregarded by Albania.

British warships were seriously damaged and members of the crew were killed by mine explosions on 22 Oct. 1946 in a section of the Corfu Channel within Albanian waters, which had been swept by allied naval authorities. The UK charged Albania with having laid the mines or allowed others to do so. The case went to the UN and the Security Council recommended that it be referred to the ICJ.

The Court found that Albania was responsible for the explosions; although it may not have laid the mines, it must have known about them. On the Albanian counter claim, it held that the UK had not violated Albanian sovereignty by the innocent passage of its warships, but had done so by sending ships to mine-sweep in Albanian territorial waters after the explosions and against Albania's will. The Court ordered Albania to pay £843 947 in reparation.

Date and case	*Nature*	*Decision*
1949–51 UK v. Norway	Extent of Norwegian territorial waters involving fishery interests	18 Dec. 1951 ICJ held that 1935 baselines established by Norway were not contrary to international law

The Court's judgment ended a long controversy of fishing interests between these two states, and of concern to other maritime states.

A Norwegian decree of 1935 sought to reserve certain fishing grounds off the northern coast exclusively for its fishermen, by laying down the width of its territorial waters. The UK claimed in its application to the Court (28 Sept. 1949) that some of these closed areas were high seas and open to all fishing vessels. Because of the configuration of fjords, islands and bays, calculating the lines was particularly difficult.

The Court found that neither the method nor the baselines Norway had established by its decree of 1935 broke international law.

Date and case	*Nature*	*Decision*
1949–50 France v. Egypt	France complained of Egyptian measures against interests of French Nationals	13 Oct. 1949 case filed; 21 Feb. 1950 France informed ICJ Egypt had withdrawn the measures; 29 March 1950 case removed from list

Case settled without action by the Court.

France invoked the Montreux Convention of 1935 in its complaint that Egypt had taken measures against the rights, interests and property of French nationals and protected persons in Egypt. Subsequently Egypt withdrew the measures, France informed the Court the case was virtually settled.

Date and case	*Nature*	*Decisions*
1949–50 Advisory opinion on interpretation of Peace Treaties	GA sought advice on arbitral procedures involving Bulgaria, Hungary and Romania	30 March 1950 ICJ held the three states should nominate representatives to treaty (arbitration) commissions; 18 July 1950 ICJ held the S-G could not appoint the third member of each commission for them

Impasse.

In 1949 the GA was concerned with accusations of the suppression of human rights in the three states and called attention to their obligations under the peace treaties of 1947. They refused to cooperate in examining these charges and to nominate representatives to treaty commissions for the settlement of such disputes as provided by the treaties.

The Court found a dispute existed and the three states were obliged to nominate their representatives to the commissions, calling on them to do so within 30 days. As they failed to do so the Court then answered remaining questions, that the S-G could not appoint the third member of each commission in their place, and the treaties required commissions of three persons.

Date and case	*Nature*	*Decision*
1949–50 Advisory opinion on status of South West Africa	GA request for advice on obligations of the Union of South Africa regarding South West Africa	11 July 1950 ICJ held South Africa's mandatory obligations continued, but to the GA, and that South Africa could not unilaterally modify the status of the territory

The Court held that the Union of South Africa was obliged to account for its administration to the UN, which it failed to do.

After the First World War the administration of South West Africa was put under the mandate of the Union of South Africa by the League of Nations. All other League mandates either became independent or were put under the UN trusteeship system. In 1946, 1947 and 1948 the GA recommended South West Africa be under trusteeship, but the Union of South Africa refused and would not submit reports.

The Court held mandated territories had not been automatically transferred to the trusteeship system, but the mandate had not lapsed and the mandatory power was obliged to account to the UN (GA) for its administration. It was not required to place the territory under trusteeship, but it could not change the status unilaterally, but only with the consent of the UN.

Date and case	*Nature*	*Decisions*
1949–50 Colombia/Peru	The Colombian Embassy in Peru sought safe conduct for Haya de la Torre to whom it had granted asylum	20 Nov. 1950 ICJ clarification of rights of asylum and Havana Convention of 1928; 27 Nov. 1950 ICJ rejected, on procedural basis, a request for interpretation

Impasse.

After a military rebellion in Peru on 3 Oct. 1948 the government charged the American Peoples' Revolutionary Party with directing it and summoned its Peruvian leader, Victor Raul Haya de la Torre. On 3 Jan. 1949 the Colombian Embassy granted him asylum, and then its Ambassador asked Peru for his safe conduct out of the country as a political refugee, which Peru refused. By agreement the case was submitted to the ICJ on 15 Oct. 1949.

The Court held that the state granting asylum (Colombia) could not alone determine the nature of the offence (political or criminal), that was binding on Peru. It also held that the Pan-American Havana Convention of 1928 guarantees for refugees were applicable only when the state (Peru) demanded the refugee leave, so safe conduct did not apply.

Peru counter claimed, asking the Court to declare Colombia's grant of asylum violated the Havana Convention because Haya de la Torre was charged with a common crime, the Court rejected this as he was charged with military rebellion; but there was no cause of urgency as stipulated in the Convention.

Colombia immediately requested the Court for interpretations of its judgment, whether (a) their Ambassador had correctly imputed the offence (as political), and it should be given legal effect, (b) Peru could not legally demand the surrender of Haya de la Torre, and (c) Colombia was not bound to surrender him. The Court found the request inadmissible on procedural grounds.

Date and case	*Nature*	*Decision*
1950–51 Peru v. Colombia (sequel)	Peru sought the surrender of Haya de la Torre by the Colombian Embassy	13 June 1951 ICJ held that Peru was entitled to demand that asylum should be ended as it had been granted irregularly, but Colombia was not obliged to surrender him as there were other ways of ending an asylum

The safe conduct of Haya de la Torre was not resolved by the Court's decision. But in March 1954 Colombia and Peru signed an agreement giving him safe conduct from Peru, which he left on 16 April 1954.

The day after the previous judgment in November 1950, Peru called on Colombia to surrender Haya de la Torre, which it refused to do. Colombia made a new application to the Court on 13 Dec. 1950, asking whether it was bound to deliver Haya de la Torre to Peru.

The Court held that Colombia was not obliged to surrender Haya de la Torre, as the Havana Convention did not require this in the case of political offenders, but it held that asylum should cease. However, it was not part of the Court's duties to say how, although it noted there were other ways than by surrendering the refugee.

Date and case	*Nature*	*Decision*
1950–52 France v. US	Rights of US Nationals in Morocco	27 Aug. 1952 ICJ held that import controls were contrary to Treaty of 1836 and General Act of Algeciras; it also ruled on the extent of US consular jurisdiction and of US consent required for application of laws in French protectorate

The Court ruled on the extent of US jurisdiction over its citizens and protégés in the French Moroccan Protectorate.

A French decree of 30 Dec. 1948 imposed a system of licence control on certain imports in the Moroccan Protectorate. The US claimed this affected its rights under treaties with Morocco, and that no law or regulation could be applied without US consent. France instigated proceedings 28 Oct. 1950 on the grounds that Americans were not entitled to preferential treatment.

The Court held the import controls were contrary to the US-Moroccan treaty of 1836 and of the General Algeciras Act of 1906, as they favoured France against the US.

On the matter of US consular jurisdiction in Morocco, it held the US could exercise this in the French zone in all disputes between US citizens and protégés, or as required by the General Act of Algeciras, but not when only the defendant was one. Moreover the laws and regulations in the French zone only required US consent when they involved US consular court intervention for enforcement as against US citizens. The Court held that US nationals were not immune from taxes.

Date and case	*Nature*	*Decisions*
1951–53 Greece v. UK	Greek claim on behalf of Ambatielos that UK must arbitrate a dispute over failure to carry out contract	1 July 1952 ICJ held it could decide on the obligation to arbitrate, but not the merits of the the claim; 19 May 1953 ICJ held the UK duty bound to arbitrate

The Court held that in accordance with the Treaties of 1886 and 1926 the UK must submit the dispute to arbitration.

By a contract of 1919 with the UK Nicholas Ambatielos of Greece was to purchase ships. He claimed to have suffered damages as the UK did not carry out the contract and English courts gave judgments against him, allegedly contrary to international law. The Greek government started proceedings at the Court 9 April 1951 claiming the UK was obliged to submit to arbitration under the treaties it had with Greece of 1886 and 1926. The UK denied the Court had jurisdiction, but at the hearings in 1952, declared willingness to have the Court arbitrate if it ruled in favour of arbitration.

The Court held it had jurisdiction to decide on whether the UK should arbitrate, but not on the merits of the Ambatielos claim. It later held the UK must arbitrate according to the above treaties and the declaration of 1926.

Date and case	*Nature*	*Decisions*
1951–52 UK v. Iran	Nationalisation of Anglo-Iranian Oil Co.	5 July 1951 ICJ order indicated provisional measures to protect the rights alleged by each party, until a final judgment; 22 July 1952 ICJ held it had no jurisdiction

The Court held it had no jurisdiction.

By a decree of 1 May 1951 Iran nationalised the oil industry. The Anglo-Persian Oil Co. had an agreement involving arbitration with Persia (as it was called) in 1933. The UK took up the case for the Anglo-Iranian Oil Co. in an application of 26 May 1951, claiming that Iran must take the dispute to arbitration as provided in the 1933 agreement, and that convention was binding on Iran.

On 22 June 1951 the UK asked the Court for provisional measures of protection, which the Court granted for each party (5 July 1951) pending its judgment. On 9 July 1951 Iran withdrew its acceptance of compulsory jurisdiction, but nevertheless appeared before the Court in June 1952.

The Court held that the UK was not a party to the contract of 1933, although this had been negotiated through the good offices of the League of Nations. Further it held that any treaties cited by the UK prior to 1932 (Iran's ratification of the compulsory jurisdiction) were not covered by it.

Date and case	*Nature*	*Decision*
1951–53 UK/France	Dispute of sovereignty over islands of Minquiers and Ecrehos	17 Nov 1953 ICJ held UK entitled to the islands

The Court decided the disputed sovereignty of two islets between Jersey and the coast of France in favour of the UK.

On 6 Dec. 1951 the UK filed an agreement at the Court between France and itself asking the Court to determine sovereignty over the islets of Minquiers and Ecrehos, which had been in question since the Middle Ages (1204).

The Court held that none of the treaties submitted were specific regarding the islets, and relied on evidence of the practice of sovereignty. It concluded that Jersey and British authorities had exercised functions there much of the time, and the UK was entitled to sovereignty.

Date and case	*Nature*	*Decisions*
1951–55 Liechtenstein v. Guatemala	Liechtenstein claimed damages on behalf of F Nottebohm	18 Nov. 1953 ICJ held it had jurisdiction; 6 April 1955 ICJ held the Liechtenstein claim not admissible on the basis of Nottebohm's nationality

Liechtenstein was not entitled to make a claim as Mr Nottebohm had been naturalised to become a neutral in wartime.

Mr Nottebohm, a German by birth and connections, wanted damages due to war measures, on the grounds that Guatemala had allegedly treated him in a way contrary to international law. As a German he had lived in Guatemala from 1905. In October 1939, on a visit to Europe, he took Liechtenstein nationality. On returning to Guatemala in 1940 he resumed his business until removed under war measures in 1943. The case was submitted to the Court on 17 Dec. 1951.

The Court held it had jurisdiction, although Guatemala's acceptance of compulsory jurisdiction had expired on 26 Jan. 1952; that was after the Court had been seized of the case.

It later held the granting of nationality, to be recognised by other states, must represent a genuine link between that state and the individual, which was not so in the case of Mr Nottebohm, as his object was to become a neutral.

Date and case	*Nature*	*Decision*
1953–54 Italy v. France, UK and US	Italian claim to Albanian gold taken to Germany, and UK claim	15 June 1954 ICJ held it did not have jurisdiction

Impasse.

Gold from the National Bank of Albania was taken by the Germans in 1943 from Rome and later recovered. Under the final act of the Peace Convention on Reparation (1946), gold in Germany was to be pooled and shared by states according to their entitlement. France, UK and US were responsible for the distribution. They agreed 25 April 1951 they needed an arbiter. If the arbiter found in favour of Albania, the gold should go instead to the UK as partial satisfaction of the Corfu Channel judgment; but also that either Italy or Albania could ask the Court for an adjudication. Albania did not apply, but Italy did on 19 May 1953 on the ground of damages due to the Albanian law of 13 Jan. 1945, and that this should have priority over the UK claim. Thereupon Italy questioned the Court's jurisdiction on its (Italy's) claim against Albania, as Albania was not a party to the suit.

The Court ruled it could not adjudicate on Italy's claim because Albania had not consented, nor could it adjudicate on the UK's claim, as it was dependent on Italy's.

Date and case	*Nature*	*Decision*
1953–54 France v. Lebanon	A French claim on behalf of the Electricité de Beyrouth Co.	29 July 1954 removed from the list as parties had agreed a settlement

Settled out of Court.

France and Lebanon agreed to modify their financial and monetary relations (24 Jan. 1948), which related to concessions to French companies with capital in Lebanon. Their agreement granted jurisdiction to the Court. The French company, Electricité de Beyrouth, considered Lebanon had acted contrary to its undertakings. France applied to the Court 11 Aug. 1953.

On 13 July and 23 July 1954 Lebanon and France informed the Court that both parties had ratified a settlement, and France requested the case be removed from the list.

Date and case	*Nature*	*Decision*
1954 US v. Hungary US v. USSR	Treatment of American aircraft and crew	12 July 1954 ICJ removed the cases from list

No action.

According to the US applications of 3 March 1954 an American aircraft and crew had been forced to land in Hungary on 19 Nov. 1951. The aircraft had been seized by USSR authorities. The four crew were delivered to Hungarian authorities, tried on 23 Dec. 1951, and sentenced for premeditated crossing of the frontier. They were released 28 Dec. 1951 on US payment (under protest) of $123,605.15. The US applications asked for the two cases to be treated together if possible. It considered the jurisdiction of the Court rested on Art. 36 (1) of the ICJ Statute, providing that the Court's jurisdiction comprises all the cases which parties refer to it.

The Court found it did not have jurisdiction as it had received a letter from the USSR 30 April 1954 that submission of the case was unacceptable and claiming the US was responsible for the incident, and a letter from Hungary 14 June 1954 that it would not submit to the Court's decision.

Date and case	*Nature*	*Decision*
1954–55 Advisory opinion: South West Africa	GA sought advice on its voting procedure regarding South West Africa	7 June 1955 ICJ upheld the GA's rule for a two-thirds majority

The Court approved the GA's rule.

The GA adopted Rule F on 11 Oct. 1954 providing that its decisions on reports and petitions regarding South West Africa should be considered important questions under Art. 18(2) of the Charter and therefore required a two-thirds majority of those present and voting. The GA sought the Court's advice (23 Nov. 1954) on (1) whether this was a correct interpretation of its judgment of 11 July 1950, and (2) if not what voting procedure should be followed.

The Court considered the GA was entitled to apply its own voting procedure and that this accorded with the requirement that its supervision should conform, as far as possible, with the procedure of the Council of the League of Nations. A unanimous decision held that Rule F of the voting procedure was a correct application of the Court's 1950 opinion, and consequently it was not necessary to answer the second question.

Date and case	*Nature*	*Decision*
1955–56 US v. Czechoslovakia	Acts of Czech aircraft over US zone of occupation in Germany	14 March 1956 ICJ removed case from its list

No action.

According to a US application of 29 March 1955 to the Court, Czechoslovakia had caused on 10 March 1953 a MiG aircraft to cross the German frontier without provocation, and to attack a US aircraft on routine patrol within the airspace of the US zone of Germany, destroying the aircraft and injuring the American pilot. The US claimed Czechoslovakia had violated its international obligations and asked for reparations.

Czechoslovakia informed the Court on 6 May 1955 that it regarded such proceedings as unacceptable, and consequently the Court found it did not have jurisdiction, ordering the case off its list.

Date and case	*Nature*	*Decision*
1955–56 UK v. Argentina UK v. Chile	UK claim to certain lands and islands in Antarctica	16 March 1956 ICJ removed the cases from its list

No action.

According to UK applications of 4 May 1955 to the Court, Argentina and Chile had encroached on territories under its sovereignty. It asked the Court to recognise the validity of its titles and to declare the encroachments contrary to international law, relying on Art. 36 (1) of the ICJ Statute for the Court's jurisdiction.

In a letter of 15 July 1955 Chile claimed the application unfounded and the Court without jurisdiction. On 1 Aug. 1955 Argentina refused to accept the Court's jurisdiction in the case. The Court then removed the cases from its list.

Date and case	*Nature*	*Decision*
1955–56 US v. USSR	Acts of Russian aircraft against a US one off Hokkaido	14 March 1956 ICJ removed the case from list

No action.

According to a US application of 2 June 1955 to the Court, two Russian aircraft on 7 Oct. 1952 pursued an American aircraft over Japanese territory near Hokkaido island and shot it into the sea. The US wanted the Court to find the USSR liable for damages of $1,620,295.

The USSR informed the Court 26 Aug. 1955 that it saw no reason for the Court to deal with the question, so the ICJ could not take any action and ordered the case off its list.

Date and case	*Nature*	*Decision*
1955–56 Advisory opinion: South West Africa	GA sought Court's advice on a function of its committee	1 June 1956 ICJ held the GA's Committee on South West Africa could hear petitioners

The Court re-enforced the GA's supervisory powers.

On behalf of its Committee on South West Africa the GA asked the Court (3 Dec. 1955) whether it might grant oral hearings to petitioners, and whether this accorded with the Court's opinion on the status of South West Africa of 11 July 1950.

The Court held that, although the League of Nations had not held oral hearings, its Council had established the right and method of exercise of petitions. It, therefore, held that the GA's Committee on South West Africa could grant oral hearings to petitioners provided the GA considered them necessary for the international supervision and administration of the mandated territory for which it was responsible.

Date and case	*Nature*	*Decision*
1955–57 France v. Norway	France claimed payment in gold on bonds securing loans floated by Norway in France	6 July 1957 ICJ held it lacked jurisdiction

The Court held it had no jurisdiction.

The loans floated by Norway in France between 1885 and 1909 were secured by bonds with obligations in gold or currency convertible into gold and various national currencies. After Norway suspended the convertibility of its currency into gold the loans were serviced in Norwegian kroner. On 16 July 1955 France, on behalf of its bondholders, asked the Court to state that the debt should be discharged by payment in gold value of coupons and redeemed bonds.

The Court found it was without jurisdiction which depended on the extent that the declarations of France and Norway conferring on it actually coincided. Norway was entitled to claim, in its favour, the reservation of France's declaration made excluding the jurisdiction of the Court over differences essentially within its national jurisdiction.

Date and case	*Nature*	*Decisions*
1955–60 Portugal v. India	Portugal claimed a right of passage to and between two enclaves in India	26 Nov. 1957 ICJ held it had jurisdiction; 12 April 1960 ICJ found India had not acted against the right of passage

The Court decided the case on the grounds that India had not acted against the right of passage that had been established by 1954, which did not apply to armed forces and ammunition.

Two Portuguese possessions in India – Dadra and Nagar-Aveli – assumed autonomous administration in 1954. Portugal applied to the Court on 22 Dec. 1955 claiming that from 1954 India prevented it from exercising its right of passage to and between the areas, as necessary to its sovereignty (in this case to prevent incursion by armed bands). India challenged the Court's jurisdiction on six counts.

The Court rejected India's objections on four of these counts. It attached the other two the merits of the case. In the second judgment the Court held it had jurisdiction on these points as well. It further recognised Portugal's right of passage in 1954 but held this was limited to civilians and goods and civil officials but not to armed police or forces and weapons, so India had not broken its obligations under Portugal's right of passage.

Date and case	*Nature*	*Decision*
1957–58 Netherlands v. Sweden	Netherlands claimed Sweden had not conformed to the 1902 Convention governing the guardianship of of infants	28 Nov. 1958 ICJ held Sweden had not failed to observe the convention

The Court dismissed the claim of the Netherlands on the grounds that the Convention did not include the protection of children.

In 1954 Swedish authorities placed a Dutch infant under a Swedish regime for the protection of children. The father and deputy guardian failed in their appeal against the Swedish authorities. The Netherlands then claimed that in applying a measure of protective upbringing to a Dutch child living in Sweden and placing it in the care of a Swedish family, thus depriving the Dutch guardian of custody, Sweden did not conform with its obligation under the 1902 Hague Convention as this provided that the national law of the child should apply if the child resided elsewhere.

The Court held this Convention did not include the protection of children as understood by Swedish law, and Sweden had not failed to observe it.

Date and case	*Nature*	*Decisions*
1957–59 Switzerland v. US	Switzerland claimed the return of assets of Inter-handel as a neutral Co.	24 Oct. 1957 ICJ order found no need for interim measures of protection; 21 March 1959 ICJ held the Swiss application inadmissible

The Court decided that the remedies of the US Courts must be exhausted.

A limited company, Interhandel, was registered in Switzerland in 1928 on the iniative of I G Farben of Germany. Most of its assets were the ownership of shares of the General Aniline and Film Corp. (GAF) in the US. In 1942 the US seized the GAF shares, vesting them in the Office of Alien Property, claiming they were the property of, or held for, I G Farben. The Swiss Government argued that Interhandel's links with I G Farben had been broken in June 1940, so the shares were owned by a neutral in 1942. Having failed to get the shares restored by diplomatic means Switzerland started proceedings at the ICJ in October 1957 and immediately requested the Court for interim measures of protection against a possible transfer of the assets before adjudication of the claim.

The Court held there was no need for interim measures of protection as it had been informed that no sale of the shares could take place without an adverse end of judicial proceedings in the US. It then found that Interhandel had not exhausted the remedies in US courts and therefore the Swiss application was inadmissible.

Date and case	*Nature*	*Decision*
1957–59 Israel v. Bulgaria	An Israeli claim over the destruction of a civilian aircraft	26 May 1959 ICJ held it had no jurisdiction

The Court held that it had no jurisdiction as a Government's acceptance of compulsory jurisdiction of the Permanent Court of International Justice had lapsed when it was dissolved.

On 27 July 1955 an Israeli civilian aircraft was shot down by Bulgarian anti-aircraft forces with the loss of seven crew members and 51 passengers. After trying to get damages through diplomatic channels Israel applied to the ICJ.

The Court held that although Bulgaria had accepted the compulsory jurisdiction of the Permanent Court of International Justice in 1921, this undertaking had lapsed with the dissolution of that Court and Act. 36 (5) of the ICJ Statute was not applicable.

Date and case	*Nature*	*Decision*
1957–60 US v. Bulgaria	A US claim arising from the destruction of the Israeli aircraft (above)	30 May 1960 ICJ order to remove from list

No action.

Several US nationals were killed on the Israeli aircraft destroyed by Bulgarian anti-aircraft on 27 July 1955. The US asked the Court to find Bulgaria liable for damages.

The US requested the proceedings be discontinued and the Court removed it from the list.

Date and case	*Nature*	*Decision*
1957–59 UK v. Bulgaria	A UK claim arising from the destruction of the Israeli aircraft (above)	3 Aug. 1959 ICJ order to remove from list

No action.

Several nationals of the UK and colonies were killed on the Israeli aircraft destroyed by Bulgarian anti-aircraft on 27 July 1955. The UK claimed damages.

The UK decided to discontinue the proceedings because of the ICJ judgment of 26 May 1959 and the Court removed it from the list.

Date and case	*Nature*	*Decision*
1957–59 Belgium/ Netherlands	Claims over two plots of frontier land	20 June 1959 ICJ upheld Belgium's claim

Court established Belgium's sovereignty.

Two parcels of land were in dispute between the Belgian commune of Baerle-Duc and the Dutch commune of Baarle-Nassau. In March 1957 the two governments agreed to ask the ICJ to settle the dispute, and so notified the Court in November 1957. Belgium based its claim on the Boundary Convention and annexed map of 1843 concluded after the separation of Belgium from the Netherlands in 1830. While the Netherlands relied on a Communal Minute drawn up between 1836 and 1841 which attributed them to the Dutch Commune, and claimed that it had exercised various acts of sovereignty over them since 1843.

The Court held the Boundary Convention determined that the plots belonged to Belgium, and that the acts which the Netherlands deemed had established its sovereignty were largely routine and did not displace Belgian sovereignty.

Date and case	*Nature*	*Decision*
1958–60 Honduras v. Nicaragua	Claim for the implementation of an arbitral award	18 Nov. 1960 ICJ held award binding on Nicaragua

The Court decided that an arbitral award on boundary delimitations should be put into effect.

By a Convention of 7 Oct. 1894 Honduras and Nicaragua agreed that in certain circumstances any unsettled boundary lines between them should be decided by the government of Spain. In October 1904 the King of Spain was asked to determine a part of the frontier on which a Mixed Boundary Commission had failed to agree. On 23 Dec. 1906 the King gave his arbitral award which Nicaragua failed to effect. In line with an OAS resolution Honduras and Nicaragua agreed on 21 July 1957 the procedure for taking the dispute to the ICJ, which they did on 1 July 1958.

The Court found Nicaragua had accepted and participated in arbitration proceedings and the award was binding on it.

Date and case	*Nature*	*Decision*
1958 US v. USSR	'Willful acts' against a US naval aircraft	9 Dec. 1958 ICJ removed case from its list

No action.

The US charged the USSR with 'certain willful acts' by its military aircraft, which had brought down into the Sea of Japan a US Neptune-type plane on 4 Sept. 1954. The US applied to the Court on 22 Aug. 1958, relying on Art. 36 (1) of the ICJ Statute for its jurisdiction. The USSR considered the US responsible for the incident and that there were no questions needing to be considered by the Court.

The Court found that without acceptance by the USSR of its jurisdiction, it could not act further.

Date and case	*Nature*	*Decision*
1958–61 Belgium v. Spain	Claim of compensation for liquidated assets of the Barcelona Traction, Light and Power Co. Ltd.	10 April 1961 ICJ removed case from list

No action as proceedings suspended.

The Barcelona Traction, Light and Power Co. Ltd. was formed in Canada in 1911. Its share capital belonged largely to Belgians. In 1948 the company was declared bankrupt in Spain. Belgium started proceedings 23 Sept. 1958 on the grounds that certain Spanish actions denied justice to the Belgian owners of much of the company's share capital and were contrary to international law. It sought restoration or compensation for the liquidated assets. Spain filed preliminary objections to the Court's jurisdiction and Belgium informed the Court it would not go ahead with the proceedings.

The Case was discontinued to allow for negotiations.

Date and case	*Nature*	*Decisions*
1962–70 Belgium v. Spain (sequel)	Claim of compensation for liquidated assets of Barcelona Traction, Light and Power Co. Ltd.	24 July 1964 ICJ dismissed two objections to its jurisdiction; 5 Feb. 1970 ICJ rejected Belgium's right to make the claim

Denial of diplomatic protection to shareholders in a foreign company against measures taken in relation to the company in a third country.

Negotiations having failed after the previous case Belgium filed a new application on 19 June 1962, asking Spain to make reparation for damage to Belgian shareholders. Spain filed four preliminary objections to the Court's jurisdiction, which dismissed two and added two to the merits of the case. Spain argued that Belgium's claim was unfounded or inadmissible.

The Court held Belgium could not legally protect shareholders in a Canadian Co. against measures taken against it in Spain.

Date and case	*Nature*	*Decision*
1959–60 France v. Lebanon	French claims against Lebanon on behalf of Compagnie du Port, des Quais et des Entrepôts de Beyrouth, and the Société Radio-Orient	31 Aug. 1960 ICJ removed case from its list

Settled out of Court.

France instituted proceedings against Lebanon on 13 Feb. 1959 on behalf of the Compagnie du Port, des Quais et des Entrepôts de Beyrouth and the Société Radio-Orient, alleging that certain Lebanese measures were contrary to the 1948 agreement of France and Lebanon on concessions of French companies in Lebanon and those with capital there. Lebanon raised preliminary objections to the Court's jurisdiction.

The Court removed the Case as the parties concluded arrangements whereby a Convention of 13 April 1960 settled the situation between the Compagnie du Port, des Quais et des Entrepôts de Beyrouth and Lebanon, and the Société Radio-Orient was satisfied by a decision of the Lebanese Council of Ministers on 11 May 1960.

Date and case	*Nature*	*Decision*
1959 US v. USSR	Destruction of a US air force plane over Hokkaido	7 Oct. 1959 ICJ removed case from list

No action.

A US B-29 was shot down on 7 Nov. 1954 in Japanese territorial airspace over Hokkaido. The US brought proceedings against the USSR at the ICJ on 7 July 1959 relying on Art. 36 (1) of the ICJ Statute for the Court's jurisdiction. The USSR considered the US responsible and that there were no questions for the ICJ to solve and no basis for the application.

The Court held, as the USSR had not accepted the Court's jurisdiction, it could not take further steps.

Date and case	*Nature*	*Decisions*
1959–62 Cambodia v. Thailand	Claim to Temple of Preah Vihear	26 May 1961 ICJ held it had jurisdiction; 15 June 1962 ICJ found in favour of Cambodia

The Court determined a matter of territorial sovereignty and its consequences.

Cambodia filed proceedings at the ICJ on 6 Oct. 1959 complaining that since 1949 Thailand had occupied Cambodian territory around the ruins of a holy monastery, the Temple of Preah Vihear which was a sacred place of pilgrimage to Cambodians. It asked the Court to declare Thailand obliged to withdraw its troops allegedly stationed there since 1954. Thailand filed preliminary objections to the Court's jurisdiction.

The Court upheld its jurisdiction, and then found the Temple was on Cambodian territory and Thailand was obliged to withdraw its guards, police or military force, and to restore any sculptures or like objects taken since 1954.

Date and case	*Nature*	*Decisions*
1960–66 Ethiopia v. South Africa Liberia v. South Africa	South Africa's violation of mandatory obligations in South West Africa	20 May 1961 ICJ joined the two proceedings; 1 Dec. 1962 ICJ upheld its jurisdiction; 18 July 1966 ICJ rejected the claims of Ethiopia and Liberia

A complainant had to establish its legal right or interest in the subject matter of its claim.

In separate proceedings instituted 4 Nov. 1960 Ethiopia and Liberia asked the

Court to declare South West Africa was under a mandate and that South Africa had breached its mandatory obligations in its administration of the territory by instituting apartheid and impeding self-determination etc. as well as disregarding the UN's supervisory functions. South Africa filed preliminary objections to the Court's jurisdiction, but these were rejected by the ICJ. It contended the mandatory obligations had lapsed with the dissolution of the League of Nations and had not been replaced by similar obligations to the UN.

The Court was divided equally on the judgment, so the president made the casting vote, which found that Ethiopia and Liberia had not established any legal right or interest in the subject of their claims.

Date and case	*Nature*	*Decision*
1961–64 Cameroon v. UK	Cameroon claimed the UK had violated the Trusteeship Agreement in respect to the Northern Cameroons	2 Dec. 1963 ICJ held it could not adjudicate upon the merits of the claim

No action practicable.

The Republic of Cameroon instituted proceedings against the UK on 30 May 1961 because it considered the UK administration of the area of the Cameroons, for which it was responsible as part of Nigeria, was in breach of the Trusteeship Agreement for the Territory of the Cameroons. It alleged this had led to the attachment of Northern Cameroons to Nigeria rather than to the Republic of Cameroon. The UK objected to the Court's jurisdiction.

A plebiscite under UN supervision had been held in February 1961, as a result of which the General Assembly terminated the Trusteeship Agreement as of 1 June 1961 on Northern Cameroons joining Nigeria.

The Court held it could not adjudicate on the merits of the claim, as it could not affect the decisions of the General Assembly, nor could it give the UK any possibility of satisfying the Republic of Cameroon.

Date and case	*Nature*	*Decisions*
1967–69 West Germany/ Denmark, West Germany/ Netherlands	Delimitation of North Sea Continental Shelf	26 April 1968 ICJ joined the two proceedings; 20 Feb. 1969 ICJ held the boundary should be by agreement on the basis of a prolongation of land territory

The Court established the basis for drawing the boundaries of the continental shelf between these countries. By agreement of the parties the Court was asked to state the principles and rules applicable to the delimitation of the continental shelf, which they undertook to effect.

The Court rejected the concept that the delimitation must accord with the principle of equidistance as provided by the 1958 Geneva Convention on the Continental Shelf, which West Germany had not ratified and was not legally binding on it, nor was this a rule of customary international law or a basic concept of continental shelf rights. It held the lines should be agreed in accordance with equitable principles, so that they represented a natural prolongation of their land territory and indicated certain factors to observe.

Date and case	*Nature*	*Decision*
1970–71 Advisory opinion: Namibia	Legal consequences for states from South Africa's presence in Namibia	21 June 1971 ICJ held South Africa's presence in Namibia illegal and states should refrain from recognising or supporting its presence there

The Court established the illegality of South Africa's presence in Namibia and the legal consequences to other states, but this was disregarded.

The Security Council, on 29 July, 1970, decided to ask the Court for an opinion on the legal consequences for states from the continued occupation of Namibia by South Africa.

The General Assembly had decided on 27 Oct. 1966 the mandate of South West Africa was terminated and that South Africa had no right to administer it. On 30 Jan. 1970 the Security Council declared South Africa's presence in Namibia was illegal as were its acts concerning Namibia, since the end of the mandate in 1966. It asked states to refrain from dealings with South Africa incompatible with this.

The Court held South Africa's presence in Namibia was illegal and it should withdraw its adminstration, that UN members must recognise that South Africa's presence and acts in Namibia were illegal and refrain from any recognition or support to South Africa's administration there, and that non-members should assist in the UN actions.

Date and case	*Nature*	*Decision*
1971–72 India v. Pakistan	India's denial of overflights by Pakistani civilian planes and the jurisdiction of the ICAO Council	18 Aug. 1972 ICJ held it was competent to hear the appeal and that the ICAO Council had jurisdiction

The Court established the competence of the ICAO Council to deal with the matter.

After an Indian aircraft was diverted to Pakistan, India suspended overflights by Pakistani civilian aircraft. Pakistan alleged this breached the 1944 Convention on International Civil Aviation and the International Air Services Transit Agreement. It complained to the International Civil Aviation Organisation (ICAO) Council. India objected to the Council's jurisdiction, and when this was rejected, it appealed to the ICJ on 30 Aug. 1971. Pakistan argued the Court was not competent to hear the appeal.

The Court held it could hear the appeal and that the ICAO Council had jurisdiction to deal with the matter under the above treaties.

Date and case	*Nature*	*Decision*
1973 Pakistan v. India	Question of trial of Pakistani prisoners of war	15 Dec. 1973 ICJ removed case from list

Discontinued in view of negotiations.

On 11 May 1973 Pakistan started proceedings at the ICJ regarding 195 Pakistani prisoners of war whom, allegedly, India intended to hand over to Bangladesh to be tried for crimes against humanity. Pakistan also asked for the indication of interim measures of protection. India objected to the Court's jurisdiction. In July Pakistan asked the Court to postpone further consideration to facilitate negotiations.

The Court removed the case after Pakistan informed it negotiations had taken place.

Date and case	*Nature*	*Decisions*
1972–74 UK v. Iceland, West Germany v. Iceland	Iceland's proposed extension of exclusive fisheries jurisdiction	1972 and 1973 ICJ stipulated certain measures of protection; 2 Feb. 1973 upheld its jurisdiction; 25 July 1974 ICJ found against Iceland and that the parties must negotiate

The Court held against unilateral extension of fisheries jurisdiction in a disputed area and that parties were under obligation to negotiate.

Iceland proposed extending its exclusive fishing limits from 12 to 50 nautical miles as of 1 Sept. 1972. The UK instituted proceedings on 14 April 1972 and West Germany on 5 June 1972. Iceland held the Court did not have jurisdiction. At the request of the UK and West Germany the ICJ indicated interim measures of protection in 1972 and 1973 that Iceland should not implement the extension to their vessels, and that there should be maxima limits to their annual catch in the area.

The Court held that Iceland's regulations were a unilateral extension, that it was not entitled to exclude fishing vessels from the disputed area unilaterally, and that the parties were mutually obliged to negotiate an equitable solution.

Date and case	*Nature*	*Decisions*
1973–74 Australia v. France, New Zealand v. France	Atmospheric nuclear tests	22 June 1973 ICJ Orders on interim measures of protection; 20 Dec. 1974 ICJ held it was not called on for a decision as France was discontinuing atmospheric tests

No decision, as the purpose of the applicants fulfilled.

In view of French atmospheric tests planned for the South Pacific, Australia and

New Zealand started proceedings at the ICJ 9 May 1973. France held the Court lacked jurisdiction. By orders of 22 June 1973 the Court indicated by interim measures of protection that France should avoid such tests causing radioactive fall-out on the territory of Australia or New Zealand pending judgment.

The Court held that a decision was not required, as there was no longer any point to the applications, since Australia and New Zealand had achieved their purpose with the French statements that atmospheric nuclear tests would not be held after the 1974 series.

Date and case	*Nature*	*Decision*
1974–75 Advisory opinion: Western Sahara	GA sought ICJ's advice on the status of Western Sahara at the time of colonisation	16 Oct. 1975 ICJ held Western Sahara's previous ties with its neighbours did not affect its right to self-determination

The Court decided the position of a state before colonisation and its present consequences.

On 13 Dec. 1974 the GA asked two questions of the ICJ: (1) 'Was Western Sahara (Rio de Oro and Sakiet El Hamra) at the time of colonisation by Spain a territory belonging to no one (terra nullius)?' if not (2) 'What were the legal ties between this territory and the Kingdom of Morocco and the Mauritanian entity?'

The Court answered in the negative to question 1, and to question 2 held that evidence showed certain legal ties with the Sultan of Morocco and with the Mauritanian entity, but they did not constitute ties of territorial sovereignty with either. The ties, it decided, did not affect the application of the GA's Declaration on the Granting of Independence to Colonial Countries and Peoples, and particularly the principle of self-determination to Western Sahara.

Date and case	*Nature*	*Decisions*
1976–78 Greece v. Turkey	Delimitation of the Continental Shelf in the Aegean Sea	11 Sept. 1976 ICJ found that indication of interim measures of protection not required; 19 Dec. 1978 ICJ held it did not have jurisdiction

The Court was without jurisdiction on the basis that had been claimed.

Greece and Turkey disputed the continental shelf around Greek Islands in the Aegean. Greece started proceedings on 10 Aug. 1976 on the grounds that the islands were entitled to their portion of the continental shelf, and asked for interim measures of protection so that neither state should explore or carry on measures of research in the area without the consent of the other pending judgment. The Court found these were not required. Turkey denied the Court's jurisdiction.

The Court found jurisdiction had not been conferred on it by either of the two instruments relied on by Greece.

Date and case	*Nature*	*Decisions*
1978–82 Tunisia/Libya	Delimitation of the Continental Shelf in the Mediterranean	14 April 1981 ICJ rejected Malta's request to intervene; 24 Feb. 1982 ICJ applied 'equitable principles' to the delimitation
1984–85	Tunisia asked for revision and interpretation of judgment	13–18 June 1985 hearings held

The Court specifically delineated, on 'equitable principles', the prolongation line dividing the two countries which abutted on a common continental shelf.

In 1978 the Court was asked to decide the principles for the delimitation of the continental shelf between Tunisia and Libya. In 1981 Malta asked to intervene on a basis of legal interest, but the ICJ decided it could not accede.

The Court concluded that physical criteria could not assist in the delimitation and that it had to apply 'equitable principles' including proportionality between the areas allocated and the length of their coastlines. It held that applying the equidistance method would not prove equitable in this particular circumstance. It determined that near the shore the line should run north-easterly at 26° angle and further out veer eastwards at a 52° bearing.

On 27 July 1984 Tunisia asked the ICJ for a revision and interpretation of its judgment of 24 Feb. 1982, the first time for such a request. The Court held hearings in June 1985.

Date and case	*Nature*	*Decisions*
1979–81 US v. Iran	Holding of the US Embassy and staff at Teheran	15 Dec. 1979 ICJ Order for restoration of Embassy and release of hostages; 24 May 1980 ICJ found against Iran; 12 May 1981 Order removed the Case from the list following discontinuance

The Court held Iran was violating its obligations to the US and under international law, but to no effect.

On 4 Nov. 1979 Iranian militants seized the Embassy in Teheran and held hostage the diplomatic and consular staff. The US filed an application at the ICJ on 29 Nov. 1979 and requested provisional measures of protection. On 15 Dec. 1979 the ICJ indicated measures for the release of the personnel and restoration of the premises. Iran asserted the Court should not entertain the case.

The Court found Iran was violating its obligations under conventions with the US and the rules of international law, and it must have the hostages released, the Embassy restored, and make reparation.

Date and case	*Nature*	*Decision*
1981–84 Canada/US	Determination of maritime boundary lines	12 Oct. 1984 a special Chamber of the ICJ decided the exact delimitation in the Gulf of Maine and Georges Bank

An ICJ Chamber drew up maritime boundary lines dividing the continental shelf and exclusive fishery zones of two abutting states, which the parties agreed to abide by in advance.

Both countries started oil exploration on the Georges Bank and disputed the area of the continental shelf in the 1960s. In 1976–77 each established a 200 mile exclusive fishing zone. They agreed in November 1981 to submit the case to the ICJ, and did so. They requested use of a special Chamber of the ICJ, a procedure not tried before, and agreed to abide by its decision. The five-judge panel was formed in 1982.

The Chamber rejected claims on the scale of fishing and oil activities and largely used geographical criteria to achieve an equal division. It arrived at two segments within the Gulf of Maine and a third outside across Georges Bank, which somewhat favoured the Canadian claim.

Date and case	*Nature*	*Decisions*
1982–85 Libya/Malta	Delimitation of the Continental Shelf	21 March 1984 ICJ rejected Italy's request to intervene; 3 June 1985 ICJ judgment

The Court determined an equitable delimitation of the continental shelf.

By an agreement of 23 May 1976 the two countries were to submit the determination of their jurisdiction on the continental shelf to the ICJ, but its implementation was not completed for many years. On 26 June 1982 Libya and Malta together notified the Court of their agreement of 1976 and the exchange of ratification on 20 March 1982. Italy applied to intervene on the grounds of a legal interest that might be affected by the decision, but this was rejected in March 1984.

In its judgment the Court stated the rules of international law applicable to delineating the continental shelf between the two states and the factors governing its adjustment of the equidistance line to reach an equitable result.

Date and case	*Nature*	*Decision*
1983– Burkina Faso/Mali	Frontier delineation	3 Oct. 1985 Memorials filed; judgment pending

Proceedings continuing.

By a special agreement of 16 Sept. 1983 Burkina Faso (formerly Upper Volta) and Mali agreed to submit their frontier dispute to the ICJ. They did this on 20 Oct. 1983 and agreed to use a Chamber of the Court. The Chamber was constituted on 3 April 1985. Their memorials were filed on 3 Oct. 1985 and the time limit for filing counter-memorials by each was set for 2 April 1986.

Date and case	*Nature*	*Decisions*
1984– Nicaragua v. US	Mining of Nicaraguan ports	10 May 1984 ICJ indicated provisional measures; 4 Oct. 1984 ICJ Order against intervention by El Salvador; 26 Nov. 1984 ICJ held it had jurisdiction; judgment pending

The Court indicated provisional measures for the protection of Nicaragua's sovereignty, and upheld its own jurisdiction. Proceedings continuing.

On 9 April 1984 Nicaragua instituted proceedings against the US for violations against its sovereignty and using force against it (i.e. the mining of its ports). It asked the Court for provisional measures under Art. 41 of the Statute 'to avoid further loss of life and destruction of property' pending a decision. Three days before, the US announced that its acceptance of the Court's compulsory jurisdiction would be suspended as regards Central American cases for two years.

In May the Court indicated provisional measures that Nicaragua's sovereignty should not be jeopardised 'by any military or paramilitary activities', particularly through laying mines, which the US announced it would observe. In November the ICJ found it had jurisdiction in the case. On 18 Jan. 1985 the US informed the Court it would not participate in the future proceedings on the grounds that Nicaragua's application was inadmissible. Hearings on the merits of the case were held 12–20 Sept. 1985.

APPENDICES

APPENDIX I

EXTRACTS FROM THE CHARTER OF THE UNITED NATIONS

Chapter I: Purposes and Principles

Article 2 (3). All Members shall settle their international disputes by peaceful means in such a manner that international peace and security, and justice, are not endangered.

Article 2 (7). Nothing contained in the present Charter shall authorise the United Nations to intervene in matters which are essentially within the domestic jurisdiction of any state or shall require the Members to submit such matters to settlement under the present Charter; but this principle shall not prejudice the application of enforcement measures under Chapter VII.

Chapter V: The Security Council

Article 24 (1). In order to ensure prompt and effective action by the United Nations, its Members confer on the Security Council primary responsibility for the maintenance of international peace and security, and agree that in carrying out its duties under this responsibility the Security Council acts on their behalf.

Article 27 (2). Decisions of the Security Council on procedural matters shall be made by an affirmative vote of nine members.

Article 27 (3). Decisions of the Security Council on all other matters shall be made by an affirmative vote of nine members including the concurring votes of the permanent members; provided that, in decisions under Chapter VI, and under paragraph 3 of Article 52, a party to a dispute shall abstain from voting.

Article 28 (2). The Security Council shall hold periodic meetings at which each of its members may, if it so desires, be represented by a member of the government or by some other specially designated representative.

Article 29. The Security Council may establish such subsidiary organs as it deems necessary for the performance of its functions.

Chapter VI: Pacific Settlement of Disputes

Article 33 (1). The parties to any dispute, the continuance of which is likely to endanger the maintenance of international peace and security, shall, first of all, seek a solution by negotiation, enquiry, mediation, conciliation, arbitration, judicial settlement, resort to regional agencies or arrangements, or other peaceful means of their own choice.

Article 33 (2). The Security Council shall, when it deems necessary, call upon the parties to settle their dispute by such means.

Article 34. The Security Council may investigate any dispute, or any situation which might lead to international friction or give rise to a dispute, in order to determine whether the continuance of the dispute or situation is likely to endanger the maintenance of international peace and security.

Article 35 (1). Any Member of the United Nations may bring any dispute, or any situation of the nature referred to in Article 34, to the attention of the Security Council or of the General Assembly.

Article 35 (2). A state which is not a Member of the United Nations may bring to the attention of the Security Council or of the General Assembly any dispute to which it is a party if it accepts in advance, for the purposes of the dispute, the obligations of pacific settlement provided in the present Charter.

Article 36 (1). The Security Council may, at any stage of a dispute of the nature referred to in Article 33 or of a situation of like nature, recommend appropriate procedures or methods of adjustment.

Article 36 (2). The Security Council should take into consideration any procedures for the settlement of the dispute which have already been adopted by the parties.

Article 36 (3). In making recommendations under this article the Security Council should also take into consideration that legal disputes should as a general rule be referred by the parties to the International Court of Justice in accordance with the provisions of the Statute of the Court.

Article 37 (1). Should the parties to a dispute of the nature referred to in Article 33 fail to settle it by the means indicated in that Article, they shall refer it to the Security Council.

Article 37 (2). If the Security Council deems that the continuance of the dispute is in fact likely to endanger the maintenance of international peace and security, it shall decide whether to take action under Article 36 or to recommend such terms of settlement as it may consider appropriate.

Article 38. Without prejudice to the provisions of Articles 33–37, the Security Council may, if all the parties to any dispute so request, make recommendations to the parties with a view to a pacific settlement of the dispute.

Chapter VII: Action with respect to Threats to the Peace, Breaches of the Peace, and Acts of Aggression

Article 39. The Security Council shall determine the existence of any threat to the peace, breach of the peace, or act of aggression and shall make recommendations, or decide what measures shall be taken in accordance with Articles 41 and 42, to maintain or restore international peace and security.

Article 40. In order to prevent an aggravation of the situation, the Security Council may, before making the recommendations or deciding upon the measures provided for in Article 39, call upon the parties concerned to comply with such provisional measures as it deems necessary or desirable. Such provisional measures shall be without prejudice to the rights, claims, or position of the parties concerned. The Security Council shall duly take account of failure to comply with such provisional measures.

Article 41. The Security Council may decide what measures not involving the use of armed force are to be employed to give effect to its decisions, and it may call upon the Members of the United Nations to apply such measures. These may include complete or partial interruption of economic relations and of rail, sea, air, postal, telegraphic, radio, and other means of communication, and the severance of diplomatic relations.

Article 42. Should the Security Council consider that measures provided for in Article 41 would be inadequate or have proved to be inadequate, it may take such action by air, sea, or land forces as may be necessary to maintain or restore international peace and security. Such action may include demonstrations, blockade, and other operations by air, sea, or land forces of Members of the United Nations.

Article 48 (1). The action required to carry out the decisions of the Security Council for the maintenance of the international peace and security shall be taken by all the Members of the United Nations or by some of them, as the Security Council may determine.

Article 48 (2). Such decisions shall be carried out by the Members of the United Nations directly and through their action in the appropriate international agencies of which they are members.

Article 49. The Members of the United Nations shall join in affording mutual assistance in carrying out the measures decided upon by the Security Council.

Article 50. If preventive or enforcement measures against any state are taken by the Security Council, any other state, whether a Member of the United Nations or not, which finds itself confronted with special economic problems arising from the carrying out of those measures shall have the right to consult the Security Council with regard to a solution of those problems.

Article 51. Nothing in the present Charter shall impair the inherent right of individual or collective self-defence if an armed attack occurs against a Member of the United Nations, until the Security Council has taken measures necessary to maintain international peace and security. Measures taken by Members in the exercise of this right of self-defence shall be immediately reported to the Security Council and shall not in any way affect the authority and responsibility of the Security Council under the present Charter to take at any time such action as it deems necessary in order to maintain or restore international peace and security.

Chapter VIII: Regional Arrangements

Article 52 (1). Nothing in the present Charter precludes the existence of regional arrangements or agencies for dealing with such matters relating to the maintenance of international peace and security as are appropriate for regional action, provided that such arrangements or agencies and their activities are consistent with the Purposes and Principles of the United Nations.

Article 52 (2). The Members of the United Nations entering into such arrangements or consitituting such agencies shall make every effort to achieve pacific settlement of local disputes through such regional arrangements or by such regional agencies before referring them to the Security Council.

Article 52 (3). The Security Council shall encourage the development of pacific settlement of local disputes through such regional arrangements or by such regional agencies either on the initiative of the states concerned or by reference from the Security Council.

Article 52 (4). This Article in no way impairs the application of Articles 34 and 35.

Article 54. The Security Council shall at all times be kept fully informed of activities undertaken or in contemplation under regional arrangements or by regional agencies for the maintenance of international peace and security.

Chapter XV: The Secretariat

Article 99. The Secretary-General may bring to the attention of the Security Council any matter which in his opinion may threaten the maintenance of international peace and security.

APPENDIX II

EXTRACTS FROM UNITED NATIONS RESOLUTIONS

'Uniting for Peace', General Assembly resolution of 3 Nov. 1950.

If the Security Council, because of lack of unanimity of the permanent members, fails to exercise its primary responsibility for the maintenance of international peace and security in any case where there appears to be a threat to the peace, breach of the peace, or act of aggression, the General Assembly shall consider the matter immediately with a view to making appropriate recommendations to Members for collective measures, including in the case of a breach of the peace or act of aggression the use of armed force when necessary.

Middle East, Security Council resolution 242 of 22 Nov. 1967.

The Security Council

1. Affirms that the fulfilment of Charter principles requires the establishment of a just and lasting peace in the Middle East which should include the application of both the following principles:

   (i) Withdrawal of Israeli armed forces from territories occupied in the recent conflict;

   (ii) Termination of all claims or states of belligerency and respect for and acknowledgement of the sovereignty, territorial integrity and political independence of every State in the area and their right to live in peace within secure and recognized boundaries free from threats or acts of force.

2. Affirms further the necessity

   (i) For guaranteeing freedom of navigation through international waterways in the area;

   (ii) For achieving a just settlement of the refugee problem;

   (iii) For guaranteeing the territorial inviolability and political independence of every State in the area, through measures including the establishment of demilitarized zones;...

Middle East, Security Council resolution 338 of 22 Oct. 1973.

The Security Council

1. Calls upon all parties to the present fighting to cease all firing and terminate all military activity immediately, no later than 12 hours after the moment of the adoption of this decision, in the positions they now occupy;
2. Calls upon the parties concerned to start immediately after the ceasefire the implementation of Security Council resolution 242 (1967) in all of its parts;

3. Decides that, immediately and concurrently with the ceasefire, negotiations start between the parties concerned under appropriate auspices aimed at establishing a just and durable peace in the Middle East.

Namibia, Security Council resolution 385 of 30 Jan. 1976.

The Security Council

7. Declares that, in order that the people of Namibia may be enabled freely to determine their own future, it is imperative that free elections under the supervision and control of the United Nations be held for the whole of Namibia as one political entity;
8. Further declares that, in determining the date, time-table and modalities for the elections in accordance with paragraph 7 above, there shall be adequate time, to be decided by the Security Council, for the purpose of enabling the United Nations to establish the necessary machinery within Namibia to supervise and control such elections, as well as to enable the people of Namibia to organize politically for the purpose of such elections;
9. Demands that South Africa urgently make a solemn declaration accepting the foregoing provisions for the holding of free elections in Namibia under United Nations supervision and control, undertaking to comply with the resolutions and decisions of the United Nations and with the advisory opinion of the International Court of Justice of 21 June 1971 in regard to Namibia, and recognizing the territorial integrity and unity of Namibia as a nation;
10. Reiterates its demand that South Africa take the necessary steps to effect the withdrawal, in accordance with Security Council resolutions 264 (1969), 269 (1969) and 366 (1974), of its illegal administration maintained in Namibia and to transfer power to the people of Namibia with the assistance of the United Nations;
11. Demands again that South Africa, pending the transfer of power provided for in paragraph 10 above:

    (a) Comply fully in spirit and in practice with the provisions of the Universal Declaration of Human Rights;

    (b) Release all Namibian political prisoners, including all those imprisoned or detained in connexion with offences under so-called internal security laws, whether such Namibians have been charged or tried or are held without charge and whether held in Namibia or South Africa;

    (c) Abolish the application in Namibia of all racially discriminatory and politically repressive laws and practices, particularly bantustans and homelands;

    (d) Accord unconditionally to all Namibians currently in exile for political reasons full facilities for return to their country without risk of arrest, detention, intimidation or imprisonment;...

Namibia, Security Council resolution 435 of 29 Sept. 1978.

The Security Council

2. Reiterates that its objective is the withdrawal of South Africa's illegal administration of Namibia and the transfer of power to the people of Namibia with the assistance of the United Nations in accordance with resolution 385 (1976);

3. Decides to establish under its authority a United Nations Transitional Assistance Group (UNTAG) in accordance with the above-mentioned report of the Secretary-General for a period of up to 12 months in order to assist his Special Representative to carry out the mandate conferred upon him by paragraph 1 of Security Council resolution 431 (1978), namely, to ensure the early independence of Namibia through free and fair elections under the supervision and control of the United Nations;

4. Welcomes SWAPO's preparedness to cooperate in the implementation of the Secretary-General's report, including its expressed readiness to sign and observe the ceasefire provisions as manifested in the letter from the President of SWAPO dated 8 Sept. 1978 (S/12841);

5. Calls on South Africa forthwith to cooperate with the Secretary-General in the implementation of this resolution;

6. Declares that all unilateral measures taken by the illegal administration in Namibia in relation to the electoral process, including unilateral registration of voters, or transfer of power, in contravention of the Security Council resolutions 385 (1976), 431 (1978) and this resolution are null and void;...

Falklands, Malvinas, Security Council resolution 502 of 3 April 1982.

Recalling the statement made by the President of the Security Council at the 2345th meeting of the Council of April 1 1982 calling on the Governments of Argentina and the United Kingdom to refrain from the use or threat of force in the region of the Falkland Islands (Islas Malvinas);

Deeply disturbed at reports of an invasion on 2 April 1982 by armed forces of Argentina;

Determining that there exists a breach of the peace in the region of the Falkland Islands (Islas Malvinas):

1. Demands an immediate cessation of hostilities;

2. Demands an immediate withdrawal of all Argentinian forces from the Falkland Islands (Islas Malvinas);

3. Calls on the Governments of Argentina and the United Kingdom to seek a solution to their differences and to respect fully the purposes and principles of the Charter of the United Nations.

Falklands, Malvinas, Security Council resolution 505 of 26 May 1982.

Concerned to achieve as a matter of the greatest urgency a cessation of hostilities and an end to the present conflict between the armed forces of Argentina and of the United Kingdom of Great Britain and Northern Ireland:

1. Expresses appreciation to the Secretary-General for the efforts which he has already made to bring about an agreement between the parties, to ensure the

implementation of Security Council resolution 502 (1982), and thereby to restore peace to the region;

2. *Requests* the Secretary-General, on the basis of the present resolution, to undertake a renewed mission of good offices bearing in mind Security Council resolution 502 (1982) and the approach outlined in his statement of 21 May 1982;

3. *Urges* the parties to the conflict to cooperate fully with the Secretary-General in his mission with a view to ending the present hostilities in and around the Falkland Islands (Islas Malvinas);

4. *Requests* the Secretary-General to enter into contact immediately with the parties with a view to negotiating mutually acceptable terms for a ceasefire, including, if necessary, arrangements for the dispatch of United Nations observers to monitor compliance with the terms of the ceasefire;

5. *Requests* the Secretary-General to submit an interim report to the Security Council as soon as possible and in any case not later than seven days after the adoption of this resolution.

APPENDIX III

EXTRACTS FROM THE UN DECLARATION ON THE GRANTING OF INDEPENDENCE TO COLONIAL COUNTRIES AND PEOPLES

Adopted 14 Dec. 1960

Convinced that all peoples have an inalienable right to complete freedom, the exercise of their sovereignty and the integrity of their national territory,

Solemnly proclaims the necessity of bringing to a speedy and unconditional end colonialism in all its forms and manifestations;

And to this end

Declares that:

1. The subjection of peoples to alien subjugation, domination and exploitation constitutes a denial of fundamental human rights, is contrary to the Charter of the UN and is an impediment to the promotion of world peace and cooperation.

2. All peoples have the right to self-determination; by virtue of that right they freely determine their political status and freely pursue their economic, social and cultural development.

3. Inadequacy of political, economic, social or educational preparedness should never serve as a pretext for delaying independence.

4. All armed action or repressive measures of all kinds directed against dependent peoples shall cease in order to enable them to exercise peacefully and freely their right to complete indepedence, and the integrity of their national territory shall be respected.

5. Immediate steps shall be taken, in trust and non-self-governing territories or all other territories which have not yet attained independence, to transfer all powers to the peoples of those territories, without any conditions or reservations, in accordance with their freely expressed will and desire, without any distinction

as to race, creed or colour, in order to enable them to enjoy complete independence and freedom.

6. Any attempt aimed at the partial or total disruption of the national unity and the territorial integrity of a country is incompatible with the purposes and principles of the Charter of the UN.

7. All states shall observe faithfully and strictly the provisions of the Charter of the UN, the Universal Declaration of Human Rights and the present Declaration on the basis of equality, non-interference in the internal affairs of all states and respect for the sovereign rights of all peoples and their territorial integrity.

MANILA DECLARATION ON THE PEACEFUL SETTLEMENT OF INTERNATIONAL DISPUTES

Adopted November 1982

The General Assembly

Reaffirming the principle of the Charter of the United Nations that all States shall settle their international disputes by peaceful means in such a manner that international peace and security, and justice, are not endangered,

Conscious that the Charter of the United Nations embodies the means and an essential framework for the peaceful settlement of international disputes, the continuance of which is likely to endanger the maintenance of international peace and security,

Recognizing the important role of the United Nations and the need to enhance its effectiveness in the peaceful settlement of international disputes and the maintenance of international peace and security, in accordance with the principles of justice and international law, in conformity with the Charter of the United Nations,

Reaffirming the principle of the Charter of the United Nations that all States shall refrain in their international relations from the threat or use of force against the territorial integrity or political independence of any State, or in any other manner inconsistent with the purposes of the United Nations,

Reiterating that no State or group of States has the right to intervene, directly or indirectly, for any reason whatsoever, in the internal or external affairs of any other State,

Reaffirming the Declaration on Principles of International Law concerning Friendly Relations and Cooperation among States in accordance with the Charter of the United Nations,

Bearing in mind the importance of maintaining and strengthening international peace and security and the development of friendly relations among States irrespective of their political, economic and social systems or levels of economic development,

Reaffirming the principle of equal rights and self-determination of peoples as enshrined in the Charter of the United Nations and referred to in the Declaration on Principles of International Law concerning Friendly Relations and Cooperation among States in accordance with the Charter of the United Nations and in other relevant resolutions of the General Assembly,

Stressing the need for all States to desist from any forcible action which deprives peoples, particularly peoples under colonial and racist regimes or other forms of alien domination, of their inalienable right to self-determination, freedom and independence, as referred to in the Declaration on Principles of International Law concerning Friendly Relations and Cooperation among States in accordance with the Charter of the United Nations,

Mindful of existing international instruments as well as respective principles and rules concerning the peaceful settlement of international disputes, including the exhaustion of local remedies whenever applicable,

Determined to promote international cooperation in the political field and to encourage the progressive development of international law and its codification, particularly in relation to the peaceful settlement of international disputes,

Solemnly declares that:

I

1. All states shall act in good faith and in conformity with the purposes and principles enshrined in the Charter of the United Nations with a view to avoiding disputes among themselves likely to affect friendly relations among States, thus contributing to the maintenance of international peace and security. They shall live together in peace with one another as good neighbours and strive for the adoption of meaningful measures for strengthening international peace and security.
2. Every State shall settle its international disputes exclusively by peaceful means in such a manner that international peace and security, and justice, are not endangered.
3. International disputes shall be settled on the basis of the sovereign equality of States and in accordance with the principle of free choice of means in conformity with obligations under the Charter of the United Nations and with the principles of justice and international law. Recourse to, or acceptance of, a settlement procedure freely agreed to by States with regard to existing or future disputes to which they are parties shall not be regarded as incompatible with the sovereign equality of States.
4. States parties to a dispute shall continue to observe in their mutual relations their obligations under the fundamental principles of international law concerning the sovereignty, independence and territorial integrity of States, as well as other generally recognized principles and rules of contemporary international law.
5. States shall seek in good faith and in a spirit of cooperation an early and equitable settlement of their international disputes by any of the following means: negotiation, inquiry, mediation, conciliation, arbitration, judicial settlement, resort to regional agencies or arrangements or other peaceful means of their own choice, including good offices. In seeking such a settlement, the parties shall agree on such peaceful means as may be appropriate to the circumstances and the nature of their dispute.
6. States parties to regional arrangements or agencies shall make every effort to achieve pacific settlement of their local disputes through such regional arrangements or agencies before referring them to the Security Council. This does not preclude States from bringing any dispute to the attention of the Security Council or of the General Assembly in accordance with the Charter of the United Nations.

7. In the event of failure of the parties to a dispute to reach an early solution by any of the above means of settlement, they shall continue to seek a peaceful solution and shall consult forthwith on mutually agreed means to settle the dispute peacefully. Should the parties fail to settle by any of the above means a dispute the continuance of which is likely to endanger the maintenance of international peace and security, they shall refer it to the Security Council in accordance with the Charter of the United Nations and without prejudice to the functions and powers of the Security Council set forth in the relevant provisions of Chapter VI of the Charter.
8. States parties to an international dispute, as well as other States, shall refrain from any action whatsoever which may aggravate the situation so as to endanger the maintenance of international peace and security and make more difficult or impede the peaceful settlement of the dispute, and shall act in this respect in accordance with the purposes and principles of the United Nations.
9. States should consider concluding agreements for the peaceful settlement of disputes among them. They should also include in bilateral agreements and multilateral conventions to be concluded, as appropriate, effective provisions for the peaceful settlement of disputes arising from the interpretation or application thereof.
10. States should, without prejudice to the right of free choice of means, bear in mind that direct negotiations are a flexible and effective means of peaceful settlement of their disputes. When they choose to resort to direct negotiations, States should negotiate meaningfully, in order to arrive at an early settlement acceptable to the parties. States should be equally prepared to seek the settlement of their disputes by the other means mentioned in the present Declaration.
11. States shall in accordance with international law implement in good faith all the provisions of agreements concluded by them for the settlement of their disputes.
12. In order to facilitate the exercise by the peoples concerned of the right to self-determination as referred to in the Declaration on Principles of International Law concerning Friendly Relations and Cooperation among States in accordance with the Charter of the United Nations, the parties to a dispute may have the possibility, if they agree to do so and as appropriate, to have recourse to relevant procedures mentioned in the present Declaration, for the peaceful settlement of the dispute.
13. Neither the existence of a dispute nor the failure of a procedure of peaceful settlement of disputes shall permit the use of force or threat of force by any of the States party to the dispute.

II

1. Member States should make full use of the provisions of the Charter of the United Nations, including the procedures and means provided for therein, particularly Chapter VI, concerning the peaceful settlement of disputes.
2. Member States shall fulfil in good faith the obligations assumed by them in accordance with the Charter of the United Nations. They should, in accordance with the Charter, as appropriate, duly take into account the recommendations of the Security Council relating to the peaceful settlement of disputes. They should also, in accordance with the Charter, as appropriate, duly take into

account the recommendations adopted by the General Assembly, subject to Articles 11 and 12 of the Charter, in the field of peaceful settlement of disputes.

3. Member States reaffirm the important role conferred on the General Assembly by the Charter of the United Nations in the field of peaceful settlement of disputes and stress the need for it to discharge effectively its responsibilities. Accordingly, they should:

   (a) Bear in mind that the General Assembly may discuss any situation, regardless of origin, which it deems likely to impair the general welfare or friendly relations among nations and, subject to Article 12 of the Charter, recommend measures for its peaceful adjustment;

   (b) Consider making use, when they deem it appropriate, of the possibility of bringing to the attention of the General Assembly any dispute or any situation which might lead to international friction or give rise to a dispute;

   (c) Consider utilizing, for the peaceful settlement of their disputes, the subsidiary organs established by the General Assembly in the performance of its functions under the Charter;

   (d) Consider, when they are parties to a dispute brought to the attention of the General Assembly, making use of consultations within the framework of the General Assembly, with the view to facilitating an early settlement of their dispute.

4. Member States should strengthen the primary role of the Security Council so that it may fully and effectively discharge its responsibilities, in accordance with the Charter of the United Nations, in the area of the settlement of disputes or of any situation the continuance of which is likely to endanger the maintenance of international peace and security. To this end they should:

   (a) Be fully aware of their obligation to refer to the Security Council such a dispute to which they are parties if they fail to settle it by the means indicated in Article 33 of the Charter;

   (b) Make greater use of the possibility of bringing to the attention of the Security Council any dispute or any situation which might lead to international friction or give rise to a dispute;

   (c) Encourage the Security Council to make wider use of the opportunities provided for by the Charter in order to review disputes or situations the continuance of which is likely to endanger international peace and security;

   (d) Consider making greater use of the fact-finding capacity of the Security Council in accordance with the Charter;

   (e) Encourage the Security Council to make wider use, as a means to promote peaceful settlement of disputes, of the subsidiary organs established by it in the performance of its functions under the Charter;

   (f) Bear in mind that the Security Council may, at any stage of a dispute of the nature referred to in Article 33 of the Charter or of a situation of like nature, recommend appropriate procedures or methods of adjustment;

   (g) Encourage the Security Council to act without delay, in accordance with its functions and powers, particularly in cases where international disputes develop into armed conflicts.

5. States should be fully aware of the role of the International Court of Justice which is the principal judicial organ of the United Nations. Their attention is drawn to the facilities offered by the International Court of Justice for the settlement of legal disputes especially since the revision of the Rules of the Court.

States may entrust the solution of their differences to other tribunals by virtue of agreements already in existence or which may be concluded in the future.

States should bear in mind:

(a) That legal disputes should as a general rule be referred by the parties of the International Court of Justice, in accordance with the provisions of the Statute of the Court;

(b) That it is desirable that they:

(i) Consider the possibility of inserting in treaties, whenever appropriate, clauses providing for the submission to the International Court of Justice of disputes which may arise from the interpretation or application of such treaties;

(ii) Study the possibility of choosing, in the free exercise of their sovereignty, to recognize as compulsory the jurisdiction of the International Court of Justice in accordance with Article 36 of its Statute;

(iii) Review the possibility of identifying cases in which use may be made of the International Court of Justice.

The organs of the United Nations and the specialized agencies should study the advisability of making use of the possibility of requesting advisory opinions of the International Court of Justice on legal questions arising within the scope of their activities, provided that they are duly authorized to do so.

Recourse to judicial settlement of legal disputes, particularly referral to the International Court of Justice, should not be considered an unfriendly act between States.

6. The Secretary-General should make full use of the provisions of the Charter of the United Nations concerning the responsibilities entrusted to him. The Secretary-General may bring to the attention of the Security Council any matter which in his opinion may threaten the maintenance of international peace and security. He shall perform such other functions as are entrusted to him by the Security Council or by the General Assembly. Reports in this connection shall be made whenever requested to the Security Council or the General Assembly.

Urges all States to observe and promote in good faith the provisions of the present Declaration in the peaceful settlement of their international disputes,

Declares that nothing in the present Declaration shall be construed as prejudicing in any manner the relevant provisions of the Charter or the rights and duties of States, or the scope of the functions and powers of the United Nations organs under the Charter, in particular those relating to the peaceful settlement of disputes,

Declares that nothing in the present Declaration could in any way prejudice the right to self-determination, freedom and independence, as derived from the Charter, of peoples forcibly deprived of that right and referred to in the Declaration on Principles of International Law concerning Friendly Relations and Cooperation among States in accordance with the Charter of the United Nations, particularly peoples under colonial and racist regimes or other forms of alien domination nor the right of these peoples to struggle to that end and to seek and receive support, in accordance with the principles of the Charter and in conformity with the above-mentioned Declaration,

Stresses the need, in accordance with the Charter, to continue efforts to strengthen the process of the peaceful settlement of disputes through progressive development and codification of international law, as appropriate, and through enhancing the effectiveness of the United Nations in this field.

APPENDIX IV

EXTRACTS FROM THE STATUTE OF THE INTERNATIONAL COURT OF JUSTICE

Article 1
The International Court of Justice established by the Charter of the United Nations as the principal judicial organ of the United Nations shall be consituted and shall function in accordance with the provisions of the present Statute.

Chapter I: Organization of the Court

Article 2
The Court shall be composed of a body of independent judges, elected regardless of their nationality from among persons of high moral character, who possess the qualifications required in their respective countries for appointment to the highest judicial offices, or are jurisconsults of recognized competence in international law.

Article 3

1. The Court shall consist of fifteen members, no two of whom may be nationals of the same state.
2. A person who for the purposes of membership in the Court could be regarded as a national of more than one state shall be deemed to be a national of the one in which he ordinarily exercises civil and political rights.

Article 4

1. The members of the Court shall be elected by the General Assembly and by the Security Council from a list of persons nominated by the national groups in the Permanent Court of Arbitration, in accordance with the following provisions.
2. In the case of Members of the United Nations not represented in the Permanent Court of Arbitration, candidates shall be nominated by national groups appointed for this purpose by their governments under the same conditions as those prescribed for members of the Permanent Court of Arbitration by Article 44 of the Convention of The Hague of 1907 for the pacific settlement of international disputes.
3. The conditions under which a state which is a party to the present Statute but is not a Member of the United Nations may participate in electing the members of

the Court shall, in the absence of a special agreement, be laid down by the General Assembly upon recommendation of the Security Council.

Article 26

1. The Court may from time to time form one or more chambers, composed of three or more judges as the Court may determine, for dealing with particular categories of cases; for example, labor cases and cases relating to transit and communications.
2. The Court may at any time form a chamber for dealing with a particular case. The number of judges to constitute such a chamber shall be determined by the Court with the approval of the parties.
3. Cases shall be heard and determined by the chambers provided for in this Article if the parties so request.

Article 27

A judgment given by any of the chambers provided for in Article 26 and 29 shall be considered as rendered by the Court.

Article 36

1. The jurisdiction of the Court comprises all cases which the parties refer to it and all matters specially provided for in the Charter of the United Nations or in treaties and conventions in force.
2. The states parties to the present Statute may at any time declare that they recognize as compulsory *ipso facto* and without special agreement, in relation to any other state accepting the same obligation, the jurisdiction of the Court in all legal disputes concerning:
   (a) the interpretation of a treaty;
   (b) any question of international law;
   (c) the existence of any fact which, if established, would constitute a breach an international obligation;
   (d) the nature or extent of the reparation to be made for the breach of an international obligation.
3. The declarations referred to above may be made unconditionally or on condition of reciprocity on the part of several or certain states, or for a certain time.
4. Such declarations shall be deposited with the Secretary-General of the United Nations who shall transmit copies thereof to the parties to the Statute and to the Registrar of the Court.
5. Declarations made under Article 36 of the Statute of the Permanent Court of International Justice and which are still in force shall be deemed, as between the parties to the present Statute, to be acceptances of the compulsory jurisdiction of the International Court of Justice for the period which they still have to run and in accordance with their terms.
6. In the event of a dispute as to whether the Court has jurisdiction, the matter shall be settled by the decision of the Court.

Article 38

1. The Court, whose function is to decide in accordance with international law such disputes as are submitted to it, shall apply:

   (a) international conventions, whether general or particular, establishing rules expressly recognized by the contesting states;

   (b) international custom, as evidence of a general practice accepted as law;

   (c) the general principles of law recognized by civilized nations;

   (d) subject to the provisions of Article 59, judicial decisions and the teachings of the most highly qualified publicists of the various nations, as subsidiary means for the determination of rules of law.

2. This provision shall not prejudice the power of the Court to decide a case *ex aequo et bono*, if the parties agree thereto.

Article 41

1. The Court shall have the power to indicate, if it considers that circumstances so require, any provisional measures which ought to be taken to preserve the respective rights of either party.

2. Pending the final decision, notice of the measures suggested shall forthwith be given to the parties and to the Security Council.

Article 53

1. Whenever one of the parties does not appear before the Court, or fails to defend its case, the other party may call upon the Court to decide in favor of its claim.

2. The Court must, before doing so, satisfy itself, not only that it has jurisdiction in acccordance with Articles 36 and 37, but also that the claim is well founded in fact and law.

Article 59

The decision of the Court has no binding force except between the parties and in respect of that particular case.

Article 60

The judgment is final and without appeal. In the event of dispute as to the meaning or scope of the judgment, the Court shall construe it upon the request of any party.

Article 61

1. An application for revision of a judgment may be made only when it is based upon the discovery of some fact of such a nature as to be a decisive factor, which fact was, when the judgment was given, unknown to the Court and also to the party claiming revision, always provided that such ignorance was not due to negligence.

2. The proceedings for revision shall be opened by a judgment of the Court expressly recording the existence of the new fact, recognizing that it has such a character as to lay the case open to revision, and declaring the application admissible on this ground.

3. The Court may require previous compliance with the terms of the judgment before it admits proceedings in revision.

4. The application for revision must be made at latest within six months of the discovery of the new fact.

5. No application for revision may be made after the lapse of ten years from the date of the judgment.

Article 62

1. Should a state consider that it has an interest of a legal nature which may be affected by the decision in the case, it may submit a request to the Court to be permitted to intervene.

2. It shall be for the Court to decide upon this request.

Chapter IV: Advisory Opinions

Article 65

1. The Court may give an advisory opinion on any legal question at the request of whatever body may be authorized by or in accordance with the Charter of the United Nations to make such a request.

2. Questions upon which the advisory opinion of the Court is asked shall be laid before the Court by means of a written request containing an exact statement of the question upon which an opinion is required, and accompanied by all documents likely to throw light upon the question.

PRINCIPAL SOURCES

Everyman's United Nations, published by the UN Office of Public Information 6th, 7th, 8th editions and supplement.

Everyone's United Nations, published by the UN Department of Public Information 9th edition, 1978.

UN Information Centre, London: Weekly summaries, special reports and press releases, agendas and resolutions of the General Assembly sessions.

UN Monthly Chronicles and UN Chronicles, published by the UN Office and Department of Information, Vol. 1 No. 1 May 1964 through Vol. XXII No. 9 October 1985.

Synopses of UN Cases in the Field of Peace and Security 1946–67, compiled by Catherine G. Teng for the Carnegie Endowment for International Peace 1968.

The International Court of Justice, UN publications 8th and 9th editions, by the UN Office of Public Information and the Department of Public Information, and *press releases*.

SELECT BIBLIOGRAPHY

Andemicael, Berhanykun (1972) *Peaceful settlement Among African States: Roles of the UN and the Organization of African Unity*. A UNITAR (UN Institute for Training and Research) Study PS No. 5.

Bailey, Sydney D. (1971) *Peaceful Settlement of Disputes: Ideas and Proposals for Research*. A UNITAR Study PS No. 1.

Bailey, Sidney (1982) *How Wars End: The United Nations and the Termination of Armed Conflict 1946–64*. Two volumes. Clarendon Press.

Burton, John (1969) *Conflict and Communication*. MacMillan.

Chai, F.Y. (1971) *Consultation and Consensus in the Security Council*. A UNITAR Study PS No. 4.

Clark, Grenville and Louis B. Sohn (1960) *World Peace Through World Law*. Second ed. Harvard University Press.

Claude, Inis L. Jr (1964) *Swords Into Ploughshares: The Problems and Progress of International Organization*. Second ed. Random House.

David Davies Memorial Institute of International Studies (1966) *Report of Study Group on the Peaceful Settlement of International Disputes*.

Edmead, Frank (1971) *Analysis and Prediction in International Mediation*. A UNITAR Study PS No. 2.

Gardner, Richard N. (ed) (1966) *Blueprint for Peace*. McGraw-Hill.

Gross, Ernest A. (1962) *The United Nations Structure for Peace*. Harper & Brothers.

Harbottle, Michael (1970) *The Impartial Soldier*. Oxford University Press.

Harbottle, Michael (1971) *The Blue Berets*. Leo Cooper.

Higgins, Rosalyn, *United Nations Peace Keeping*. Oxford University Press, Vol I 1969, Vol II 1971.

Hiscocks, Richard (1973) *The Security Council: A Study in Adolescence*. Longman.

Hollins, Elizabeth J. (ed.) (1966) *Peace is Possible*. Grossman Publishers.

James, Alan (1969) *The Politics of Peace-Keeping*. Chatto & Windus.

Lall, Arthur (1966) *Modern International Negotiation*. Columbia University Press.

Luard, D. and T. Evan (1970) *Conflict and Peace in the Modern International System*. University of London Press.

Luard, D. and T. Evan (1982) *A History of the United Nations: The Years of Western Domination 1945–55*. MacMillan.

Northedge, F.S. and M.D. Donelan (1971) *International Disputes: The Political Aspects*. Europa Publications.

Parsons, Sir Anthony and Alan James (1986) *The United Nations and the Quest for Peace*. Welsh Centre for International Affairs, Special paper No. 11.

Pechota, Vratislav (1971) *Complementary Structures of Third-Party Settlement of International Disputes*. A UNITAR Study PS No. 3.

Pechota, Vratislav (1972) *The Quiet Approach: A Study of the Good Offices Exercised by the Secretary-General in the Cause of Peace*. A UNITAR Study. No. 6.

Rikhye, Indar Jit, Michael Harbottle and Bjørn Egge (1974) *The Thin Blue Line*. Yale University Press.

Suter, Keith D. (1981) *Alternative to War: The Peaceful Settlement of International Disputes*. Women's International League for Peace & Freedom, Australian section.

Teng, Catherine G. (1968) *Synopses of UN Cases in the Field of Peace and Security 1946–67. Compiled for the Carnegie Endowment for International Peace*.

Thant, U (1978) *View from the UN*. David and Charles.

Urquhart, Brian E. (1973) *Hammarskjöld*. Alfred Knopf.

Yost, Charles (1968) *The Insecurity of Nations: International Relations in the Twentieth Century*. Pall Mall Press.

INDEX OF UN CASES

SEE FOLLOWING INDEXES FOR ICJ CASES

INDEX OF ICJ CASES

BY COUNTRY

INDEX OF ICJ CASES

BY SUBJECT